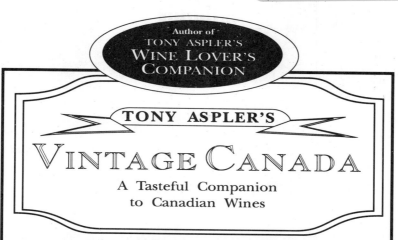

Author of
TONY ASPLER'S
WINE LOVER'S
COMPANION

TONY ASPLER'S

VINTAGE CANADA

A Tasteful Companion
to Canadian Wines

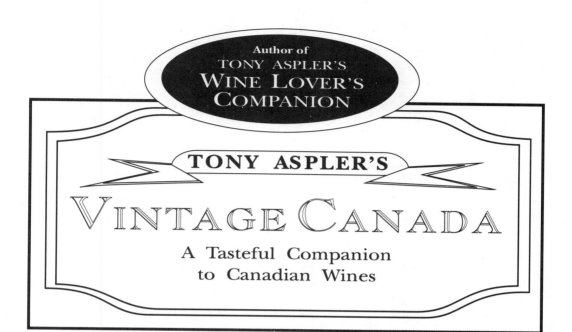

Author of
TONY ASPLER'S
WINE LOVER'S
COMPANION

TONY ASPLER'S

VINTAGE CANADA

A Tasteful Companion
to Canadian Wines

McGraw-Hill Ryerson
Toronto Montreal

TONY ASPLER'S VINTAGE CANADA

Copyright © 1993 by Tony Aspler

First published in 1993 by
McGraw-Hill Ryerson Limited
300 Water Street
Whitby, Ontario
L1N 9B6

1234567890 AP 2109876543

Canadian Cataloguing in Publication Data
    Aspler, Tony, 1939–
        Tony Aspler's vintage Canada : a tasteful
companion to Canadian wines

    Includes index.
    ISBN 0-07-551499-0

    1. Wine industry – Canada – History. 2. Wineries –
Canada. 3. Wine and wine making – Canada.
I. Title. II. Title: Vintage Canada.
TP559.C3A86 1992   338.4'76632'0971
                                    C92-095328-X

The author is represented by MGA Agency Inc., 10 St. Mary Street, Suite 510, Toronto, Ontario M4Y 1P9.

COVER AND INTERIOR DESIGN: MATTHEWS COMMUNICATIONS DESIGN
COVER PHOTO: GARY CRAILLÉ · THE IMAGE BANK

Printed and bound in Canada

For my late father
who drank wine for
sacramental purposes only,
but shared his life as if
he were a winemaker.

ABOUT THE AUTHOR

Tony Aspler is the most widely read wine writer in Canada. He has been active on the international wine scene since 1964. As a consultant and a wine judge, he makes frequent trips to the vineyards and wine fairs of Europe and is recognized as the leading authority on Canadian wines.

His previous books include *Tony Aspler's International Guide to Wine, Vintage Canada (1982), The Wine Lover Dines* and *Tony Aspler's Wine Lover's Companion*. He is a wine consultant to restaurants and hotels in Canada and the United States.

Tony Aspler has lectured extensively on wine in Canada, and has been accorded international honours for wine writing. The wine columnist for *The Toronto Star* since 1981, Aspler has also contributed to *Toronto Life, City & Country Home, Wine Tidings, Canadian Business, Food Service & Hospitality, The Wine Spectator* and *Wine & Spirit*.

CONTENTS

ACKNOWLEDGEMENTS

Sharing is second nature to wine lovers. Show interest and a winemaker will lead you to the cellar and introduce you to all his children.

Over the past sixteen years I have been privileged to meet virtually all Canada's winemakers and through their generosity I have tasted an unprecedented number of Canadian wines. I thank them for that opportunity and for their continuing dedication. And I would like to pay a special tribute here to all those people who are not winemakers but whose efforts behind the scenes to turn Canada into a globally recognized wine-producing country have made this book possible. I refer specifically to such institutions as The Canadian Wine Institute, The Wine Council of Ontario, The Vintner's Quality Alliance, The Ontario Grape Growers Marketing Board, The Association of British Columbia Grape Growers, The Grape Growers Association of Nova Scotia and the Association of Winemakers of Quebec.

I would also like to thank some special individuals who have made my research much easier and more pleasurable: wine writer Maurice Chenier in Montreal; Thomas Bachelder of *Wine Tidings* magazine; Dave Gamble, editor of *British Columbia Wine Trails*; Natalie Lévesque of Tourism Québec; Chris Coletta of BC's VQA; Connie Beilert of the BC Grape Growers; and particularly Peter Gamble, director of Ontario's VQA.

INTRODUCTION

Ten years ago I wrote a book called *Vintage Canada*. It was a history of winemaking in Canada, complete with profiles of the thirty-four wineries in five provinces that existed then (including Andrew Wolf of Alberta who makes wine from frozen California grapes). The book also contained tasting notes on all the wines—still, sparkling and fortified—that were available in provincial liquor stores at the time.

While researching that book I travelled across the country, visiting wineries, grape growers, liquor boards and government research stations and I sampled over 600 products. Only a handful impressed me then as being of international standard and my critical assessments, I admit now, leaned towards the charitable—rather like the statements you make after sitting through a school concert in which your kids are performing. I really wanted Canadian wines to be good and I did everything I could in that book and through subsequent wine columns and magazine articles to encourage our wineries to make wines Canadians could take pride in.

So much has changed in the industry in the last ten years that it is time for another assessment. Pressures of the Free Trade Agreement and GATT have radically altered the oenological landscape—geographically, financially and psychologically. Over that decade major wineries with long histories have disappeared, while many others have sprung up to take their place. There is no shortage of entrepreneurs who believe that Canada is a wine-growing country. Currently, there are 66 wineries in four provinces making wine from locally grown grapes (which is the focus of this book, not those operations in Quebec that bottle imported wines).

No excuses have to be made for Canadian wines today. They stand on their own merits in the global wine world. They win prizes in international competitions. They are exported to Europe, the Far East and the United States. They appear on the wine lists of fine dining-rooms and, more importantly, Canadian consumers have begun to realize that wines of quality are at last being produced in their own backyards.

Permit me to quote myself. Ten years ago, I wrote in *Vintage Canada*:

> Today the Canadian wine industry is on the verge of producing products in the blended table wine range that can stand up against those from any wine-producing country in the world. Canada may never produce a Château Lafite, a Richebourg or a Hermitage, but a fine Chardonnay or Johannisberg Riesling is certainly within reach—as well as wines that have nothing to do with a European taste tradition, like Seyval Blanc, Vidal, Baco Noir and Maréchal Foch. Given our climate and the delicacy of the vines which produce the noble wines of Europe we can only hope that through clonal selection the wineries can find varieties sturdy enough to withstand winter cold and fungal diseases and, equally important, to find the right soil and microclimate in which to plant them.
>
> It must not be forgotten that the Canadian wine industry—in terms of the production of table wines — really only began after World War II. It took the French and the Germans 2,000 years of trial and error to achieve their Lafites and Bernkasteler Doktors. With modern technology and European know-how the Californians, blessed with a better climate than Niagara or the Okanagan Valley, took 200 years to produce their excellent Cabernets and Chardonnays. Today, the Canadian wine industry is where California was in the late 1960s. We have nowhere to go but up. As long as it remembers it is a wine industry and not a commodities market where the bottom line is all that counts, it can win the respect and admiration of wine lovers across Canada.

Perhaps I was a little optimistic in my timeframe. In ten years we have not developed the way the Californians have. Our wineries have moved cautiously, even timidly. The second generation of small boutique operations (after Inniskillin and Château des Charmes in Ontario and the now defunct Claremont in British Columbia) have become the engine, dragging the old established firms reluctantly behind them into a bright new dawn.

Ironically, what has awakened the consumers' interest in Canadian wines both at home and abroad is not Chardonnay or Riesling, Cabernet or Pinot Noir but a luxury product as rare as it is expensive—Icewine. Icewine made in Ontario and British

2

Columbia from frozen grapes is the one wine that no wine lover can resist and we make it as well if not better than the Germans who invented it. Overseas buyers are beginning to clamour for our Icewine.

However, the industry cannot sustain itself on Icewine alone. It needs a solid consumer base for its inexpensive table wines, white and red, as well as its single vineyard, vintage-dated bottlings. More importantly, our wineries cannot rely on an export market for their financial health. Canadians have to drink Canadian wine and have it available to us in all provinces. Right now we experience the ludicrous situation of having free trade with the United States, but inter-provincial tariffs on our own wines. Surely it is not beyond the wit of our politicians to allow us to have British Columbia and Quebec wines in Ontario.

And what of the future? The optimism of our young winemakers is infectious. Taste their wines blind against comparable bottles from Europe and you will be amazed by the result. There is no question now that Canada is a wine-growing country even if the rest of the world has not woken up to that fact (wine books published in Britain still neglect to mention Canadian regions and major wine magazines such as *Decanter* have yet to publish articles on Ontario or British Columbia).

Then again, perhaps it is not a bad thing that Canadian wines have yet to be discovered. That means the best that we produce still remains within our borders for our own delectation and delight.

In the Beginning

*W*inemaking is the world's second oldest profession. According to a Persian legend it was a woman who first discovered the delights of the fermented grape. This unnamed heroine was a concubine in the harem of King Jamsheed. Her royal master had a weakness for grapes and ordered bunches to be stored in jars so that he could enjoy them at his table all year round (presumably as raisins).

One of the jars began to ferment and the raisins lost their sweetness. The king supposed that the juice was poisonous and had the container labelled as such. One day, our unknown benefactress, who suffered from constant migraines, decided to put herself out of her misery. Finding the jar marked "poison" she drank deeply and immediately fell asleep. She awoke feeling on top of the world and returned to the jar to finish it off. Summoned before the king to explain her odd, euphoric behaviour she confessed her misdemeanour. Intrigued, King Jamsheed ordered a quantity of wine to be made for the delection of his entire court. The fabled king is said to have lived for 700 years—the earliest testimonial we have to the salutary effects of the fermented grape.

William Younger, in *Gods, Men and Wine*, argues that winemaking may date back 10,000 years or more to the Magdalenian rock painters of southern France. "During the Upper Palaeolithic Age which marks the emergence of 'modern man', some of the conditions existed for the deliberate making of wine, although they did not exist for the deliberate growing of grapes."

It is a pleasing thought that those primordial artists working in the bowels of the earth with their charcoal and vegetable dyes might have stepped back to admire their work by the light of the fire, with a bowl of wine in their hands.

Certainly they would have had grapes to eat, if not to ferment, since wild vines have existed since the Tertiary Period, a million to 60 million years ago. But the first vigneron, who deliberately cultivated grapes, was Noah. According to the Book of Genesis (IX, 20), "Noah began to be an husbandman, and he planted a vineyard: And he drank of the wine, and was drunken; and he was uncovered in his tent." Scholars have placed that first vineyard near Erivan in Armenia, though they have yet to agree on what "uncovered" meant.

The Old Testament is replete with references to vineyards, grapes and wine. Perhaps the best-known has provided the logo for the Israeli Tourist Board—Moses' spies returning from Canaan, the land of milk and honey: "...and they came upon the Brook of Eschol and cut down from thence a branch with one cluster of grapes and they bare it between two upon a staff" (Numbers XII, 23). One bunch of grapes requiring two men to carry it! Grape growers through the ages must share this same sense of hyperbole when it comes to describing the quality of their harvest!

The story of Moses' spies has its echo in the first documented discovery of grapes growing in Canada.

In the summer of 1001 A.D., Leif Ericsson set sail from Norway in a Viking longboat. According to the two sagas written from oral sources around 1250, Leif, a newly baptized Christian, was "a big strapping fellow, handsome to look at, thoughtful and temperate in all things." But this did not prevent him from provisioning his crew of 35 with beer and mead to help them survive the rigours of the journey.

The expedition sailed first to Baffin Island which Leif named "The Country of Flat Stones," and then on to Labrador ("Land of Forests"). Historians still argue about where the intrepid explorer made his final landfall on the American continent — the place he was to call "Vinland." As Samuel Eliot Morrison says in *The European Discovery of America*, "There are few local histories of seaport towns between Newfoundland and the Virginia capes which do not open with a chapter asserting 'Leif Ericsson was here!' In the Latin translation of the sagas published by Thormodus Torfaeus at Copenhagen in 1705, the author identified Vinland unequivocally as Newfoundland.

In 1960 Helga Ingstad, a Norwegian archeologist, pinpointed Leif's landfall at L'Anse aux Meadows in northern Newfoundland. Morrison is convinced that this is the spot "where Leif Ericsson spent one winter and where members of his family founded a short-lived colony." The exact location is significant because of what the sagas tell us in the narrating of the "history" of the voyage to Vinland. According to a tale in the "Greenlanders Saga," one member of the party—Leif's foster father, a German named Tyrker—wandered off. Search parties were organized, but before they could set out Tyrker emerged triumphantly from the woods "rolling his eyes and babbling, first in a German dialect none of his shipmates understood, then in Norse." The crew gathered round him and the excited old man broke the news: "I found grape vines and grapes!" Leif was incredulous and not a little dubious. "Certainly," replied the German. "I was born where there is no lack of either vines or grapes."

Leif ordered his men to harvest the grapes and load them aboard along with the cargo of timber they had cut. When spring allowed the expedition to sail home again, Leif had already named the unknown country Vinland—the land of the vines.

Adam of Bremen was the first chronicler of Leif Ericsson's original voyage and around the year 1075 he reported to the King of Denmark that Leif "spoke of an island in that (northern) ocean, discovered by many which is called WINLAND, for the reason that vines yielding the best of wine grows there wild."

Grapes growing in northern Newfoundland? Grapes that produce "the best of wine"? Certainly, today, the finest European grapes as well as hybrids flourish in the Annapolis Valley above the Bay of Fundy in Nova Scotia. So perhaps there is a microclimate where the hardy wild grapes might have grown around L'Anse aux Meadows in Newfoundland.

Cynics have suggested that what Leif Ericsson actually found were either blueberries, wild currants, gooseberries or, possibly, the mountain cranberry. Samuel Eliot Morrison dismisses such speculation: "If it be objected that Leif Ericsson, after whooping it up in the court of King Olaf (of Norway), must have known wine and would not have been put off by a poor substitute made from berries, one may reply that, just as his father Eric (the Red) put the 'Green' in Greenland to attract settlers, so Leif put the 'Vin' in Vinland. And with such success as to throw off all Vinland-seekers for centuries!"

But it was 500 years after Ericsson before we have more evidence of grapes and winemaking in eastern Canada. In 1535 when Jacques Cartier sailed down the St. Lawrence on his second voyage to New France, he anchored off "a great island." Here Cartier found masses of wild grape vines growing up the trees. He named it Ile de Bacchus but on reflection—thinking that this might be seem too frivolous for his masters in Paris—renamed it Ile d'Orléans after the duc d'Orléans, son of his monarch, Francis I.

From this point on the history of the grape is closely bound with the history of Canada.

The Jesuit missionaries who followed in Cartier's footsteps brought sacramental wine with them and when they ran out they tried their hands at winemaking using the native wild grape. They recorded that the grapes were plentiful but the wine they produced (probably from *Vitis riparia*) was obviously only tolerable enough to be sipped at Mass, not to be quaffed back to warm the hearts of the settlers during the long winters.

The Jesuits may have been able to supply their own sacramental needs, but their congregation required something a little more palatable. In 1648, a certain Jacques Boisdon in Quebec City applied to the Council of New France for a licence to open the first tavern. The Council agreed and even supplied Boisdon with eight barrels of French wine, free of charge, to help him start his business. But in true bureaucratic style they set down stringent regulations: "to prevent any unseemliness, drunkenness, blasphemy or games of chance," the inn had to be located in a public square within sight of the church, allowing the priest to be a one-man Liquor Control Board.

But the Church fathers, far from frowning on the practice of winemaking, actively encouraged it. Father Jacques Bruyas wrote in a letter dated 1668: "If one were to take the trouble to plant some vines and trees they would yield as well as they do in France ... and (properly pruned) the grapes would be as good as those of France"—a sentiment which would be echoed down the years to our own day by every grape grower who put a plant in the ground.

If the new settlers, accustomed to the wines of France, were less than enthusiastic about the possibility of winemaking from wild grapes, the indigenous peoples of Upper Canada were untroubled by such latent wine snobbery. Indian tribes, such as the Seneca, Tuscarora and Cayuga, are believed to have offered tributes of fermented grape juice to the gods who lived at the foot of Niagara Falls. The ceremony, during which the wine was poured into the churning waters to placate the gods, was known as the Wischgimi. The bands travelled great distances to make their offering and as Percy Rowe suggests in *The Wines of Canada*, "It is conceivable that the journey would have been a dusty one so that the Indians were sufficiently tempted to slake their throats with a portion of the 'gifts'."

If wild grapes like *Vitis riparia* and *Vitis labrusca* flourished in eastern Canada it would not be until the nineteenth century when committed amateurs tried to cultivate vines for the express purpose of producing wines fit to drink. The wild *labrusca* grapes with their small berries would have produced a wine of poor quality—harsh and acidic, with a decidedly "foxy" flavour.

Father Bruyas' suggestion of planting vines had already been tried by British colonists in Virginia and the Carolinas at the instigation of Lord Delaware who, in 1619, imported French cuttings along with French vignerons to oversee their planting. The vines they planted died, unfortunately, before a commercial wine industry based on French *vinifera* grapes could be established in the new colonies. But their presence among the native varieties was enough to create new strains. Through cross-pollination with wild grapes the first North American hybrids were created.

THE EARLY YEARS

*I*n the years to follow, the nascent Canadian wine industry in the east was to benefit from American grapes which flourished in the more conducive climate of the south.

The poor performance of imported vines forced the early American winemakers to re-evaluate the native stock. As early as 1683, William Penn called for better viticultural practices to improve the quality of the vine in the hope that "the consequence will be as good wine as any European countries of the same latitude do yield." Some 90 years later, during the American Revolution, Governor John Penn's gardener, a certain John Alexander, discovered the first accidental hybrid growing by a river near Philadelphia. He had been experimenting unsuccessfully with European varieties, and some of them survived long enough to cross with nearby wild varieties. Alexander planted a cutting and happily it took root in Governor Penn's garden. The Alexander grape became popular around 1800 as the Cape, a name which suggested South African origins.

With the blessing of President Thomas Jefferson, who had vines growing in his garden in Virginia, the Alexander enjoyed a brief moment in the sun before it was eclipsed by two new hybrids —Isabella, introduced in 1816 and Catawba in 1823.

At the same time in Ontario a retired German soldier, Corporal Johann Schiller, was tending his *labrusca* vines on 20 acres of ground by the Credit River. He had built himself a house on North Dundas Street, Cooksville (now Mississauga) on land granted to him for his military service.

By 1811 Schiller, who had previous winemaking experience in the Rhine, was fermenting grapes he had presumably grown from cuttings of wild vines and early American hybrids furnished by settlers from Pennsylvania. He made sufficient quantities to be able to service his own needs and sell to his neighbours. Johann

Schiller is generally acknowledged to be the father of the Canadian wine industry.

We have no indication as to how long Schiller's winery lasted. The property was bought in 1864 by Count Justin M. de Courtenay, who formed a company called the Vine Growers Association. He extended the original vineyards to 40 acres of Clinton and Isabella grapes, making his Clair House label the largest in Ontario.

De Courtenay was an aggressive evangelist in the cause of Canadian wine, harrying the government of the day with letters and pamphlets to proselytize its members in support of the infant industry.

The owner of Clair House had begun his wine-producing experiences in Quebec. He was convinced that European grapes could not only grow in Lower Canada but could outperform their Burgundian cousins in terms of the wine they produced: "It will be easily perceived the importance attached in Burgundy to their wines," wrote de Courtenay, "and there is no reason why we should not produce better ones on the borders of the St. Lawrence."

To prove his point de Courtenay sent some bottles to the Premier of Lower Canada, L.V. Sicotta, on January 15th, 1863, with a covering letter:

> I have now the honour to present you with samples of wine furnished by the cultivated wild grape, and am persuaded that, making allowances for the green taste which it possesses in common with almost all new wines, you will consider it equal to ordinary Burgundy which it resembles not only in flavour but in its qualities and colour ... The fact that a good, sound wine can be produced in this country, I consider has been by me practically demonstrated.

The Honourable L.V. Sicotta was not won over by such confident huckstering and passed the bottles over to a government consultant, a Mr. McDougall, who pronounced the wine sour.

But de Courtenay would not take this criticism of his wine lying down. He shot back a letter to Quebec City full of righteous indignation: "I deny the wine in question being sour, but admit it to be bitter in consequence of containing too much tannin." The age-old cry of the winemaker: "all it needs is bottle-age."

What Justin de Courtenay could not accomplish in Quebec he tried with more success in Ontario. His Clair House wines he considered of sufficient quality to be exhibited in Paris in celebration of Canada's nationhood in 1867. On July 8th the *Toronto Leader* printed the following story:

The French exposition has established the character of our Canadian wines. The jury on wines, which would naturally be composed of the best judges to be found in Europe, speak in very high terms of the wines sent from the Clair House Vineyards, Cooksville. They find in them a resemblance to the Beaujolais wine, which is known to be the best produced in France. They say of those wines that they resemble more the great French table wines than any other foreign wines they have examined, and that the fact of the wine being so *solide* as to bear the sea voyage, and the variations of heat and cold without losing anything of either its quality or limpidity, should be a question of great consideration even to our own producers.

This authoritative opinion of the quality of Ontario wine will do more than anything else that could possibly occur, at present, to bring this wine into general use.... The time will come, we hope and verily believe, when grape-growing and wine-making will be one of the principal employments of our population; and when it does come, the cause of temperance will be advanced to a degree which could be reached by no other process.

De Courtenay had been vindicated. His red wine, at an alcoholic strength of 13%, was the talk of Toronto. But the newspaper's predictions failed to come about. In 1878, no longer able to secure a grant from the Parliament of Upper Canada, de Courtenay was forced to close his winery.

Justin de Courtenay, the flamboyant count who dashed off letters of blistering irony to parliamentarians, quoting Pliny and Virgil, overshadowed the efforts of those stolid Ontario farmers of lesser education who laboured quietly in the background. For example, Porter Adams was shipping grapes to the Toronto market from the Queenston area in the same year that de Courtenay was shipping his wines to France. John Kilborn—as early as 1862—won a prize of $3 at the Provincial Exhibition in Toronto for the "best bottles of wine made from the grape." Kilborn owned 17 acres of land on Ontario Street in Beamsville. In 1860 he reported to *The Canadian Agriculturalist* that his wine was fetching $1.75 a gallon locally "and probably would bring in more if we asked for it. At all events it is worth four times as much as the miserable stuff sold by our merchants under the name of wine."

Winemaking in the late nineteenth century was more of a basement hobby than a business. When it was not sold through the kitchen door it would have been available at the local drug store. Farm wineries such as those owned by John Kilborn and W.W. Kitchen of Grimsby were, however, large enough to advertise their products. Kitchen's broadsheet declared that his wines were "in use by some Hundreds of Churches for sacramental services." In addition, "It is sold by most of the principal Chemists in Canada East and West."

The problem for those early winemakers, whether they made it for their own consumption or profit, was the alcohol strength. The native hybrids like Catawba and Isabella were low in sweetness and high in acidity so sugar had to be added to the fermentation to bring up the alcohol level. The grapes would be pressed a second time after water or sugar syrup had been added to the skins to get every last ounce of juice out of the grape.

The first growers along that Niagara Peninsula, like Porter Adams, planted their vines basically to service the fresh fruit trade. One of the best table varieties, as well as an excellent taste for jams and jellies, was the Concord grape whose flavour is unmistakable to us today as the essence of virtually all grape-flavoured products. The grape was named after the Massachusetts town where it was propogated by a man who rejoiced in the splendid name of Ephraim Wales Bull.

As a boy growing up in New York's Hudson River Valley, Bull became interested in grape growing. In 1836, he moved to Concord to pursue his hobby more vigorously. And to make wine. In his quest for a grape which would survive the New England winter better than the Isabella, he planted the seeds of some wild *labrusca* grapes. The one that succeeded best he named Concord in honour of the town where it was raised.

In 1854, Bull offered his Concord vines to nurseries at a hefty price of $5 a vine. But the nurserymen managed to propogate the vine for themselves and Bull saw little remuneration for his gift to the North American wine industry. He died penniless in Concord's Home for The Aged in 1895. His tombstone bears the forlorn legend: "He sowed, but others reaped."

When the Concord grape was exhibited at the Massachusetts Horticultural Society, it was an instant winner. In his book *American Wines and How to Make Them*, Philip Wagner explains why. "It produces so cheaply and abundantly that it makes a dismal joke of all competition: it is virtually indifferent to climate, growing rankly in both hot and cold regions, and flourishes in practically any soil; it is immune to most of the vine diseases and thrives under neglect; it travels well and withstands storage moderately well; it does not winter kill..."

The only problem is that Concord grapes make awful wine. As grape juice it can be enjoyable or when its "foxy" taste is camouflaged as sherry or port, but as wine I'd rather drink the gum they used to stick on the label. Yet the Concord was to become the backbone of the Canadian wine industry up until the 1940s—and as the major constituent in the "Duck" range of pop wines it provided 90% of the company profits until the late 1970s.*

Not only did the Americans send their grapes north, they also dispatched their entrepreneurs whose presence would give the youthful industry a nudge toward the twentieth century. In the 1860s most of the operations in Ontario were small-volume businesses, a sideline for farmers who had crops other than grapes to harvest.

In 1866, "a company of gentlemen from Kentucky," according to a letter in the *Canadian Farmer*, "who have been in the grape business for 14 years, have purchased a farm on Pelee Island and planted 30 acres this spring, and intend to plant 20 acres next spring." Pelee Island—the most southerly part of Canada, on the same latitude as northern California—stands 12 miles to the north of Kelly's Island in Lake Erie. In 1860, Catawba grapes were successfully planted there to supply the wineries at Sandusky, Ohio, one of the oldest winemaking centres in the United States. (In 1893, Brights bought Catawba from Pelee Island to produce a sweet table wine.)

The southern gentlemen were D.J. Williams, Thomas Williams and Thaddeus Smith, who formed a company called Vin Villa to create the first commercial winery on Pelee Island. Before they had built a house on their land, they excavated a wine cellar, forty feet by sixty feet and twelve feet deep, which showed that this was to be no bathtub operation.

But Vin Villa was not to be without competition. A few months after the Kentuckians acquired land on Pelee Island, two English brothers, Edward and John Wardoper, purchased 15 acres and planted a rival vineyard. Today the Pelee Island Vineyards boast the largest *vinifera* planting in Canada—Riesling, Gewürztraminer, Chardonnay and Pinot Noir—planted by Walter Strehn in 1980.

An enterprising grocer in Brantford named Major J.S. Hamilton bought the grapes as well as finished wine from the Pelee vineyards. Hamilton had opened his store in 1871 and in the same year was granted a royal charter to sell wine and liquor. Three

---

*Ten years after it started its grape-breeding program in 1913, the Horticultural Research Institute of Ontario at Vineland had given up using the Concord as a "parent." In 1942, the Institute stated in its report that the goal of the grape-breeding program was to produce hybrids that no longer had the *labrusca* taste characteristics and resembled more those of the European *viniferas*.

years later he met Thaddeus Smith and was impressed by the yield of his vineyards (four to five tons per acre of Delaware and Catawba) and the quality of his wine. He asked Smith if he could sell Vin Villa wine for him in the eastern United States.

Hamilton also wanted to market these wines in Canada and to do so he entered into an agreement with the Pelee Island growers to transfer the winemaking operation from the island to the city of Brantford.

The assets of J.S. Hamilton and Company Limited, which absorbed the Pelee Island Wine and Vineyard Company in 1909, would be sold in 1949 to London Winery, giving that company the longest pedigree in the venerable art of Canadian winemaking.

In the same decade that Major Hamilton was shipping casks of wine over from Pelee Island, some 2,000 miles away, the Oblate fathers' tiny vineyard at their mission seven miles south of Kelowna in British Columbia's Okanagan Valley was reaching maturity. In British Columbia, as in Quebec, it was the Church that first fostered and encouraged the cultivation of the grape for winemaking.

If Justin de Courtenay moved from Quebec to Ontario to find more favourable microclimates in which to grow vines to produce better burgundies than those of France, other English-speaking farmers remained to battle the winters. A certain Mr. Menzies of Pointe Claire, Quebec, created a vineyard "on a larger scale than usual in the province" which he called The Beaconsfield Vineyard. Two years later he was joined by a partner but the association was brief. After a few months Mr. Menzies was forced to publish a pamphlet warning his clients that his former associate had set up a farm a mile from his own from which the rascal had been selling American wines under the name of The Beaconsfield Vineyard.

But the lustiest child in the nation's vinicultural nursery was Ontario. From the 1860s vineyards flourished in the Beamsville-Vineland-Grimsby area. Grape growers experimented in their own backyards to find a new variety that was disease resistant and winter hardy. The process was long and difficult. It takes at least three years for a vine to produce a commercial crop, let alone the years it takes to develop a successful crossing. So when a new variety was introduced the effect was rather like a coronation or the arrival of a royal baby.

In 1868, in Lockport, New York, two growers created what they were to call the Niagara grape by crossing the Concord with a relatively little known variety called the Cassady. It was to be the white wine equivalent of the unkillable purple Concord. The two growers, mindful of what had happened to Ephraim Bull, sold their vines at $1.25 a piece with a written understanding that the purchaser would return all cuttings to them so the vines could not be pirated.

In 1882 the Niagara grape was introduced to Ontario and, like the Concord, it is still with us.

By 1890 there were 41 commercial wineries across Canada, 35 of which were situated in Ontario. The great majority of these, fully two-thirds, were centred around Essex county, which in 1904 boasted 1,784 acres of vines. The pre-eminence of Essex as Canada's grape-growing centre was to last 20 years. By 1921 the grape vines had been torn out in favour of such cash crops as tobacco and soft fruit. A mere 50 acres remained, but this concentration was still greater than anywhere else in Canada.

In 1873, two years after Major James Hamilton had shaken the hand of the gentlemen from the South to confirm their business arrangement, George Barnes, a relative of Porter Adams by marriage, started a winery at St. Catharines. With the literalness of a German wine label, he embraced every function of the company in its name so there could be no mistaking its purpose: the Ontario Grape Growing and Wine Manufacturing Company, Limited. What it lacked in imagination, it made up for in longevity because it operated until 1988 as Barnes Wines.

George Barnes' vines had been in the ground one year when Thomas Bright and his partner, F.A. Shirriff, opened a winery in Toronto. In naming it they must have subconsciously realized they would have to move closer to their grape supply. They called it the Niagara Falls Wine Company and move they did 16 years later, in 1890, to the outskirts of the town. In 1911 they changed the name to T.G. Bright and Company.

Those years at the end of the nineteenth century showed a remarkable growth for Ontario, and for the grape-growing areas south and southwest of the province. At the turn of the century there were some 5,000 acres under vine along the Niagara Peninsula.

But two events were to check the new wine industry and to set it off on a path of incipient self-destruction: World War I and Prohibition.

PROHIBITION

*I*n the early days of this century what passed for the Canadian wine industry resided in Ontario. And those companies that survived into the 1900s were targets for the growing number of drum-beating temperance societies in the province, particularly in the rural areas. Some farmers refused to sell their grapes to winemakers, and by 1892 the public outcry against alcoholic beverages had reached such a crescendo that even the idea of planting more vineyards in Niagara came under scrutiny.

When World War I broke out the government's need for industrial alcohol to make explosives synchronized with the popular sentiment for prohibition. Once the Temperance Act had been passed the distilleries could be converted to the production of industrial alcohol for the war effort.

On September 15, 1916, the government of Sir William F. Hearst, himself an active Methodist layman and dedicated temperance advocate, passed the legislation known as the Ontario Temperance Act. Under its statutes all bars, clubs and liquor shops would be closed for the duration of the war. No one could sell any intoxicating liquor unless authorized to do so by the province and no one could "have, keep, give, or consume liquor except in a private dwelling house."

In 1916 and 1917 all but one of the provinces went dry. Quebec, which marches to a different drum in these matters, held out until 1919 and then proscribed the sale of liquor, but not wine or beer.

The Women's Christian Temperance Union of Ontario, the vanguard of the movement, had triumphed but political realities began to nibble away at their victory. Pressure from the strong grape growers' lobby caused the Conservative government to exempt native wines from the provisions of the act. Section 44 stated that wines made from Ontario-grown grapes could be produced by manufacturers who held permits from the Board of Licence Commissioners. This political sleight of hand was to elicit a raised eyebrow—if somewhat belated—from the editorial page of the *Toronto Telegram* (April 21, 1921): "There may be political reasons for protecting wine and banning beer. But there is no moral or social reason. There is no inherent vice in barley which does not also lodge in grapes."

When the Ontario Temperance Act became law there were ten operating wineries in the provinces. While they were able to vinify legally during Prohibition the government saw to it that consumers had a difficult time getting hold of it. Each winery was allowed one store outlet and that on its premises. Customers could only buy a five-gallon quantity or its equivalent in bottles—two cases. An extraordinary piece of double-think by a government dedicated to the proposition that the people must be denied alcoholic beverages!

Another bizarre anomaly of Prohibition in Canada was that while it might have been illegal to sell liquor, it was not against the law to manufacture it. Alcohol was readily available for "Sacramental, industrial, artistic, mechanical, scientific and medicinal purposes." And it was the medical profession that was to become the barman of the nation. A doctor could prescribe alcohol to a patient if he felt that patient might benefit from such "medicine." Peter Newman writes of those days in *The Bronfman Dynasty*: "As well as selling straight liquor through the drug stores to patients with doctors sympathetic enough to prescribe it, the booze was sold to processors who concocted a variety of mixtures for the drug trade, including a Dandy Bracer—Liver and Kidney Cure—which when analyzed, was found to contain a mixture of sugar, molasses, bluestone and 36% pure alcohol, plus a spit of tobacco juice."

Stephen Leacock summed up the social situation with the observation that "to get a drink during Prohibition it is necessary to go to the drug store ... and lean up against the counter making a gurgling sigh like apoplexy. One often sees there apoplexy cases lined up four deep."

Nevertheless, during the eleven years of Prohibition in Ontario the only alcoholic beverage that could be sold legally was wine. The natural effect was to spark off a mad scramble by European immigrants who had some brush with winemaking in the old country to get in on the act. And even those native-born Ontarians who could not tell wine from vinegar jumped on the bandwagon.

Wineries were started up in basements, at the back of grocery stores, in garages—and one even in the converted pig shed of a Beamsville farm.

The Board of Liquor Commissioners handed out permits with heady abandon to placate the vociferous grape growers' lobby. Between 1917 and October 31, 1927, no fewer than 57 licences for new wineries were issued, in addition to the ten that were already established.

The three major centres for these wineries were the Niagara Peninsula—at the source of the grapes; Toronto—as the largest urban population; and Windsor—to take advantage of the great thirst across the Detroit River. But distance from the vineyards was of little consequence to those early wine-producers. There were two successful wineries in the lakehead cities of Fort William and Port Arthur (Twin City Wine Company and Fort William Wine Co.), one at Kitchener (in the basement of Fred J. Kampmann's house), one at Belleville (John Tantardini who started in Guelph, eventually selling out to the Belleville Wine Company in 1926) and yet another in Sudbury (the Sudbury Wine Company). There were even two Toronto rabbis who made kosher wines: Rabbi M.H. Levy of Bathurst Street was granted a licence in 1921. His company was purchased in 1925 by Canada Wine Products Ltd., which in turn was swallowed by Jordan in 1938. The other was Rabbi Jacob Gordon, who manufactured Passover wine in the cellar of his home at 116 Beverly Street. In 1928 the rabbi's winery licence was purchased by the Oporto Wine Company on Danforth Avenue, which sold medicated wine. After a series of takeovers the rabbinical company—originally called the Concord Wine Co. Ltd. in 1923—ended up as part of Chateau-Gai in 1978.

Only those companies that made a drinkable product survived this extraordinary era —companies like Brights who introduced the first bottling line in Canada, Jordan Wines (a company formed to take over Canadian Grape Products Ltd., in 1926), the London Winery (which purchased a three-year-old licence from Giovanni Paproni in 1925) and the Turner Wine Company. This last enterprise dated back to 1885 when it was founded by a Brantford grocer—no doubt in competition with the enterprising Major J.S. Hamilton. They distributed a product known as "Turner's Tonic Bitters" which was heavy on alcohol and quinine.

As far as most winemakers were concerned there were no quality controls, no government interference and in many cases, little of the basic knowledge of the craft. American equipment and cooperage, hastily bought by the newly formed companies, was calibrated in US gallons as opposed to Imperial measurements; but this meant nothing to some unscrupulous manufacturers who were simply out to line their pockets at the expense of the public thirst. They squeezed their grapes—literally—till the pips squeaked and with added water they were getting as much as 600 gallons of wine from every ton of grapes. (Today the negotiated limit is 818 litres per tonne.) Sugar was poured into the vats by the sackful during fermentation to bring up the alcohol level. If the colour wasn't right after so much dilution there was always coal tar or vegetable dyes like cochineal to deepen it. Blocks of sulphur were pitched into the vats to kill bacteria and one enterprising vintner even used aspirins to control his fermentation.

For all those who made wretched wine under licence there were countless others who did so without the bureaucratic blessing of a permissive government. Unlike moonshine whisky, homemade wine was legal and the hobbyist who had a few hundred gallons of wine could always plead that he had made it for the home consumption of his entire family rather than for selling through the back door. Few such cases ever came to court and the government took a lenient view of new immigrants who wished to make their own wine when the LCBO was created in 1927. All they would require was a home winemaking licence and they could produce up to 100 gallons for their own use. (Today no such permit is required.)

In spite of the abysmal quality of most wines available during the eleven-year hiatus, the mere fact of Prohibition had focused the attentions of Canadians on their domestic wine industry. And Prohibition more than anything else turned Canadians into a nation of wine drinkers. During 1920–21 Canada consumed 221,985 gallons of domestic wine. A decade later the figure was 2,208,807 gallons—for Ontario alone! And 80% of it was a red port-style wine of maximum alcoholic strength made from the Concord grape.

After eleven years of social dislocation Canada passed through the wilderness of Prohibition. Even those who were loudest in its support saw that Prohibition had failed. Sanity finally prevailed. It was seen by most conservative politicians as a victory for "British values" over "all the evils...wished on Canada by agitators who took their ideals not from the motherland but from that hot-bed of political experiment, the American Middle West."

If the politicians could not stop the fermented juice of the forbidden fruit from finding its way down the throats of the people at least they could regulate its use.

Eventually, province after province would adopt a form of government control over the sale and distribution of alcohol—a system which involved a state monopoly, based on the Scandinavian model, and more importantly, control over the quality of the product. The new system meant that each province would decide, individually, which wines of the world they would make available to their consumers and how much they would tax them for that privilege.

With the advent of government liquor stores, consumers now had a focus for their complaints if the wines they purchased were substandard—and they had a lot to complain about. During Prohibition the mere ideal of beating the regulations in acquiring wine made the drinker overlook its dubious quality; but now it was legal and the government was held responsible for every bottle that tasted of vinegar, was black with sediment or contained such foreign bodies as spiders and flies. Some bottles never reached the consumer as they exploded on the liquor store shelves owing to a secondary fermentation—much to the consternation of the employees who felt as if they were working in a minefield. And the bottles themselves could be any shape. A.N. Knowles, Vice President of London Winery, recalls seeing the same label of his father's company on three or four different types of bottle. "Winery employees used to visit the junk yards," he said, "buy up boxes of old bottles, wash them out and fill them with wine. Bottles were hard to get in those days."

In Ontario, the government acted after 1928 by bringing in a rudimentary quality control for the products it accepted for sale from the wineries. The new Liquor Control Board under Sir Henry Drayton, a former federal minister of finance, administered the new regulations which set a maximum of 250 gallons per ton of grapes, limiting the amount of water that could be added to the wine. The new restrictions stressed cleanliness of operations above all and fixed the permissible level of volatile acid at 4%, which was still enough to make a wine taste of vinegar. (Even this generous limit was beyond the capabilities of most basement vintners.) But the bureaucrats had to move cautiously since the Depression was looming and the vocal farmers' lobby was concerned about the dropping price of grapes. King Concord had fallen as low as $12 a ton.

In an effort to improve the quality of winemaking, the Board's chief analyst, Bert Bonham, suggested that the Provincial Department of Health set up a winemaking school at the laboratory in the east block of Queen's Park. When the more marginal companies found their products were being refused for listing at the liquor stores their winemakers flocked to attend. Many were new immigrants whose command of English was limited and they decided that winemaking in the new world was not for them. The courses lasted for two years but they had the desired effect. The bathtub school of winemaking as a commercial proposition quietly died.

Encouraged by the government, viable companies such as Brights and Jordan began buying up the licences of these precarious operations lock, stock and barrel at prices as low as $5,000 to $10,000. Over the years Brights acquired 13 such licences, not for the wine which was generally sent to the distillers, nor for the equipment, but for the privilege of owning another retail store. The wineries still had their own single outlet and the government now allowed them to locate these stores away from the facility in the cities of their choice. By this expedient the government eventually reduced the number of Ontario wineries from 51 to eight.

The next problem was to rationalize the sale of tonic wines and patent medicines which were readily available over grocery store counters. Doubtful products such as Dandy Bracer (Liver & Kidney Cure) were extraordinarily high in alcohol and of questionable therapeutic value. The Liquor Control Board came up with an elegant solution. The sale of medicated wines could continue but the makers had to blend in a "certain additive." If the tonic in question were taken without reference to the stated dosage the additive induced vomiting in the would-be patient. Needless to say such nostrums quickly disappeared from the shelves for all time.

But the well-intentioned government did not address the fundamental question of what Ontarians were drinking. Wines made from the Catawba and Concord grapes were selling for 30 cents a bottle. They were sweet and highly alcoholic—twice the strength of European table wines. (In 1932 the government established a 20% limit.) In an effort to help the wine industry and the growers, the Ontario government removed the 50 cent a gallon tax on wines in January 1929 to enable the Liquor Board to sell Ontario products at such a low price. These beverages were known as "Block-and-Tackle" wines—you drank a bottle, walked a block and you could tackle anybody!

Further representations from the grape growers and the wine lobby convinced the Department of National Revenue to allow the fortification of domestic wines. By adding pure grape spirit the producers could now manufacture fortified wines. The new legislation was a godsend for the industry which could now use wine that was badly oxidized. Before, they would have had to pour it into the sewer. Now they could distill it for grape alcohol.

The Ontario grape growers, too, were happy because they could sell more grapes and doubly so when in 1931 the government banned the importation of grapes from outside the province. The Liquor Board also insisted that the wineries pay a minimum of $40 a ton for those they bought.

Concerned about the rocketing sales of these new fortified wines—42% of all wines sold in 1933—the government appointed a Wine Standards Committee in an attempt to wean Canadians from such heady products towards lighter wines to be drunk with meals. In its report the Committee suggested that it was the industry's responsibility to supply the marketplace with a range of "good quality light wines." It stated that, "The distribution of pamphlets fully describing the merits and low alcoholic content of table wines will unquestionably materially assist in promoting the sale of same."

But the Canadian public was not yet ready for wines of 9 to 12% alcohol; their palates had become accustomed to fortified products which were closer to whisky than wine in their alcoholic strength. It would take another 25 years before the industry would suddenly be caught offguard by the demand for the style of wines consumed by the Europeans. In the meantime, port and sherry would be the mainstays of the Canadian industry, especially during the Depression when disenchantment and despair found solace in cheap alcohol.

The brand leaders at this time were Brights' Catawba sherry, (affectionately known as "Brights' Disease") and Jordan's Bran-Vin.

Without the ability to advertise or promote their products—a legacy of the Prohibition mentality—the Wine Standards Committee loftily reported that "many people in this province associate drinking of any kind of alcoholic beverage with fostering drunkenness"—the wineries struggled through the 1930s to keep their industry alive. No new winery licences were to be granted in Ontario to allow those currently operating to stay afloat.

But in those dismal years between the two world wars a dedicated group of individuals laboured in their respective vineyards to produce wines of quality and if this goal proved to be beyond the capabilities of the native grapes such men were determined to find varieties that could do so.

In the early thirties, Harry Hatch, the new owner of Brights, brought a young French chemist and winemaker from Montreal to his Niagara Falls winery. A French aristocrat by birth, Viscomte Adhemar de Chaunac de Lanzac was working at Brights' Quebec plant in Lachine at the time. Nurtured on the wines of his native land, he had little time for the company's ports and sherries and set about to make experimental batches of dry table wines from Catawba and Delaware grapes he found in Bright's Concord vineyards. Harry Hatch was so impressed by the results that he gave de Chaunac his head to experiment further, setting aside funds for his winemaker to buy vines from New York State to be planted in the company's experimental plot. In 1937, de Chaunac went to France to find out more about the hybrids the French were experimenting with.

At the same time the Horticultural Research Institute at Vineland was conducting similar experiments to provide the wineries with hardy varieties to resist winterkill. Patiently, the scientists at Vineland had been crossing vines to produce the magic grape free of *labrusca* flavour. William Rannie writes in *The Wines of Ontario* that the Institute planted and evaluated 57,000 seedlings between 1913 and 1928 and retained only six as "promising for table grapes and five wine making!"

World War II interrupted this quiet revolution, the fruits of which would eventually change the nation's wine-drinking habits.

Cut off from Europe during the war, the wineries retrenched. All experimentation ceased; it was enough to keep the companies going until the servicemen returned home. As members of a non-essential industry winemakers found themselves short of bottles and were forced to recycle those they could find.

During the war wineries were rationed by the government as to how much wine they could sell; the figure varied between 75% and 80% of their production in the base of year 1939. Wine drinkers used to line up for three hours outside the liquor stores until they opened at 10 a.m.

The Canadian wine industry marked time and waited for the peace that would signal its renaissance.

Post WW II

When the war was over, Adhemar de Chaunac of Brights was determined to upgrade the quality of his company's table wines. In 1946 he visited France again and ordered 40 European vine varieties—hybrids and such noble *viniferas* as Pinot Chardonnay (the grape of white burgundy) and Pinot Noir (red burgundy). The vines were planted in the spring of that year, some on their own roots, others grafted onto a European rootstock known as Couderc 3309.

Ten varieties, including the two *vinifera*, adapted reasonably well to their new surroundings. In 1952, Harry Hatch, the owner of Brights, ordered 600 acres of Concord and Niagara vines torn out between Lake Ontario and the Niagara Escarpment to make way for the new varieties. Among them was a hybrid called Seibel 9549 which would be rechristened De Chaunac in 1972 as an accolade to the Frenchman for his contribution to the Canadian wine industry.

De Chaunac also selected a list of varieties for the Horticultural Research Institute at Vineland after discussion with J.R. Van Haarlem who was in charge of grape development at the time. These vines were planted in the spring of 1947. HRIO's initial experiments suggested that a hybrid called Chelois would be the grape of the future. It took ten years before they found that Chelois was susceptible to a disease called "dead arm."

Other commercial concerns were also experimenting. Parkdale Winery, based in Toronto, brought in vines from Hungary in 1947. Although they proved to be a "dead loss" they did have some success with Gamay Beaujolais on their test farm and with Johannisberg Riesling and a muscat-flavoured Couderc, which de Chaunac had brought in as well. (A young nurseryman in Niagara-on-the-Lake, Donald Ziraldo, would eventually propogate these vines from cuttings and, in 1971, would sell them to other wineries.)

Of all the hybrids planted at Vineland, it was the Seibel 9549 which would prove to be the leading commercial variety for red wines in Ontario during the 1960s and '70s, or as we know it today, the De Chaunac.

If Brights thought back in the 1950s that their Pinot Noir vines would give them wine to rival the best of Burgundy—as Justin de Courtenay had dreamed about—they were disappointed. The vines produced a mere ton per acre, well below commercial viability; in fact, a "nuisance volume."

But the initial step to plant better grapes had been taken and Brights' former Director of Viticultural Research, George Hostetter (the first vintner to be awarded The Order of Canada), could justifiably claim that their 1946 experiment predated the introduction of the finest French grapes to the Eastern United States by that outspoken champion of *vinifera*, Dr. Constantin Frank.

In 1955 Brights produced the first 100% Canadian Pinot Chardonnay from the vines de Chaunac brought back from France. And now every Canadian winery worth its salt has a Chardonnay among its premium varietal wines.

De Chaunac also brought to Canada 88 vines of a red hybrid called Maréchal Foch, (a cross between Pinot Noir and Gamay). Nine years later, having propogated them and allowed them to reach maturity, Brights put on the market a wine called Canadian Burgundy in 1958, much to the disgust of the French who were unhappy that their finest wines should be impugned with such an adjective.

Brights shared their research willingly with the rest of the industry and when de Chaunac retired in 1961 the wineries were nudging their growers to replant their vineyards with more acceptable hybrids varieties like Seibel, Foch and Verdelet and, where possible, *viniferas*. They were now in a position to produce the style of products the Wine Standards Committee had called for back in 1933. Only this time, it was the consumers' voice they heard demanding drier wines that resembled those of France and Germany—if not in complexity and finesse, at least in alcoholic strength and without the overriding "foxy" *labrusca* taste. But old Mr. Fox would be a long time a-dying and a new craze would give him a breath of life again.

Social behaviour is governed by the law of the pendulum and wine drinking like everything else has its cycles, it fads and its fashions. In the affluent sixties young people became a formidable force in the marketplace and the wine companies began to take notice of this new section of society. In the late sixties, at the request of a Detroit tavern owner, a German winemaker in Michigan created a blended sparkling wine named "Cold Duck" which immediately took off.* Everyone started making Cold Ducks—a 12% alcohol, sparkling wine made from *labrusca* grapes with sugar and water added.

In 1952 when Brights purchased the Fred Marsh Wine Company one of the products Marsh was working on was a 7% sparkling wine. De Chaunac overcame the problems of instability and developed Brights Winette which was originally sold in a 13 ounce pop bottle. Since it was a sparkling product the champagne tax of $2.50 per gallon was applied. M.F. Jones of Brights argued successfully with the LCBO to lower the tax and the mark-up because of the product's low alcohol level. The tax per gallon was fixed at 25 cents.

The 7% wine was an inspiration: not only did it score Brownie points with those pressure groups who wanted to see less alcohol consumed, but it saved the company vatfuls of money. The *labrusca* grapes which were—and still are—used are the cheapest on the market. The crush is stretched with water and the excise tax is half that of table wines.

For several years Brights had the market to themselves with Winette and Du Barry Sparkling Vin Rosé.

However, out in British Columbia, Andrew Peller at Andrés was looking for a new product line and, realizing that there were high profits to be made from this style of beverage, he and his company took the plunge.

Andrés created a range of Chanté wines (as in *enchanté*) and one of these evolved as the "wine" that would create a revolution in Canadian taste—Baby Duck. At its peak, two years after its 1971 launch, one out of every 24 bottles of wine sold in Canada was Andrés' Baby Duck.† The rest of the trade—and by now it

---

*There is a European tradition, convivial though unsanitary, which calls for the guests to pour their glasses into a common bowl at the end of the party. The mixture of wines of whatever hue are then sampled. This is called in German *das caulde Ende*—"the cold end." The German word *Ente* meaning duck, very similar in sound, is a pun which gave the winemaker his name.

†As Winston Collins wrote of the Baby Duck phenomenon: "Most Canadian grow up on soft drinks, and prefer to consume their alcoholic beverages flavoured, sweetened, carbonated, chilled, and diluted—rum and Coke, rye and

was corporate business run by marketing men and Harvard-trained MBAs—scrambled to make a light, sparkling wine. A whole menagerie of pop wines descended on the liquor board shelves as a consequence; their names suggested Noah's ark rather than a wine shop: Little White Duck, Luv-a-Duck, Fuddle Duck, Baby Bear, Baby Deer, Pink Flamingo, Gimli Goose, and Pussycat, were just some of them.

The generation of postwar Canadians may have turned their backs on the whisky-substitutes of the Depression era, but there were few Canadian wines of sufficient quality to fill the gap between the ports and sherries and the Ducks. The provincial liquor boards, seeing there were hefty profits to be made by catering to the growing demand for wine, began to increase their imports of European products until in 1975, 3,315 imports were listed across the country as opposed to 1,875 domestic products. This posed a new problem for the indigenous wineries that had to contend with a public who knew what it didn't want from Canadian wineries and went elsewhere for what it thought it ought to be drinking—the wines of France, Italy and Germany.

Alarmed by the influx of inexpensive wines from overseas, the grape growers and the wineries appealed to the Ontario government.

In 1976, Queen's Park instituted the Ontario Wine Industry Assistance Programme. The LCBO sent around a memo to all its stores saying "Delist imported wines that are not meeting their sales quotas and thereby make room for Ontario wines ... Urge store managers and wine consultants to mention Ontario wines ... Store managers will rearrange present shelf-facings and thereby make room for additional brands of Ontario wines...." The government also initiated a program for the growers to help them change over from *labrusca* to the more desirable hybrids and *viniferas* so that the wineries could produce European-style wines. The program provided interest-free loans for five years.

The "Big Four" wineries of Ontario—Andrés, Brights, Chateau-Gai and Jordan—in searching for ways to sell more of their prod-

ginger. Baby Duck was an easy transition from soft drinks to not-too-hard alcohol for the baby-boom generation, young people who may have been attracted to wine but were put off by its "come-alive-for-a-dollar-five" image, or else intimidated by the overly sophisticated aura of something with an unpronounceable foreign name." (*Saturday Night*, June 1982) ucts began to build bottling plants and blending facilities in non-grape growing provinces. The initial capital outlay would soon be ameliorated by a grateful province which would now list all that company's products in its stores. Their investment was welcomed because the new facilities provided jobs locally. And the companies gained the added benefit of being able to manufacture wines without the regulations that restricted them in Ontario and, to a lesser extent, in British Columbia.

The mid-1970s were a watershed for the Canadian wine industry. The large companies were desperately searching for a table wine that would appeal to the nation's palate to compete with such imported blends as Black Tower, Blue Nun, Colli Albani and Donini.

Indications from south of the border suggested that Americans were drinking white wine instead of red and the same thing would happen here. The sherry and port market virtually collapsed. Diet- and health-conscious Canadians switched their allegiance from red to white and there were hardly enough quality white hybrid grapes in the ground to satisfy the demand.

The Baby Duck drinkers had graduated to Mateus Rosé and the blended wines of Europe. Imports enjoyed a cachet on the strength of their label alone, irrespective of the quality of what was in the bottle.

In 1976, Calona wines in British Columbia entered the field with a wine to compete with the top-selling Black Tower called Schloss Laderheim. It looked suspiciously like a Rhine Riesling in its brown bottle and German gothic script. In 1978, Chateau-Gai launched Alpenweiss in Ontario—the first of that company's wines to contain California grapes blended with the locally grown Seyval. The success of these two wines sent the other companies off in the direction of brand names and labels which were unashamedly European in appearance and style. The age of the packaged wine had arrived. The way the bottle looked was as important as what was in it.

The "Big Four," with their modern plants strung out across the country, not only had to contend with burgeoning imports but also with the arrival of a new source of competition—the boutique wineries. The last licence issued by the Ontario government was in 1930, but the young nurseryman, Donald Ziraldo, so impressed Major-General George Kitching, Chairman of the Liquor Board of Ontario, with his concept of a cottage winery that he and his winemaker Karl Kaiser were given the green light to produce 10,000 gallons of wine from the 1974 vintage. Inniskillin Wines was born that year.

A few months earlier, a Hungarian winemaker named Karl Podamer had been granted a licence to create the Podamer Champagne Company at Clinton, Ontario. These two small wineries were the first since the bad old days of Prohibition and paved the way for other such adventuresome entrepreneurs as Alan Eastman at Charal (now defunct), Paul Bosc at Château des Charmes, Joe Pohorly at Newark (subsequently renamed Hillebrand Estates Winery), and Enzo DeLuca and his winemaker Carlo Negri at Colio Wines in Harrow.

In British Columbia the first estate winery, Claremont, was opened in 1979. This opened the doors for Uniacke Cellars, Sumac Ridge and Gray Monk. And in 1980 the tiny Grand Pré Winery began fermenting grapes grown on its own property near Wolfville in Nova Scotia.

These cottage enterprises were dedicated to producing labour-intensive wines of quality from *vinifera* and hybrid grapes and would nudge the big wineries in both grape-growing provinces to follow their lead. The public, in the belief that small is better, snapped up the wines of Inniskillin and Château des Charmes and overenthusiastic nationalists held blind tastings against European products to prove that Canadian wines could hold their own in the international marketplace.

There is no question that since the early 1980s Canadian wines have improved out of all recognition to what was offered to the consuming public in the past. Tasted blind in competition against wines of similar style and character from Europe or other New World regions they have more than held their own. Slowly, a style is evolving in Ontario and British Columbia that is unique to these growing regions and has nothing to do with California taste profiles, let alone those of France, Italy or Germany. Canadian white wines, both dry and sweet, have come of age. The reds are improving steadily and some Pinot Noirs, Merlots and Cabernets are very find indeed. If, over the next ten years, our winemakers can continue to perfect their cold fermentation techniques and their use of barrel ageing we will have a wine industry to rival those whose products currently take up the majority of space on our restaurant wine lists and provincial liquor board racks.

ONTARIO

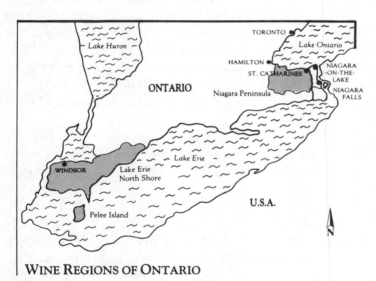

WINE REGIONS OF ONTARIO

Ontario's vineyards, which produce 90% of Canadian wines, lie in the same latitudes as Languedoc-Roussillon in southern France, the Chianti Classico zone of Italy and Spain's Rioja region. From a geographer's perspective, the Niagara Peninsula, the north shore of Lake Erie and Pelee Island are smack in the middle of the northern hemisphere's wine belt.

True, cities such as Hamilton and London, Ontario, may not enjoy the same climate as Cannes and Florence. But Lakes Erie and Ontario smooth the rough edges of our harsher weather—reflecting sunshine and storing heat in the summer, acting like hot water bottles during the winter—making it possible to grow wine grapes of quality in Ontario.

Today there are 17,000 acres of vines in the province, down from the 24,000 that existed prior to the Free Trade Agreement with the United States. That political reality, coupled with a GATT ruling in 1988, has radically changed the Ontario wine industry—ironically, for the better though at the time winery executives and farmers joined in a collective tearing of hair, convinced that the end of the world was at hand.

In Ontario, politics and wine go hand in hand and to appreciate the dramatic change in the style and quality of its products we have to understand the history involved. The year 1988 will go down in the annals as a watershed year for Ontario wine. On September 1st that year the Ministry of Agriculture and Food revamped The Wine Content Act. Under pressure from the estate wineries, the government banned the use of *labrusca* grapes (native North American varieties such as Concord and Niagara) in table wines. They also lowered the amount of wine that could be made from a tonne of grapes from 1,022 litres to 818 (products at the upper limit owed as much to the local reservoir as they did the vineyard) and they allowed the wineries to raise the amount of imported wine they could use in any one of their own blended products from 30% to 70%. (Today the figure is 75%.) In order to protect the growers, the wineries were committed to buy a minimum 25,500 tonnes of Ontario grapes each year for 12 years starting with the 1988 harvest.

But from the wineries' viewpoint, if they were forced to purchase expensive local grapes and then compete on a level playing field with international giants such as Ernest & Julio Gallo (who annually make two-and-a-half times the amount of wine all Canadians consume in one year) they had to have some break on the price of the raw material. Ontario, incidentally, is the only wine region in the world where grape prices are negotiated before the harvest.

The formula arrived at was typically Canadian: it's called the Grape Price Support Program. It takes the average price per tonne grown in California and relates it to the same grape or its equivalent variety grown in Ontario. For example, no Seyval Blanc is grown in California, but the equivalent varieties are Chenin Blanc and French Colombard. The average laid-in cost per tonne of Chenin Blanc or French Colombard delivered in Ontario when the regulation was set was $381; the Ontario Grape Growers Marketing Board price for Seyval Blanc that year was $661 per tonne. Under the program the wineries paid the landed California price and the government gave the difference to the grower in the form of a transition subsidy that decreases with the years and will be eliminated in the year 2000.

However, even these "reforms" were not going to turn the industry around by themselves. Apart from personal pride, there was no real incentive to make quality wines since the Ontario government cushioned the local industry against foreign imports with a mark-up differential of 65% (and that included the wines of British Columbia as well as those of Europe and the new world). Spurred on by the deal that Ottawa was cooking up with Washington that would give preferential treatment to Californian wines in Canadian markets, exasperated members of the European Community ruled that provincial liquor boards contravened GATT regulations by discriminatory mark-ups against their wines. Under the Free Trade Agreement, the mark-up on American wines was cut by half on January 1, 1990 and the remaining tariff phased down to parity with Canadian wines over the following five years. Under the GATT deal that International Trade Minister John Crosbie's team brought back from Brussels in December 1988, the preferential mark-up given to Canadian products against European and Australian products was to be phased out entirely over a period of seven years for blended wines and 10 years for wines made from 100% Canadian-grown grapes. This distinction is significant because it gave the growers and wineries an economic incentive to concentrate on purely Canadian wines. (The growers had asked for a 15 year phase-down period.)

Given the harsh reality of foreign competition and Canadians' traditional indifference to the locally grown product, farmers were faced with the prospect of unwanted grapes. To ease the burden, the federal and provincial governments stepped in with a hefty financial assistance package to the tune of $156 million. Fifty million of that was earmarked for the contentious vineyard "pullout" program. In order to compete in the global wine world the Ontario industry had to downsize. Some 7,000 acres of unwanted *labrusca* and hybrid vines were pulled (in BC under a similar program nearly one-third of the vineyards were ripped out). The scheme, however well intentioned, basically rewarded failure. Those growers who had insisted on maintaining *labrusca* vineyards when there was no call for those grapes (the government bought any surplus so they always had a market for them) received fat cheques to cease and desist, while more committed farmers who had struggled to create Chardonnay, Riesling, Pinot Noir and Cabernet Sauvignon vineyards got no support at all.

The most significant occurrence in 1988 was the creation of the Vintners Quality Alliance (for details of the regulations see the last section of this book). The VQA is Ontario's appellation system, and it has also been embraced by the BC wine industry. Negotiations are currently underway with Nova Scotia and Quebec to bring these regions under the umbrella.

Every wine growing region around the world has its own appellation system which is a set of minimum production standards followed by a bureaucratic tasting for typicity. The fledgling VQA rules are designed to establish conditions to create quality wines although as yet they do not address the concerns of grape yields per acre or the amount of wine produced from a given number of vines.

Eventually, the geographic designations of Niagara Peninsula and Lake Erie North Shore will be fragmented into smaller subzones, just as Bordeaux is broken down into communes such as St-Émilion, Pauillac, Graves, etc. There is a case, for instance, for wines grown on the bench of the Niagara Escarpment to be differentiated from those grown on the lakeshore plain since their taste profiles are perceptibly different.

There can be no question that the banning of *labrusca* and the creation of the VQA have been the two major factors that have signalled a dramatic leap forward for the quality of Ontario wines. Exposing the industry to global competition has also positively affected the thinking of winery executives. They soon realized that they could not compete with the economies of scale practiced by the major Californian houses when it comes to house blends. But they could compete with varietal wines of quality—a situation that fits nicely with the current consumer preferences for less but better.

One interesting sidelight on the phoenix-like rebirth of the Ontario wine industry is the subtle shift of power from the large commercial wineries—Andrés, Brights, Cartier and London—to the new kids on the block. Since the inception of the Vintners Quality Alliance the philosophies and marketing strategies of the major estate wineries, Inniskillin, Château des Charmes and Hillebrand, have become the motivating force of the industry. These enterprises, which had all started as cottage wineries in the middle and late 1970s, became the engine for the industry, fuelled by aggressive competition from smaller, newer companies such as Cave Spring Cellars, Vineland Estates, Reif, Henry of Pelham, Konzelmann and Stoney Ridge. Their voices are the ones that people are listening to and it is their wines that began to turn up on restaurant wine lists. The large commercial concerns, in an effort not to be left behind, jumped on the VQA bandwagon and started to produce wines of sufficient quality to merit the appellation.

It's one thing to produce better products, but quite another to convince jaded consumers with long memories that Ontario wines can now rival some of the best white wines around the world, both in the dry and sweet categories. For years the wineries had taken an apologetic stance, dressing their products in labels that suggested that they came from a castle on the Rhine or a chateau in Bordeaux rather than an industrial park in Niagara-on-the-Lake, Oakville or Woodbridge, Ontario. Since 1988, all that has changed. When the dust of free trade settled, the wineries repositioned themselves to withstand the cold blast of competition. Niche marketing became the watchword of the industry and a new self-confidence was born.

Somehow the message had to be gotten out. But after years of vilification and consumer neglect the industry had forgotten how to blow its own horn. In 1991, a $5 million government-financed advertising campaign was undertaken to convince Ontario consumers to try the wines again. "We're ready when you are" was the ambiguous copy line. Two television commericals and a series of print ads had the desired effect because in that fiscal year sales of VQA wines rose 1.1% while imports fell 3.8%. (According to VQA's director, Peter Gamble, that increase in market share translates into over 750,000 bottles sold at a value of $5 million.) These figures become more significant when you realize that in the three previous years Ontario wine sales had declined by 7 ½% each year! Early sales figures for 1992 are even more dramatic. In the month of April VQA wines were up nearly 100% over the previous year.

The industry received another shot of adrenalin when Inniskillin won the Citadel d'Or, prix d'honneur, at Vinexpo at Bordeaux in June 1991 for its Vidal Icewine 1989. Only 19 wines out of 4,100 entries from around the world were accorded this signal honour. Now Ontario Icewine has an international profile and is much in demand as a cult wine. Those expensive half bottles of honey-sweet nectar have become the calling card of the industry as some 20 wineries currently produce it.

The next phase in the development of Ontario's wine culture is the emergence of farm wineries—growers who had once been content to tend their vineyards and sell their grapes to wineries are now going into business for themselves. John Marynissen of Marynissen Estate, Eddy Gurinskas of Lakeview Cellars and Roberto Quai of Quai du Vin are examples of this new trend. With the proliferation of small wineries the obvious next step is to create a form of agri-tourism in southern and southwest Ontario to encourage visitors just as they do in California. Who knows, the Niagara Peninsula just might become Napa East.

ONTARIO WINERIES

ANDRÉS WINES

P.O. Box 550
Winona, Ontario
L0R 2L0
phone: (416) 643-4131
fax: (416) 643-4944

Andrew Peller was 58 when he founded Andrés Wines in Port Moody, British Columbia in 1961. He would have opened up in Ontario but provincial bureaucrats turned down his winery licence application because of his flagrant beer advertising on radio under the guise of selling his ice. (Under the Peller name he owned a brewery and an ice factory.) After an early success, facilities in Calgary and Truro, Nova Scotia, were opened to get listings in those provinces, but business reversals forced Andrew's son, Dr. Joseph Peller to take over the financial reins of the company. In 1969, Andrés bought their winery in Ontario and five years later a winery in St-Hyacinthe, Quebec, followed by the Rouge Valley Winery in Morris, Manitoba.

The mid-1970s was Andrés era with the success of Baby Duck followed by the German-sounding Hochtaler. But the company got left behind in the *vinifera* revolution when the small wineries began to dictate public taste. It was not until 1991 that they realized the Andrés name—synonymous with Baby Duck—was not going to sell Chardonnay and Riesling. They introduced the Peller Estates label to market their varietals that conform to VQA regulations. In 1991, they made their first Icewine and have limited amounts of Cabernet Sauvignon.

Winemaker: Barry Poag

Production: 750,000 cases

Average tonnage crushed: 5,000

Annual imported tonnage: 3,000

Winemaking philosophy: "To answer broad consumer needs with a selection of superior quality 'commercial' wines and the more upscale market with a selection of wines that are unique in character and premium in quality."

LCBO wines: *white*—Auberge, Boisseau, Botticelli, Cellar Cask, Cellar Cask Reserve, Cellar Cask Reserve Dinner, Domaine D'Or, Domaine D'Or Chardonnay, Domaine D'Or Supérieur, Grand Canadian Chablis, Hochtaler, Hochtaler Dry, Hochtaler Gold Riesling, Hochtaler Light, Wintergarten

red—Botticelli, Cellar Cask Dry, Cellar Reserve, Cellar Reserve Dinner, Domaine D'Or, Domaine D'Or Supérieur

Own stores: Seyval Blanc★
Peller Estates wines—French Cross★, Chardonnay★, Vidal★, Chambourcin★, Cabernet; Andrés Aurore, Johannisberg Riesling★

Sparkling wines: *Charmat process*—Canadian Champagne Dry★, Blush Champagne, Kurhauser Trocken Sekt, Select Brut; *7% sparklers*—Baby Champagne, Baby Duck, Baby Duck White, Chante Blanc, Moody Blue, Sangria, Spumante

Sherries: Almond Cream, Club House Gold, Medium Dry, Regency Fine Old, Richelieu Golden Cream

Specialty products: Madrigal Dessert NV; *under licence*—Stone's Ginger Wine, Bulmer's Strongbow Cider

Stores: at wineries

Barrie:	Bayfield Centre, 320 Bayfield
Bramalea:	Miracle Mart (Highway 7 & Dixie)
Brampton:	A & P Centennial Mall Westbram Food City (400 Queen St. W.) Food City MacKay Plaza Food City Conestoga Square Plaza
Cambridge:	Zehr's, 180 Holiday Inn Rd. Zehr's, South Cambridge Mall
Collingwood:	Blue Mountain Mall, 55 Mountain Rd.
Dundas:	Miracle Ultra Mart, 119 Osler Dr.
Etobicoke:	IGA, 600 The East Mall Garden Market, 245A Dixon/Islington
Guelph:	Zehr's, Willow West Mall Zehr's, 297 Eramosa Rd.
Hamilton:	Lloyd D. Jackson Square, 2 King St. W. Fortinos, Kenridge Plaza Fortinos, 50 Dundurn St. Fortinos, 65 Mall Rd. Fortinos, Eastgate Square
Kitchener:	Zehr's HiWay Market, 1375 Weber St. E. Zehr's, 700 Strasburg
London:	A & P, Adelaide Centre A & P, 387-401 Wellington Rd. S. A & P, Byron Village Zehr's, Treasure Island Plaza
Mississauga:	A & P, King Ten Plaza Miracle Mart, Westdale Plaza Food City, Deer Run Plaza Food City, 6040 Glen Erin Dr. A & P, 1240 Eglinton Ave. W.
Nepean:	Loblaws, 1460 Merivale Rd.
Oakville:	Food City, Maple Grove Plaza
Orangeville:	Zehr's, Heritage Mall, 54-4th Ave.
Oshawa:	Loblaws, Kingsway Village A & P, 285 Taunton Rd. E.
Owen Sound:	Heritage Place, 135-16th St. E.
St. Catharines:	Zellers, 366 Bunting Rd.

A & P, Midtown Plaza, 126 Welland Ave.
A & P, 275 Geneva St.
Food Terminal, 318 Ontario St.
A & P, 149 Hackzel Rd.

Scarborough: Miracle Mart, 5085 Sheppard Ave. E.
A & P, 2131 Lawrence Ave. E.

Stoney Creek: Fortinos, Fiesta Mall, 102 Highway 8

Waterloo: Zehr's, Beechwood Plaza

Willowdale: Miracle Mart, 4775 Yonge St.

Winery store hours: Monday through Friday, 10 am – 5 pm
Saturday & Sunday, 12 pm – 5 pm

Tours: minimum 10 persons, $1.50 per person, tasting 7 products; Deluxe Tour $4.95; Wine & Cheese Experience $9.95

Public tastings: during store hours

BRIGHTS WINES

P.O. Box 510
4887 Dorchester Road
Niagara Falls, Ontario
L2E 6V4

phone: (416) 358-7141
fax: (416) 358-7750

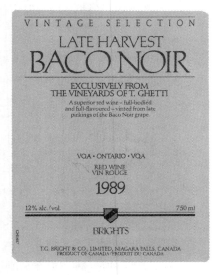

With the demise of Barnes, Brights is now Ontario's oldest winery dating back to 1874 when it was called The Niagara Falls Wine Company and operated out of Toronto! As Canada's largest winery (after acquiring Jordan), it has a long and distinguished history, especially in its research and development of grape varieties suitable for Ontario winters. Thanks to its long-time oneologist Adhemar de Chaunac who worked for the company from the late thirties to the early sixties, Brights was the first company to produce a non-*labrusca* table wine (Manor St. Davids Claret from Chelois grapes), the first *vinifera* varietal (Chardonnay 1956), the first 7% sparkling wine (long before Baby Duck uttered its first quack), the first bottle-fermented sparkling wine (Brights President 1949), the first "champagne" made exclusively from Chardonnay grapes and the first Canadian sherry to be made by the Spanish method using flor yeasts and the solera system.

The company has a huge portfolio of products, yet still manages to produce small parcels of varietal wines under the Experimental Cellars label and Vidal Icewine of excellent quality. Their Sawmill Creek label takes advantage of the Wine Content Act which allows for the blending of up to 75% off-shore material into Ontario wines.

In 1991, Brights underwent a $10 million expansion of its Niagara Falls plant to consolidate all its winemaking operations under one roof. The company exports to the USA, Cuba and Trinidad.

Winemaker: Jamie Macfarlane

Acreage: none

Average tonnage crushed: 10,000 tonnes

Grapes bought in: 10,000 tonnes

Winemaking philosophy: "Quality, yesterday, today and tomorrow."

LCBO wines: *white*—White House, Dry White House, House Chablis, Maria Christina White, Maria Christina Dry White, Maria Christina Light White, Cuvée du Berceau, Warnerhof, Entre-Lacs White, Ste-Michelle Selection, Liebesheim, Toscano White, Mon Village White, Manor St. Davids Medium Dry, Sauterne, Vidal, Le Cruchon

red—Red House, Dry Red House, Cuvée du Berceau, Maria Christina Red, Maria Christina Dry Red, Entre-Lacs Red, Toscano Red, Cresta Roja, Still Cold Duck, Mazel Tov, Baco Noir★

Sawmill Creek label white—Chardonnay (Yugoslavia/Ontario), Fume Blanc (Washington/Ontario)★, Dry Riesling (Washington/Ontario), Semillon Chardonnay (Bordeaux/Ontario), Zinfandel-Gamay (California/Ontario), Sawmill Creek White, White Reserve

Sawmill Creek label red—Red Reserve, Red Merlot-Baco, Cabernet-Baco

Own stores: *white*—Town of Tweed White, Village of Eganville, Riesling, Gewürztraminer★★, Vidal★★, Vidal Icewine★★, Sawmill Creek Sauvignon-Riesling, Sawmill Creek Sauvignon-Chardonnay, Sawmill Creek Vidal Icewine★, President's Choice, Chairman's Choice

red—Cabernet Franc★, Late Harvest Baco Noir★, Merlot★★, Cabernet Sauvignon★★, Sawmill Creek Zinfandel-Gamay★

Sparkling: Spumante Bambino, Spumante Bambino Berry, Peach, Lonesome Charlie, Jordan Crackling Rosé; President Chardonnay Canadian Champagne★, President Pink Champagne, President Brut, Gold Seal Pink Canadian Champagne, Gold Seal Dry Canadian Champagne, Sunquest Champagne

Sherry: Cream Sherry, Pale Dry Select, President Sherry, '74 Sherry, Dry Sherry, Napoleon Sherry, Hermit Sherry, '67 Sherry, St. Georges Sherry, Branvin Sherry, Sippin Sherry

Port: President Port, '74 Port, '67 Port

Specialty wines: Durouget, Dry Vermouth, Sacramental

Ciders: Valley Premium Dry, Growers Extra Dry, Growers Dry

Stores (68):

Ajax:	Harwood Mall
Barrie:	(coming soon)
Burlington:	Supercentre Fairview Rd.
Cambridge:	John Galt Centre
Chatham:	Chatham Centre
Coburg:	Northumberland Mall
Cornwall:	Eastcourt Mall
Guelph:	Silvercreek Parkway Bullfrog Mall Stone Road Mall
Hamilton:	Centre Mall Stoney Creek Limeridge Mall Miracle Food Mart (James St.)

Kingston:	Herbie's
Kitchener:	Dutch Boy (King St. E.) Fairview Park Mall
London:	Sherwood Forest Mall (A&P) White Oaks Mall Masonville Place Wonderland Mall
Midland:	Mountainview Mall
Oakville:	Miracle Food Mart Hy & Zel's
Orillia:	Orillia Square Mall
Ottawa:	Carlingwood Mall Lincoln Heights Galleria Zellers (Cyrville Rd.) George St.
Pembroke:	West End Mall
Peterborough:	Portage Place Shopping Centre Zellers
Pickering:	Supercentre
St. Catharines:	The Pen
Sarnia:	Clearwater
Stratford:	Sobey's
Tillsonburg:	Town Centre
Thornhill:	Hy & Zel's
Toronto East:	Woodside Square Fairview Mall Zellers (Lawrence & Midland)
TorontoCentral:	Knobhill (Lansdown Ave.) Dominion (Parkwood Village) Knobhill (Weston Rd. & 401) Zellers (Jane & Finch) Don Mills Shopping Mall King St. W.
Toronto West:	Knobhill (Dixie & QEW) Zellers (Dixie & Dundas)

Bramalea City Centre
Central Parkway Mall

Waterloo:	Zellers
Whitby:	Whitby Mall
Windsor:	Central Mall
	University Mall
	Devonshire Mall
	Grand Marais Rd.
	Eastowne Plaza
Woodstock:	Zellers

Store hours: vary with locations

Tours: May 1 to October 31: Monday through Saturday, 10:30 am/2 pm/3:30 pm; Sunday, 2 pm/3:30 pm

November 1 to April 30: Monday through Friday, 2 pm; Saturday & Sunday, 2 pm/3:30 pm. Group tours for 20 or more on request.

CARTIER WINES & BEVERAGES

2625 Stanley Avenue
Niagara Falls, Ontario
L2E 6T8

phone: (416) 354-1631
fax: (416) 354-0161

In 1989 the management team of Chateau-Gai and its sister winery Casabello in BC bought out the enterprise (including the holding company Ridout Wines) from Labatts and renamed it Cartier Wines & Beverages. Chateau Cartier (orignally Parkdale Wines of Toronto) was one of the companies Labatts took over in 1973.

The new owners, Rick Thorpe, Don Triggs, former winemaker Allan Jackson, Allan George and Peter Granger styled their operation as "the largest employee-owned manufacturer and marketer of wine and modern adult beverages." As a large commercial winery existing since 1928, Chateau-Gai had placed most of its emphasis on blended brand name table wines and had introduced Canada's first wine cooler as well as the first wines in tetrapaks and a wine-based cream liqueur.

The company operates 42 stores around the province called "The Wine Rack."

Winemaker: Mira Ananicz

Average tonnage crushed: 5,500 tonnes (all grapes bought in on long-term contracts)

Production: 1,000,000 cases (wine & wine-based drinks)

Winemaking philosophy: "To produce constantly a well-made, high quality wine that will be widely accepted by the consumer."

LCBO wines: *white*—Adagio, Heritage Estates Chablis, L'Ambiance, Chantonné, Alpenweiss, Alpenweiss Dry, Alpenweiss Light, Capistro Dry, Capistro Light, Edelwein, Gala Dry, Gala Medium, L'Escapade, San Gabriel, Sauterne, Vintner's Choice (French), Vintner's Choice (German)

red—Chantonné, Heritage Estates Burgundy, L'Ambiance

sparkling—(all Charmat process) Alpenweiss, Spumante Bianco, Spumante Classico, Brut Champagne, Dry Champagne, Pink Champagne

Own stores: Trillium label series—Gewürztraminer; Chancellor, Villard Noir

Sherries: Hallmark Cream★, Hallmark Dry, Heritage Cream, Heritage Dry, Heritage Very Pale, Imperial, Private Stock, Stamford Park Cream, Stamford Park Dry, Old Niagara

Ports: Concord, Private Stock

Vermouth: Dry

Stores:

| Balderson: | Balderson Cheese Company, Highway #511 |
| Brampton: | Shoppers' World, Highway #10 & Steeles |

Brantford:	Lynden Park Mall, 84 Lynden Rd.
Burlington:	Burlington Mall, 777 Guelph Line
Etobicoke:	201 Lloyd Manor Rd.
Gloucester:	Gloucester Centre, 1980 Ogilvie Rd.
	Beacon Hill Shopping Centre, 2339 Ogilvie Rd.
Hamilton:	Eastgate Square, 75 Centennial Parkway N.
	A&P Store, Centre Mall, 1147 Barton St. E.
Kingston:	Kingston Shopping Centre, 1080-96 Princess St.
Kitchener:	95 King St. W.
London:	First London Centre, 1080 Adelaide St. N.
	611 Wonderland Rd. N.
Milton:	55 Ontario St. S.
Mississauga:	Dominion Store, Meadowvale Town Centre
Nepean:	Merivale Mall, 1942 Merivale Rd.
Newmarket:	Upper Canada Mall, 17600 Yonge St.
Niagara Falls:	2625 Stanley Ave.
North Bay:	Northgate Square, 1500 Fisher St.
North York:	York Gate Mall, 1 York Gate Blvd.
Oakville:	Bronte Village, 2441 Lakeshore Rd. W.
Oshawa:	Oshawa Centre, 419 King St. W.
Ottawa:	Bayshore Shopping Centre, 100 Bayshore Dr.
Richmond Hill:	Hillcrest Mall, 9380 Yonge St.
Sault Ste Marie:	Station Mall, 293 Bay St.
Scarborough:	Bridlewood Mall, 2900 Warden Ave.
	Miracle Ultra-Mart, 355 Bamburgh Circle
	Cedarbrae Mall, 3495 Lawrence Ave. E.
	Morningside Mall, 255 Morningside Ave.
	Malvern Town Centre, 31 Tapscott Rd.
Thornhill:	The Shops on Steeles, 2900 Steeles Ave. E.
Toronto:	1354 Queen St. W.
	731 Queen St. E.
	403 Parliment St.

560 Queen St. W.
Shoppers World, 3003 Danforth
77 Wellesley St. E.
Hudson's Bay Centre, 2 Bloor St. E.
2447 Yonge St. (at Erskine)
Loblaws Superstore, 17 Leslie St. (Lakeshore)
Royal Bank Plaza, Upper Mall Level
103 Cosburn Ave. (at Pape)

Store hours: 10 am – 9 pm Monday through Saturday

Tours: no

Public tastings: no

CAVE SPRING
CELLARS

3836 Main Street
Jordan, Ontario
L0R 1S0

phone: (416) 687-9633
fax: (416) 682-9171

Cave Spring is a model for what small Ontario wineries should be. The company produces a limited number of wines, but each has a style and quality that expresses what the region is capable of growing. The "farm on the bench" is owned by John and Len Pennachetti who went into partnership with Dr. Tom Muckle (who owns French Oak vineyard) and winemaker Angelo Pavan in 1986. The winery and store are located seven kilometres away in an old stone building in Jordan that used to be an apple warehouse dating back to 1870. In 1978, the Pennachettis planted the original 12 acres of vines. Much of the company's award-winning Riesling is supplied from French Oak vineyard. Cave Spring is unique among small wineries in only using *vinifera* grapes for its products. All grapes are sourced from the Beamsville Bench of the Niagara Escarpment located between Twenty Mile Creek and Thirty Mile Creek. The principals are so dedicated to the Bench as "Ontario's finest growing microclimate" that they have called their newsletter *Benchmarks*.

The company buys sixteen new barrels for each vintage. Angelo uses a rotary vacuum filter to get the cleanest possible juice from the lees.

Winemakers: Angelo Pavan, Robert Summers

Acreage: 70

Soil: Moderately well-drained clay loam soil of the benchland. A steep north-facing slope affords good natural water drainage and excellent air drainage. Close proximity to the Niagara Escarpment gives a relatively high concentration of mineral deposits from erosion which add complexity as trace elements in the wine.

Varieties: Chardonnay, Riesling, Gamay, Pinot Noir, Cabernet Sauvignon, Cabernet Franc, Merlot

Production: 15,000 cases

Average tonnage crushed: 200 tonnes

Grapes bought in: 25 tonnes

Winemaking philosophy: "100 per cent *Vitis vinifera* to produce only premium varietal wines. No house wines produced. Minimal intervention in the winemaking process with fining on juice only, never on finished wines. Filtration is kept to an absolute minimum with diatomaceous earth filtration only prior to bottling. No pad filtration."

LCBO wines: *white*—Chadonnay Bench★, Riesling Dry★, Riesling Off-Dry★, *red*—Gamay Noir

Own store: *white*—Chardonnay Musqué, Chardonnay Reserve★, Chardonnay Barrel-fermented★, Riesling Reserve, Indian Summer Riesling★, Riesling Botrytis Affected★, Riesling Icewine★★, Gewürztraminer

red—Pinot Noir, Merlot, Gamay Reserve, Gamay Rosé

Store on premises: Tuesday to Saturday, 10 am – 5 pm; Sunday 12 pm – 5 pm; closed Mondays

Tours: yes

Public tastings: by appointment

CENTRAL
VALLEY
WINES

98 Crockford Blvd.
Scarborough, Ontario
M1R 3B7
phone: (416) 752-1616

After nine years of operation Central Valley Grapes & Juices became Central Valley Wines in May 1992, when Simon DiLiddo decided to make wine from the raw material he tankered in from Lodi, California. He had a loyal following of Italian home winemakers, many from his native town of Monte Leone (Foggia) near Naples, who now buy his wines which he sells in bulk in 10 to 20 litre plastic containers. He blends a white and a red with 30% Ontario grapes. Simon eventually plans to bottle his wine in the more orthodox format of 750 mL. His winery is a 9,000 square foot facility in an industrial area of Scarborough which used to be a metal factory.

The wines are currently fermented in 1,100 gallon stainless steel tanks, but some oak will be brought in for aging. Only two blends are made at present, a red and a white, but Simon has ordered Californian Pinot Noir, Johannisberg Riesling, Gray Riesling and Cabernet Sauvignon to extend the range.

Winemaker: Simon DiLiddo

Production: 300 hectolitres

Winemaking philosophy: "Selling bulk wine for everyday people."

Wines: Own store: *white*—(70% Californian Chenin Blanc and French Colombard with 30% Ontario Seyval Blanc)

red—(70% Californian Ruby Cabernet, 30% Ontario De Chaunac)

Store hours: Monday to Friday, 9 am – 6 pm
Saturday, 9 am – 5 pm

Tours: yes

Public tastings: 9 am – 5 pm, Monday to Saturday

**CHÂTEAU DES
CHARMES WINES**

P.O. Box 280
St. Davids, Ontario
L0S 1P0

phone: (416) 262-4219
      1-800-263-2541
fax: (416) 262-5548

Paul Bosc trained at the University of Dijon and made wine in Algeria before emigrating to Canada. A stint as winemaker with Chateau-Gai (now Cartier) convinced him there was an opportunity to make fine wines in Niagara. In 1978, he opened his own winery with its 60-acre vineyard with lawyer Rodger Gordon as a partner. Paul did much to convince the industry that the future lay in *vinifera* varieties and his early Rieslings and Chardonnays were models for other wineries.

His winemaking style is totally Burgundian, especially in his penchant for the difficult Aligoté grape and his insistence in making a Gamay Beaujolais Nouveau every year (the best in Ontario). He also makes the best champagne method sparkling wine in Canada.

Paul's wife Andree and his son, Paul Jr., are both very active in the company. The black-labelled Estate refers to the original farm with its concrete bunker of a winery, while Paul Bosc Estate refers to the property purchased in St. Davids in 1989 with its dramatic French chateau-style home. The Boscs own a 93-acre vineyard on St. David's Bench, as yet unnamed. Paul, Sr., will not submit hybrids for the VQA designation. He uses Allier oak barrels for his range of Chardonnays.

Winemaker: Paul Bosc, Sr.

Acreage and Soil: Château des Charmes Estate—60 acres, Chardonnay, Riesling, Gamay, Pinot Noir, Aligoté, Auxerrois. Four different soil types, 70% sandy loam, some clay.

Paul Bosc Estate Vineyard (1985)—50 acres (30 planted), Chardonnay, Pinot Noir, Gamay, Riesling, Cabernet Sauvignon,, Cabernet Franc, Merlot. Vineyard features extensive drainage

St. David's Bench Vineyard—93 acres (14 planted), Chardonnay, Pinot Noir, Auxerrois, Gamay, Aligoté, Sauvignon Blanc. Heavily under-drained. Pinot Noir and Chardonnay are ear-marked for champagne production and this will be the site of a new winery facility.

Varieties: Chardonnay, Riesling, Pinot Noir, Gamay, Aligoté, Cabernet Sauvignon, Cabernet Franc, Merlot

Production: 50,000 cases

Average tonnage crushed: 700

Grapes bought in: approxiately 250 tonnes

Winemaking philosophy: "Paul Bosc produces wines which are the closest to the French style by virtue of his heritage (fifth generation French winegrower) and education. His experience in Burgundy has allowed him to enjoy his greatest success with those varieties (Chardonnay, Pinot Noir, Gamay, Aligoté) and he has produced a range of styles (Champagne, Nouveau, Blanc de Noir, dry whites, dry reds) with these varieties."

LCBO wines: *white*—Chardonnay, Cour Blanc, Estate Chardonnay★, Gamay Blanc, Riesling, Sentinel Blanc, Seyval Blanc

red—Cour Rouge, Gamay Noir, Gamay Cabernet, Pinot Noir★, Sentinel Rouge

sparkling—Sec Canadian Champagne★★

Own stores: *white*—Estate Riesling TBA★, Estate Aligoté★,

Estate Auxerrois, Nokara Estate Chardonnay, Late Harvest Riesling★★, Estate Pinot Blanc de Noir, Paul Bosc Estate Chardonnay★, Estate Gewürztraminer, Riesling Icewine

red—Estate Pinot Noir★, Paul Bosc Estate Chardonnay★, Paul Bosc Estate Late Harvest Riesling★, Paul Bosc Estate Cabernet, Paul Bosc Estate Cabernet Sauvignon, Paul Bosc Estate Merlot, Paul Bosc Estate Cabernet Franc★

sparkling—Brut Canadian Champagne★

Stores (4): At winery

Ottawa:	Minto Place, Laurier and Lyon
Oakville:	Bronte Harbour, Bronte & Lakeshore Rd.
Toronto:	Minto Plaza, Bay St.

Hours: Monday through Sunday 9:30 am – 5:30 pm at winery store; 10 am – 6 pm at other locations.

Tours: by appointment

Public tastings: during store hours

**COLIO WINES
OF CANADA**

1 Colio Drive
Harrow, Ontario
N0R 1G0

phone: (519) 738-2241
fax: (519) 738-3070

Colio, as its name suggests, was founded by a group of Italian businessmen in 1978. They brought over a winemaker from Trentino Alto-Adige, Carlo Negri, for their first crush in 1980. The style of wines from the beginning was unrepentantly commercial, but Carlo's natural ability has given them a flair generally lacking in competitively priced brand-name wines. The winery is located in their village of Harrow and its exterior belies the extent of the investment in stainless steel within.

In March 1992, Colio purchased the vineyard acreage of the former Kingsville Estate winery.

Carlo not only produces Icewine but he has gone back to his roots to produce a Vin Santo wine he first called Nobile and their Vin de Curé (made from grapes dried in a greenhouse.) Colio is the only winery to use grapes from all three of Ontario's designated viticultural areas in its blends and American oak.

Winemaker: Carlo Negri

Acreage: 35 (plus 110 acres of the Kingsville Estate property for the 1993 vintage)

Variety: Vidal

Production: 80,000 cases

Average tonnage crushed: 900 tonnes

Grapes bought in: 600 tonnes

Winemaking philosophy: "To produce dry wines which not only are Italian in style but also coincide with all major wine-producing countries. To be proud of the entire production, not only of a small percent of the production that would be written up from wine tastings. All the wines Colio enters in wine tastings and competitions are produced in quantities available to the public, mostly through general listings."

LCBO wines: *white*—Bianco, Bianco Secco, Carlo Negri Chardonnay★, Castle Cellar, Extra Dry, Pinot Blanc★, Riesling Dry★, Riserva Bianco

red—Cabernet Franc, Maréchal Foch★, Riserva Rosso★, Rosso Secco, Winemaker's Reserve★

sparkling—Chateau D'Or Canadian Champagne★ (Charmat process), Spumante

Own stores: Barone Bianco, Chablise, Chardonnay, White Wine; Barone Rosso, Castle Cellar Red, Red Wine, Blanc de Noir, Vin de Curé★, Icewine, Port, Sherry

Stores: at winery

Amherstburg: Fort Malden Mall, 400 Sandwich St.

Leamington: Country Fair Mall, 250 Erie St.

Tecumseh: Green Valley Plaza, 13300 Tecumseh Rd.

Windsor: A&P Store, 6740 Wyandotte St.

Bright's Grove: 2600 Lakeshore Rd.

London: 1166 Commissioner's Rd.

Port Colborne: Port Colborne Mall, 287 West Side Rd.

Waterloo: Westmount Plaza, 50 Westmount Rd.

Neapean: 250 Greenbank Rd.

Oakville: 125 Cross Ave.

Store hours: 10 am – 6 pm. Late hours some nights.

Tours: Wednesday 1 pm, Saturday from 12 pm to 4 pm. Groups and bus tours welcome Monday to Saturday by appointment.

Public tastings: during store hours

CULOTTA WINES

1185 North Service
Road East
Oakville, Ontario
L6H 1A7

phone: (416) 844-7912
fax: (416) 844-2228

In 1984 Peter Culotta officially turned the California grape business he inherited from his father into a winery. He had incorporated the company five years before and 1983 was his first vintage. Culotta's location between Toronto and Niagara-on-the-Lake (opposite the Ford plant on the QEW) suggests the industrial nature of the enterprise. The original Columbus labels suggested the Italian style of the wines made by a German winemaker, Rudi Müller who had worked for Chateau-Gai, Andrés and Barnes.

The current winemaker, Bob Claremont, used to run his own estate winery in the Okanagan. The style of the company is geared towards easy-drinking table wines, using imported juice to flatter Ontario grapes. The first production of Vidal Icewine was in 1991. Some wines are aged in "Yugoslavian oak ovals—off premises." The wine for their "champagne" is sent to Montravin for secondary fermentation by the Charmat process.

Winemaker: Bob Claremont

Grapes bought in: Approximately 60% of Culotta's grape requirement is imported either as juice or finished wine. The rest is Ontario product.

Production: 25,000 cases

Winemaking philosophy: "The philosophy of Culotta is to produce an affordable everyday wine in the style and character enjoyed by our European ancestors. It is also our goal to enhance our image and reputation by utilizing the expanded availability of premium off-shore varieties to complement superior Ontario hybrids and limited local *viniferas*."

LCBO wines: *white*—Riesling Special Reserve★, Chardonnay★, Chablis, Seyval Blanc

red—Cabernet Sauvignon★

Own stores: DeChaunac/Foch, Petite Sirah, Merlot, Gewürztraminer, Champagne, Gluhwein, Maréchal Foch, Vidal Icewine

Winery store hours: 9 am – 6 pm

**D'ANGELO
VINEYARDS**

5141 Concession 5
R.R. #4
Amherstberg, Ontario
N9V 2Y9

phone: (519) 736-7959
fax: (519) 736-8788

Salvatore D'Angelo planted his vineyard in 1983. As an accomplished amateur winemaker his ambition was to open his own winery—which he did seven years later. Located south of Windsor and just east of Amherstberg, in the heart of Essex County, the winery bears the Lake Erie North Shore appellation. Only grapes grown on the estate are used in Sal's wines which are vinted in his temperature-controlled fermenting room.

Winemaker: Salvatore D'Angelo

Acreage: 12

Soil: clay loam; vineyard at the centre of Essex County, surrounded by Lake St. Clair and Lake Erie. Well drained, with breezes off Lake Erie six kilometres away.

Varieties: Chardonnay, Riesling, Pinot Blanc, Seyval Blanc, Vidal, Cabernet Sauvignon, Pinot Noir, Merlot, Gamay, Maréchal Foch

Production: 2,000 cases

Average tonnage crushed: 50 tonnes

Grapes bought in: none

Winemaking philosophy: "To produce the best wines from our own vineyards. We make wine the old-fashioned way. We grow it."

LCBO wines: Vidal

Own store: *white*—Seyval Blanc, Riesling, Chardonnay, Pinot

Blanc, Gamay Blanc de Noir, Premium Select Late Harvest Riesling, Vidal Icewine

red—Maréchal Foch, Pinot Noir, Merlot, Cabernet Sauvignon, Gamay Rosé

Store hours: 10 am – 6 pm

Tours: yes

Public tastings: during store hours

DE SOUSA
CELLARS

3753 Quarry Road
Beamsville, Ontario

phone: (416) 563-7269

John and Mary De Sousa are Canadian farmers who remember the wines of their native Portugal. In 1987, they decided to turn the grapes they grew high on the Bench of the Niagara Escarpment into Portuguese style wines. They hired Dieter Guttler, formerly a partner and winemaker at Vineland Estates, to produce a red, a white and a limited edition Riesling under the Dois Amigos label.

Wines: *white*—Dois Amigos (Vidal, Riesling and Chardonnay) Riesling Limited Edition

red—Dois Amigos (De Chaunac, Maréchal Foch and Pinot Noir)

ESTATE

HENRY OF PELHAM

1469 Pelham Road
R.R. #1
St. Catharines, Ontario
L2R 6P7

phone: (416) 684-8423
fax: (416) 684-8444

Empire Loyalist Henry of Pelham whose lugubrious hand-drawn features grace the winery's labels is an ancestor of the Speck family, owners of this historic property. Henry's father, Nicholas Smith, was a bugle boy in the Revolutionary War of 1776. The graveyard next to the winery attests to the fact that the property has been in Smith family in an uninterrupted line.

The modern, well-equipped winery, located on the Bench of the Escarpment, is housed behind the ancient coaching inn (1842) with its atmospheric cellars, now the tasting room, wine shop and cooperage storage. When Paul and Bobbi Speck and their three sons took over the property in 1988 there was already a 20-acre vineyard that had been planted 75 years ago. They have planted 55 more acres of vines with a further 100 acres at their disposal.

A restaurant and wine school are planned.

Winemaker: Ron Giesbrecht (formerly with Brights)

Acreage: 70

Soil: Heavy clay/loam soil called Smithville Till Clay, high in calcerous content which contributes to low yields. Good air drainage and water run off. Lower humidity than the lakeshore below and marginally higher heat accumulation.

Varieties: Chardonnay, Riesling, Cabernet Sauvignon, Baco Noir, Seyval Blanc

Production: 11,000 cases

Average tonnage crushed: 145 tonnes

Grapes bought in: 80 tonnes (mainly from the Bench)

Winemaking philosophy: "To provide handcrafted wines which mirror the qualities and potential of our unique conditions in Niagara, and in particular the Niagara Bench. Our philosophy of winemaking embraces innovation, enabling the creation of what tradition and nature have inspired."

LCBO wines: *white*—Regal House White, Vidal★, Riesling, Chardonnay, Proprietor's Reserve Chardonnay★

red—Loyalist House Red★, Gamay Noir

Own store: *white*—Seyval Blanc, Proprietor's Reserve Riesling★, Riesling Icewine★★, Gewürztraminer, Barrel Fermented Chardonnay★

red—Baco Noir★, Merlot, Pinot Noir, Blanc de Pinot Noir, Cabernet Sauvignon

Store on premises: 10 am – 6 pm, seven days a week

Public tastings: store hours

Tours: yes

HERNDER ESTATES WINERY

1607 8th Avenue
St. Catharines, Ontario
L2R 6P7

phone: (416) 682-6543

Fred Hernder has been growing grapes since 1967 and supplying juice to the home winemaking fraternity from a company first called Champagne Heights and then The Wine Barn. This stone structure dating back 120 years has been refurbished for the creation of Ontario's newest farm winery which was licenced at Christmas 1991. It is located near Henry of Pelham and the 20 vineyard plots are located between the QEW and 8th Avenue, stretching between 1st and 13th Streets.

The first wine (Vidal) made from the 1991 vintage was fermented and aged in stainless steel. Fred has recently purchased French oak staves in Austria.

Winemaker: position to be filled

Acreage: 400

Soil: heavy clay to fine sand

Varieties: Chardonnay, Riesling, Seyval Blanc, Vidal, 235-12, De Chaunac, Concord, Niagara. Planted in 1992—Pinot Gris, Cabernet Franc.

Production: 600 cases

Tonnage crushed: 10

Grapes bought in: none

Winemaking philosophy: "To make the best wine in the country, true to the variety."

Winery store: Vidal, dry and semi-dry

Tours: by appointment

Public tastings: yes

HILLEBRAND ESTATES

R.R. #2, Highway 55
Niagara-on-the-Lake,
Ontario, L0S 1J0

phone: (416) 468-3201
fax: (416) 468-4789

Joe Pohorly created a winery in 1979 called Newark but three years later debt problems forced him to sell to Underberg, the giant Swiss bitters company which held a controlling interest in Peter Mielzynski, the Toronto-based wine and spirit importers. The name was changed to Hillebrand Estates. Underberg also controls the Scholl & Hillebrand winery in Rüdesheim and Schlumberger sparkling wine in Austria. The company's winemaking expertise was brought to bear on early brands such as Schloss Hillebrand and the initial Rieslings. No winery in Canada has grown as quickly as Hillebrand thanks to the injection of capital from Switzerland. Their equipment and facilities are the envy of their colleagues. In 1990, they built a new building to house the offices above a bottling line which is itself over a new sparkling wine cellar for their Mounier label, created by Robert Mielzynski.

Hillebrand, though large, concentrates on quality in its varietals, especially Chardonnay (24,000 cases), Cabernet and Riesling of which there are a bewildering number of labels.

Heavy emphasis is placed on barrel fermenting and aging with oak from Nevers, Vosges, Troncais and Alliers as well as American.

The company encourages visits and offers the best tour in Ontario.

They are also relying on their forty-two stores around the province to act as local wine merchants, educating the public. Hillebrand also offers a wine club with special tastings and offerings for members.

Winemakers: Jean Laurent Groux, Benoit Huchin

Acreage: 30

Soil: clay

Varieties: Chardonnay, Riesling, Pinot Noir, Pinot Gris, Cabernet Franc

Production: 230,000 cases

Average tonnage crushed: 2,800 tonnes

Grapes bought in: 2,000 tonnes

Winemaking philosophy: "Varietal wines of quality are created in the vineyards, the cellar and by the philosophy of the winemaker. Together these determine the quality of our Chardonnays, Rieslings, Cabernet Sauvignon, Merlot, Gamays, Pinot Noirs and many others. In Hillebrand's cellars, the birth of clean, complex and fine quality wines originates from unpretentious working principles. The principles create the foundation for future generations of Hillebrand wine producers and consumers."

LCBO wines: *white*—Chablis, Chardonnay, Cuvée 1812 Chablis, Etienne Brulé Blanc, Le Baron Blanc, Peterhof, Riesling, Schloss Hillebrand, Seyval Blanc, Vidal

red—Cuvée 1812 Burgundy, Maréchal Foch★

sparkling—Canadian Champagne★

Own stores: *white*—Chardonnay Huebel Vineyard★, Chardonnay Buis Vineyard★, Collectors Choice Chardonnay★★, Harvest Chardonnay★, Trius Chardonnay★, Trius Riesling Dry, Gewürztraminer, Riesling Classic★, Harvest Riesling★, Riesling Inspirations★, Morio Muscat, Gamay Blanc★, Late Harvest Vidal★, Vidal Eiswein★★

red—Gamay Noir, Gamay Nouveau, Baco Noir, Collectors Choice Cabernet Sauvignon Merlot, Trius Glenlake Vineyard (Bordeaux blend), Pinot Noir Huebel Vineyard

sparkling—Riesling Cuvée Brut★, Mounier (champagne method)

Stores: Winery

Barrie: Georgian Mall, 509 Bayfield St. N.

Brampton:	Kingspoint Plaza, 370 Main St. N.
Burlington:	Lakeside Shopping Village, 5353 Lakeshore Rd.
	Burlingwood Centre, 2400 Guelph Line
Etobicoke:	Shipp Centre, 3300 Bloor St. W.
Hamilton:	Westdale Village, 1018 King St. W.
Kanata:	Van Leeuwen Centre, 420 Hazeldean Rd.
Kingston:	Cataraqui Town Centre, 945 Gardiners Rd.
Kitchener:	Highland Hills Mall, 46-875 Highland Rd.
London:	Oakridge Mall, 1201 Oxford St. W.
	Sebastian's, 539 Richmond St.
	Westminster Centre, 332 Wellington Rd. S.
Markham:	Markham Supercentre, 1661 Denison
	Loblaws, 8601 Warden Ave.
Mississauga:	Clarkson Village, 1865 Lakeshore Rd. W.
	Erin Mills Town Centre, 5100 Erin Mills Parkway
	South Common Mall, 2150 Burnhamthorpe W.
Newmarket:	The New Marketplace, 155 Yonge St. N.
North Bay:	North Bay Mall, 300 Lakeshore Dr.
Oakville:	131 Lakeshore Rd. E.
	Abbey Plaza, 1500 Upper Middle Rd. W.
Oshawa:	Five Points Mall, 285 Taunton Rd. E.
Ottawa:	Rideau Centre, 50 Rideau St.
	Orleans Garnes Shopping Centre, 1615 Orleans Blvd.
	Southgate Shopping Centre, 2515 Bank St.
Peterborough:	Peterborough Square, 360 George St. N.
Richmond Hill:	Loblaws (Supercentre), 9325 Yonge St.
St. Catharines:	Port Plaza, 600 Ontario St.
Scarborough:	Golden Mile Supercentre, 1880 Eglinton Ave. E.
	Markington Square, 3227 Eglinton Ave. E.
Toronto:	1689 Bayview Ave.
	2144 Queen St. E.
	2273 Bloor St. W.

	College Park, 444 Yonge St.
	Pusateri's, 1539 Avenue Rd.
	Standard Life Centre, 121 King St.W.
Vaughan:	Loblaws, 1054 Centre St.
Waterloo:	Waterloo Square, 75 King St.
Welland:	Seaway Mall, 800 Niagara St. N.

Six more stores are planned including sites in Guelph, Waterloo and Hamilton, bringing the number to forty-two.

Winery tours: 11 am, 1 pm, 3 pm, 4 pm daily

Public tastings: during store hours, 10 am – 6 pm

INNISKILLIN WINES INC.

R.R. #1, Line 3
Niagara-on-the-Lake
Ontario, L0S 1J0

phone: (416)468-2187
    468-3554
fax: (416) 468-5355

The credit must go to Donald Ziraldo and Karl Kaiser for rejuvenating the Ontario wine industry at a time when it could easily have foundered in the swamps of *labrusca*. They received their boutique winery licence — a new concept in 1975 when the industry was dominated by large commercial wineries ferociously competing with Baby Duck-style products and imitation Liebfraumlich—and they determined to make only quality wines. For a decade it was an uphill battle, but they have earned their place in the sun with a range of single vineyard Chardonnays, Pinot Noir, Cabernet Sauvignon and Vidal Icewine and along the way they have raised the profile of Ontario wines in Canada and around the world. The tireless Donald Ziraldo was the prime mover in setting up the Vintners Quality Alliance, Canada's appellation system, and getting the provincial government to create a wine route through the Peninsula. Inniskillin's 1989 Vidal Icewine won a gold award at Vinexpo in 1991, an accolade which has drawn global attention to Ontario as a wine region.

The winery itself, beautifully situated just off the Niagara Parkway, has a California look and feel. The Brae Burn barn which acts as the store and champagne loft is well worth a visit.

Given Karl Kaiser's Austrian background, you'd expect to find Grüner Veltliner and Zweigeltrebe in the vineyard—and you do.

Each year he buys from 40 to 80 new barrels from France. Inniskillin wines are sold in the United States, the United Kingdom, France, Japan and Hong Kong.

Winemaker: Karl Kaiser

Acreage: 60

Soil: Medium-light to medium-heavy sandy loam with some clay.

Varieties: Pinot Noir, Gamay, Cabernet Sauvignon, Cabernet Franc, Merlot, Zweigeltrebe, Maréchal Foch, Baco Noir, Leon Millot, Chambourcin, De Chaunac; Chardonnay, Riesling, Gewürztraminer, Vidal, Seyval Blanc, Pinot Grigio, Pinot Blanc, Grüner Veltliner, Auxerrois

Production: 100,000 cases

Average tonnage crushed: 1,000 to 1,200 tonnes

Grapes bought in: 70%

Winemaking philosophy: "Our basic philosophy of expanding varietal planting in Ontario has not changed since 1974. In winemaking our goal is to establish a style for whites that will be remembered for their balance and finesse, offering the appropriate flavours for our region's cool autumn climate."

LCBO wines: *white*—Auxerrois, Brae Blanc, Braeburn, Chardonnay, Gamay Blanc, Gewürztraminer*, Late Harvest Riesling*, Late Harvest Vidal, Proprietor's Reserve Riesling/Chardonnay, Riesling, Riesling B.A.**, Seyval Blanc, Vidal

red—Brae Rouge, Gamay Noir, Maréchal Foch*, Millot-Chambourcin, Pinot Noir, Proprietor's Reserve Cabernet Sauvignon/Zweigeltrebe

sparkling—L'Allemand* (Riesling, Charmat process)

Winery stores: *white*—Chardonnay Reserve★, single vineyard Chardonnays (Schuele★, Seeger★, Montague★), Riesling Reserve★, Pinot Grigio, Pinot Blanc, Grüner Veltliner, Vidal Icewine★★ (the most decorated Canadian wine)

red—Pinot Noir Reserve★, Cabernet Sauvignon/Cabernet Franc★, Zweigeltrebe, Maréchal Foch Reserve, Baco Noir

sparkling—Canadian Champagne

Specialty wine: Fleur d'Ontario★ (Pineau de Charentes style, Vidal and grape spirit)

Stores (4): Winery

Toronto: First Canadian Place
2570 Yonge St. (N. of Eglinton)

Ottawa: 11 Metcalfe St.

Winery store hours: November – April, 10 am – 5 pm
May – October 10 am – 6 pm

Tours: June – October 10:30 am and 2:30 pm
November – May, 2:30 pm only Saturday & Sunday

Tastings: store hours (50 cents per serving)

KONZELMANN WINERY

R.R. #3, Lakeshore Rd
Niagara-on-the-Lake
Ontario, L0N 1J0

phone: (416) 935-2866
fax: (416) 935-2864

Herbert Konzelmann's family has been making wine in Württemberg since 1893 and a reproduction of the entrance to that winery can be seen on his Ontario labels. An oenology graduate from Weinsberg in Germany, Herbert ran the family facility for 25 years before visiting Canada on a hunting trip in 1980. He was so impressed by the potential of winemaking in Niagara that he took soil samples home with him in margarine containers and had them analyzed. Four years later he was back to purchase his 40-acre estate that backs onto Lake Ontario. He planted 32,000 vines and took his first crop off in the 1986 vintage, producing nine different varietals.

His Germanic winemaking style manages to coax subtle perfumes from his grapes, particularly Riesling, Chardonnay and Gewürztraminer. While he uses Allier, Nevers and Yugoslavian oak, especially for Chardonnay, his best results are from stainless steel, according to his own traditions. Herbert's Icewine is one of Canada's best.

In the German style, he believes in sweet reserve, back-blending fresh grape juice to the finished wines.

Winemaker: Herbert Konzelmann

Acreage: 40

Soil: Clay, sand. Ideal microclimate because of the proximity of the lake. Winds dry the vines, inhibiting fungus growth.

Varieties: Riesling, Chardonnay, Pinot Blanc, Gewürztraminer, Riesling-Traminer, Geisenheim 311, Vidal, Pinot Noir, Gamay, Zweigelt, Cabernet Sauvignon, Cabernet Franc, Merlot

Production: 80,000 cases

Average tonnage crushed: 130 tonnes

Grapes bought in: 30 tonnes

Winemaking philosophy: "Konzelmann stands for quality."

LCBO wines: Golden Vintage, Johannisberg Riesling (Sugar Code 1★, Sugar Code 2★), Chardonnay, Pinot Blanc, Pinot Noir★

Own store: *white*—Late Harvest Riesling Dry, Chardonnay Reserve Barrel-aged★★, Late Harvest Vidal, Late Harvest Riesling Medium Dry★, Late Harvest Gewürztraminer★, Pinot Noir Rosé, Peach Wine, Riesling-Traminer Icewine★★, Vidal Icewine★★

red—Pinot Noir, Gamay Noir, Baco Noir Late Harvest, Zweigelt Late Harvest

sparkling—Canadian Riesling Champagne

Store hours: Monday – Saturday, 10 am – 6 pm
Sunday 12:30 pm – 5:50 pm
January – March: Wednesday – Saturday, 10 am – 6 pm

Public tastings: during store hours

Tours: by arrangement

LAKEVIEW CELLARS
ESTATE WINERY

R.R. #1
4037 Cherry Avenue
Vineland, Ontario
L0R 2C0

phone: (416) 562-5685

Grower Eddy Gurinskas was a dedicated home winemaker who consistently won medals at national and international amateur competitions, especially for his Vidal Icewine. In 1991, he and his wife Lorraine followed in the footsteps of their friend John Marynissen in turning from grape grower to commercial winemaker when Lakeview Cellars got the second farm winery licence issued in Ontario.

From the start Eddy's intention was to bottle single vineyard wines with barrel aging for his Chardonnay and Cabernet Sauvignon. Currently he has 12 French and American barriques. The winery is a newly constructed barn with a gambrel roof.

Winemaker: Eddy Gurinskas

Acreage: 13

Soil: The vineyard is located on the first plateau of the Niagara Escarpment, better known as "the Bench," approximately three kilometres from Lake Ontario. The air drainage is very effective in the summer and provides considerable protection from extreme cold in winter. Soils are heavy clay loam.

Varieties: Cabernet Sauvignon, Chardonnay, Pinot Gris, Baco Noir, Vidal

Production: 1,250 cases

Average tonnage crushed: 20 tonnes

Grapes bought in: 10 tonnes

Winemaking philosophy: "Our aspirations are to make wine using only 100% Ontario grapes that are locally grown. We intend to cap our production at 5,000 cases with sales of our wines through our winery store along with limited sales through the LCBO."

Wines: *at winery*—Riesling (Vinc Vineyard), Welschriesling (Vinc Vineyard), Vidal (Gurinskas Vineyard), Cabernet Sauvignon, Vidal Icewine

Store on premises: Monday through Sunday, 10 am – 6 pm

Tours: yes

Public tastings: store hours

LAURO & BURDEN WINERY

991 Matheson Blvd., East
Mississauga, Ontario

phone: (416) 602-7835
fax: (416) 602-7836

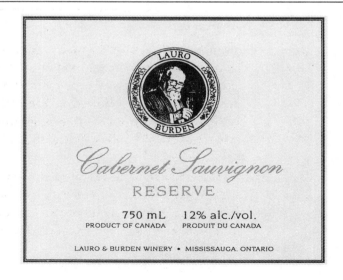

Ken Burden is a marketing man and Gaetano (Nino) Lauro is a winemaker. Together, in 1992, they opened a 3,000 square foot facility in a commercial/industrial area next to a Coffee Time Donut shop to make wines from imported grapes blended with Ontario wines. The products, apart from the basic Dry White and Dry Red, are available in screwtop 750 mL bottles or under cork and are priced to be competitive. None of the current wines are vintage dated. Ken's father drew the design for the labels.

Twenty-five French oak barrels have been purchased for aging Chardonnay in futures.

The company offers "an extensive line of custom labels."

Winemaker: Gaetano Lauro

Production: approximately 9,000 cases

Average tonnage crushed: (projected) 150 tons

Grapes bought in: (projected) 200 tons

Winemaking philosophy: "Quality wines at the most affordable price possible for our customers."

Wines: Own store only. *white*—Dry White Wines, Biancalina, Seyval Blanc

　　red—Dry Red Wine, Cabernet Sauvignon

　　rosé—Cabernet Rosé

Store hours: Monday to Friday, 10:00 am – 7:00 pm

Tours: yes

Public tastings: yes

MAJOR

LONDON WINERY

560 Wharncliffe Road
    South
London, Ontario
N6J 2N5

phone: (519) 686-8431
fax: (519) 686-2829

London Winery was founded by the Knowles brothers in 1925 and is still in the family. A traditional company, specializing in ports and sherries, mead (the only Canadian producer) and other sweet dessert wines, it also makes a range of *vinifera* table wines as well as Icewine. London boasts Canada's oldest wine, St. Augustine Communion, a sweet red of 16% alcohol made from Concord and Fredonia grapes that dates back to the time when Vin Villa on Pelee Island first made it in the 1870s.

For all its atmosphere of history and conservatism, London does have some impressive achievements in the technological advance of the Canadian wine industry: the company was the first to introduce the process for making flor sherry (invented by Ralph Crowther at Vineland's Horticultural Research Institute), the first to put on the market sherry in a decanter with a ground glass stopper (London Cream) and the first to use the millipore filter.

Of special note is the 225,000 litre barrel solera aging cellar for the company's premium sherries and ports. London does a healthy export business to the northeastern United States.

The Scottish winemaker, Jim Patience, lives up to his name. He's been making wines with the company for twenty-nine years.

London has a second label, Cedar Springs, for its 75% off-shore blends with Ontario wines.

Winemaker: Jim Patience

Acreage: 60 (sixty miles west of London at Cedar Springs, established in 1984)

69

Soil: Fox gravel loam, situated half a mile from Lake Erie.

Varieties: Riesling, Chardonnay, Merlot, Vidal, Seyval Blanc, Vivant, 23-512

Production: 300,000 cases

Average tonnage crushed: 2,100 tonnes

Grapes bought in: 1,850 tonnes

Winemaking philosophy: "To address all segments of the wine market (i.e., Sherry, Port, Vermouth, Blended Table Wines, Premium Varietals, Sparkling Wines, Champagnes, Fruit Wines, Honey Wine). To produce premium quality products in all categories and thereby provide excellent value to the wine consumer."

LCBO wines: XXX Sherry, Westminster Sherry, Supreme Sherry, Cream Sherry, Bella Spumante, Sweet Vermouth, Dry Vermouth★, Red St. Augustine Communion Wine, 410 Port, Bella Spumante, Candlelight Sherry, Chablis, Spumante Bianco, Baco Noir★, Pale Dry Sherry, Cuvée Supérieur Red, Cuvée Supérieur White, Cold Duck, XX Port, L'Oiseau Bleu, L'Oiseau Bleu Sélectionné, O'Briens, Oxford Sherry, Golden Cream Sherry, Sweet Vermouth

Own stores: Eiswein★★, Cream Port★, Edelmere, Honey Wine, Pink Flamingo, White Champagne, Pink Champagne, Peach Wine, Strawberry Wine, Cherry Wine, Ancient Meade Golden Honey Wine, Creme d'Or Sherry, Cuvée d'Or, Night Moves, Chablis Blanc, Vinroi White, Chablis Extra Dry, Summer Cooler, Chilly Willy Wine Cooler, Pink Flamingo Wine Cooler, Maréchal Foch, Seyval Blanc, Vidal, Seyval Blanc, De Chaunac, Chardonnay, Late Harvest Vidal

Stores:

Thunder Bay: 1020 Dawson Rd.
425 North Edwards St.

London: 115 Dundas St.
623 Dundas St. E.
1299 Oxford St. E.
509 Commissioners Rd. W.
1401 Ernest Ave.
130 King St.

Toronto:	1548 Bloor St. W.
	1255 The Queensway
	700 Lawrence Ave. W.
Ottawa:	1670 Heron Rd.
	1309 Carling Ave.
Orleans:	110 Place d'Orleans Dr.
Kingston:	112 Princess St.
Brockville:	2399 Parkedale Ave.
Hamilton:	15 King William St.
	655 Upper James St.
Windsor:	2430 Dougall Ave.
	7201 Tecumseh Rd. E.
Peterborough:	174 Charlotte St.
St. Thomas:	417 Wellington St.
Blenheim:	R.R. #1
Sarnia:	500 Exmouth Street
	600 Murphy Rd.

Public tastings: at retail stores (hours vary)

Tours: not at winery, only at Bleinheim retail store

MAGNOTTA
WINERY

100 Cidermill Avenue
Vaughan, Ontario
L4K 4L9

phone: (416) 738-9463
1-800-461-WINE
fax: (416) 738-5551

-and-

1.5 L   11% alc./vol.

Festa Rosso
RED WINE • VIN ROUGE

MAGNOTTA

PRODUCT OF CANADA   PRODUIT DU CANADA
MAGNOTTA WINERY • CONCORD • ONTARIO • CANADA

71

VINTAGES INTERNATIONAL

2555 Dixie Road
Unit 14
Mississauga,
Ontario
L4Y 2A1

phone:
(416) 897-5550

Gabe and Rossana Magnotta used to be in the juice business, supplying Toronto's Italian community and other interested home winemakers with imported juice. In 1990 they opened a winery in a business park in Vaughan, having purchased the stock of the defunct Charal winery in Blenheim. Taking advantage of the Ontario Wine Content Act (which then allowed 70% off-shore material to be blended with Ontario wines) their Argentinian winemaker produced a range of very inexpensive table wines for the ethnic community. Much of the imported juice is sourced from Argentina and Chilean juice or from Delicato Vineyards in California's San Joaquin Valley.

The winery uses 60 French and American barriques (Chardonnay and reds) and made its first Vidal Icewine in 1991.

The Magnottas opened up a second facility in Mississauga, Vintages International, which has a similar philosophy to the original winery. They have also bought land on Highway 55 in the Niagara Peninsula to build a winery and have planted 26 acres of *vinifera* vines on the Bench in Beamsville.

Winemaker: Alejandro DeMiguel

Production: 30,000 cases

Average tonnage crushed: 300 tons

Winemaking philosophy: "To search the world for the best quality wines and/or juices at the best possible prices, blend them with the best Ontario product and give the best possible value to our customer."

Wines: Chardonnay, Riesling Dry, Riesling Off-Dry, Icewine*; Pinot Noir, Cabernet Sauvignon Special Reserve*, Merlot

International Vintages series (75% off-shore grapes, 25% Ontario): *Italian:* Pinot Grigio, Pinot Bianco, Bardolino, Valpolicella, Merlot; *California:* Cabernet Sauvignon Rosé, California Burgundy, California Chablis; *Chile:* Cabernet Sauvignon, Merlot, Chardonnay, Sauvignon Blanc; *Argentina:* Cabernet Sauvignon, Merlot, Syrah, Chardonnay; *Limited Editions:* Cabernet Sauvignon L.E., Merlot L.E., Chardonnay L.E.; *Bulk wines:* California Burgundy, California Chablis

Store on premises: Monday – Friday, 9 am – 7 pm
    Saturday, 9 am – 5 pm
    No LCBO listings

Tours: yes

Public tastings: during store hours

MARYNISSEN
ESTATES

R.R. #6
1208 Concession #1
Niagara-on-the-Lake
Ontario, L0S 1J0

phone: (416) 468-7270
fax: (416) 468-5784

▼

MARYNISSEN
E S T A T E S

1990
CHARDONNAY
BARREL FERMENTED

Estate Grown and Bottled
Marynissen Estates Ltd., RR 6, Niagara On The Lake, Ontario
PRODUCT OF CANADA   PRODUIT DU CANADA
750 ml WINE • VIN   11.5 % alc./vol.

As an amateur winemaker, grower John Marynissen has a cabinet full of trophies for his Chardonnays, Rieslings, Cabernet Sauvignons and Icewines won in national and international competitions. His family talked him into creating Ontario's first farmgate winery and with some backing from Tony Doyle (who used to own Willowbank, the stock was sold to Brights and the equipment went to Marynissen's barn) he started his own operation in 1990. A farmer for over forty years, he sources his fruit from his two vineyards located between the Niagara Escarpment and the lake. His Chardonnay planted in the mid-1970s and his Cabernet (1978) are some of the oldest in the Niagara region.

John is a believer in carbonic maceration for Ontario reds and favours the use of oak for fermenting and aging. He currently uses Troncais, Allier, Nevers and some American oak.

Winemaker: John Marynissen

Acreage: 70

Soil: Lot 31 sandy loam; Lot 66 more stoney, loam and gravel.

The vineyards are protected from the more extreme air currents near the lake and from the escarpment.

Varieties: Chardonnay, Riesling, Gewürztraminer, Cabernet Sauvignon, Cabernet Franc, Merlot, Gamay Noir, Seyval Blanc, Vidal

Production: 6,000 cases

Average tonnage crushed: 100 tonnes

Grapes bought in: 3 tonnes of Pinot Noir in 1991

Winemaking philosophy: "We emphasize working with nature and producing wines as natural as possible. Growing all of our grapes for wine production here gives us an advantage in that we cut back our yields in order to produce a more concentrated, premium grape and wine. We also use crop control depending on the weather, etc."

LCBO wines: Cabernet Sauvignon/Merlot Blend

Own store: Riesling, Chardonnay Barrel Fermented, Merlot Barrel Select, Cabernet Sauvignon Barrel Select, Vidal Icewine★, Riesling Icewine★

Store hours: Monday through Sunday, 10 am – 6 pm

Tours: yes, large parties by appointment only

Public tastings: during store hours

MONTRAVIN
CELLARS

1233 Ontario Street
P.O. Box 968
Beamsville, Ontario

phone: (416) 563-5313
fax: (416) 563-8804

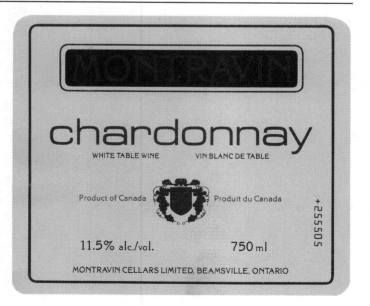

Hungarian sparkling winemaker Karl Podamer opened his winery and received his licence two weeks after Inniskillin got theirs in 1975. His *méthode champenoise* wines were good but expensive and the winery that bore his name ran into financial trouble. Viennese oenolgist Ernst Fischer, formerly with Chateau-Gai, was called in by the new owners to create a line of table wines under the Montravin label. The sparkling wines still appear as Podamer products though some of them are now made by the Charmat process. The company is currently undergoing reconstruction and statisical information is not yet available.

Wines: Aristeo White, Chardonnay, Sauvignon/Chardonnay; Aristeo Red

Sparkling: (champagne method) Podamer Brut, Podamer Blanc de Blancs, Podamer Extra Dry, Podamer Special Reserve (Charmat process)

PELEE ISLAND WINERY

455 Highway # 18 East Kingsville, Ontario N9Y 2K5

In 1980, Austrian winemaker Walter Strehn planted Riesling and Chardonnay and other German varietals on Pelee Island, the first such planting since the 1860s and 1870s when Canada's first commercial winery was founded on the island, called Vin Villa. Vineyards here are the most southerly in Canada, enjoying the longest growing season and most heat units. The cottage-style crushing facility (built in 1984) is on the mainland, but now there is a newly opened tasting pavilion on the vineyard site complete with restaurant and picnic facilities, petting zoo and playground.

Another Austrian, Walter Schmoranz, took over the winery in 1986.

The barrel cellar tasting room is worth the long drive to Kingsville—and so are the wines.

Walter Strehn produced Ontario's first Icewine in 1983 and Walter Schmoranz made Ontario's first red Icewine in 1989 (from Lemberger and Blaufränkisch). Through the Opimian Society, Pelee Island offers a range of wines blended with California and Oregon fruit (from the William Hill winery). The vineyards on the island and at Kingsville are the most extensive *vinifera* plantings of any estate winery.

Winemaker: Walter Schmoranz

Acreage: 200

Soil: Limestone bedrock close to surface; moderating effect of Lake Erie.

Varieties: Chardonnay, Riesling, Gewürztraminer, Zweigelt, Riesling Italico, Gamay, Pinot Noir, Scheurebe, Kerner, Merlot, Cabernet Franc

Production: 50,000 cases

Average tonnage crushed: 6,500 tonnes

Grapes bought in: 300 tonnes

Winemaking philosophy: "Our winemaking philosophy is to combine our extensive oenological and viticultural skills with our significant estate vineyards located in the most favoured climatic grape-growing region to produce quality wines as unique as the appellation of Pelee Island."

LCBO wines: *white*—Blanc de Blanc, Chardonnay★, Ducks Unlimited Chardonnay, Hulda's Rock Chardonnay, Pelee Island Dry, Gewürztraminer, Italico Riesling, Riesling Dry, Riesling Late Harvest, Scheurebe, Vin Villa

red—Ducks Unlimited Gamay Noir, Pelee Island Rouge, Fenian's Cuvée★, Pinot Noir★

sparkling—Battle of Lake Erie

Own stores: Gamay Nouveau, Eiswein, Scheurebe BA

Stores: at winery and two on Pelee Island (West Dock for tax-free export sales)

Hours: April to December, 9 am – 6 pm daily
January to March, 9 am – 6 pm Monday to Saturday
Tours: noon, 2 pm, 4 pm

Public tastings: Kingsville—noon, 2 pm, 4 pm
Wine Pavilion (Pelee Island) 10 am – 7 pm

QUAI DU VIN ESTATE WINERY

R.R. #5
St. Thomas, Ontario
N5P 3S9

phone: (519) 775-2216

Roberto Quai, like Jim Warren of Stoney Ridge and John Marynissen, was an accomplished prize-winning amateur winemaker who went professional. He created his small winery in 1988 with the determination to keep his operation small so that he could control all of its aspects. His father, Redi, had planted the vineyard 20 years ago and used to sell the grapes to Colio.

The winery itself is spartan and its unique philosophy of offering a 25-cent return deposit on bottles may be the future of an industry that is becoming more environment-conscious. (It's also a good marketing ploy to keep customers coming back.)

When asked if he used any special winemaking equipment in his bijou operation, Roberto replied: "Big feet." No oak barrels or stainless steel tanks, all the wines are made in 500 gallon polyethylene tanks. He also makes limited amounts of "port" and "sherry."

Quai du Vin must be the only winery on this planet situated in a "dry" zone, a hangover from Prohibition era.

Winemaker: Robert Quai

Acreage: 20

Soil: Clay-loam, gravel base. Highest point in Elgin County, five kilometres from Lake Erie.

Varieties: Vidal, Chardonnay, Aurore, Seyve-Villard 23-512, Riesling, De Chaunac

Production: 5,000 cases

Average tonnage crushed: 36.6 tonnes

Grapes bought in: 16 tonnes

Winemaking philosophy: "To produce good quality wine at reasonable prices. Simple winemaking techniques, no sophisticated equipment. Low overheads, no employees, 'profit driven'."

Wines: Winery store only—Aurore (Semi-Dry), Riesling Semi-Dry, Late Harvest Riesling, New York Muscat Blush, Chardonnay, SV23-512; De Chaunac

Store hours: Tuesday – Saturday, 10 am – 5 pm
Sunday, 1 pm – 5 pm (closed Monday)

Tours: yes (no set hours)

Public tastings: yes (no set hours)

REIF ESTATE
WINERY

R.R. #1
Niagara Parkway
Niagara-on-the-Lake
Ontario, L0S 1J0

phone: (416) 468-7738
fax: (416) 468-5878

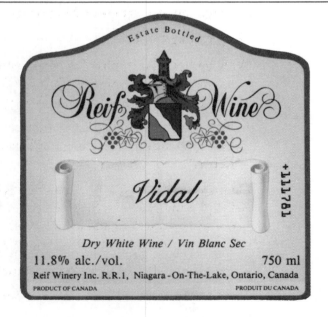

Ewald Reif purchased his vineyard on the Niagara Parkway in 1977, uprooting *labrusca* and hybrids in favour of Riesling, Chardonnay,

Gewürztraminer, Kerner and Gamay. Five years later he started his winery. The equipment was sent from his brother's winery in Neustadt in the Rheinpfalz. His nephew Klaus (a thirteenth generation vintner who trained at Geisenheim) took over the winemaking duties in 1987, and since then Ewald concentrates on the vineyards.

The winemaking style is Germanic, using large old oak barrels and back-blending off-dry and late harvest wines with sweet reserve. Reif, a neighbour of Inniskillin, is beautifully situated on the Niagara Parkway. Wines are exported to the United States and the Orient.

Winemaker: Klaus Reif

Acreage: 135

Soil: Sand and loam. The moderating effects of Lake Ontario and the Niagara River provide the vineyards with optimum growing conditions.

Varieties: Riesling, Chardonnay, Gewürztraminer, Vidal, Seyval Blanc, Kerner, Cabernet Sauvignon, Merlot, Pinot Noir, Gamay

Production: 16,000 cases

Average tonnage crushed: 230 tonnes

Grapes bought in: none

Winemaking philosophy: "A combination of tradition and new technology. All wines are 100% estate bottled. Absolutely no imports of grapes, juice or wine. Winemaking starts in the grape."

LCBO wines: Rheingold★, Chardonnay★, Johannisberg Riesling Dry★, Johannisberg Riesling Off Dry, Seyval Blanc, Vidal★, Kerner★

Own store: *white*—Chardonnay Reserve★, Gewürztraminer (Dry★ and Off Dry★), Siegfried Rebe, Vidal (Late Harvest, Select Harvest★★ and Select Harvest Dry), Riesling Late Harvest★, Vidal Icewine★★, Riesling Icewine★

red—Gamay Rosé, Pinot Noir, Cabernet Sauvignon, Baco Noir★

Store hours: winter 10 am – 5 pm; summer 10 am – 6 pm

Tours: summer: Saturday 1:30 pm/3 pm/4:30 pm Sunday 11 am winter: Sunday 11 am

Public tastings: during store hours

SOUTHBROOK FARMS WINERY

1061 Major McKenzie
Drive (west of Bathurst)
Vaughan, Ontario
L0J 1E0

phone: (416) 832-2548
fax: (416) 832-9811

Founded in 1991, Southbrook Farms is a farm winery with a difference. There are no vineyards, and the Redelmeier family trucks in grapes from Niagara (mainly from the Reif estate) and vinifies them in an old barn. Brian Croser from Petaluma in Australia helped the family to set up the operation and gave consulting assistance in the first crush (1991). That operation was carried out at the Reif winery. In future, the company will vinify at the farm as well as buying in finished wines from Ontario and California.

Eighty per cent of the wines are 100% Ontario grapes (under the Southbrook Farm Winery label); the other 20% are blends using California fruit (Southbrook Blends label). The winery purchased 180 old French and 10 American oak barrels and 18 new Nevers. A small quantity of Icewine was bottled in 1991.

During the summer months picnic facilities and food are provided. The store in the beautiful old barn offers wine books and ancient maps of European wine regions.

Winemaker: Klaus Reif

Production: 5,000 cases

Average tonnage crushed (bought in): 40 tons

Winemaking philosophy: "Southbrook Farm Winery wines are fruit focused wines. Both the 100% Ontario wines and the wines produced in the Southbrook blending program utilize the finest grapes and wines available in the market. In the end, the style of these wines is to a great degree determined by the market we serve. With cellar door sales only, market preferences are made clear daily, on a one to one basis."

Wines: Own store only. *Southbrook Farm Winery label* (100% Ontario grapes): *white*—Chardonnay, Riesling, Dry Riesling, Dry House White

Southbrook Farm Winery label: red—Pinot Noir Vin Gris

Southbrook Blends label: white—Chardonnay

Southbrook Blends label: red—Cabernet Sauvignon, Cabernet/Merlot, Blush

Shop hours: 10:30 am – 6:30 pm daily

Tours: yes

Public tastings: during store hours

STONECHURCH VINEYARDS

1270 Irvine Road
R.R. #5
Niagara-on-the-Lake
Ontario, L0S 1J0

phone (416) 935-3535
fax: (416) 646-8892

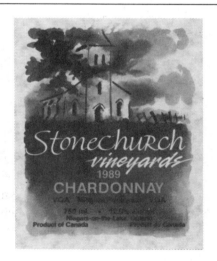

Trained at California's oenology school at Davis, David Hulley teamed up with the farming Hunse family to make their wines, after a stint with Hillebrand and Henry of Pelham. The winery was founded in 1989 as the first of the new wave of small farmgate enterprises. Lambert and Grace Hunse have farmed Stonechurch for 35 years. They now own 200 acres of fruit trees and vines in parcels near Lake Ontario and the Welland Canal. Their son, Rick, who looks after the vineyard part of the operation, leans towards organic growing and is a believer in leaf removal to improve the microclimate around the grape clusters to allow maximum sun penetration and good air circulation.

Stonechurch make Canada's most expensive barrel-fermented Chardonnay. The winery uses new Nevers, Allier, Troncais and American oak. They also make a champagne method sparkler from Pinot Noir. In spite of its size the company exports to Japan, Taiwan and Holland.

Winemaker: David Hulley

Acreage: 85

Soil: Ranging from hard-pan clay to silt to gravel depending on location which allows for planting vines in soils sympathetic to the cultivar.

Varieties: Cabernet Sauvignon, Pinot Noir, Gewürztraminer, Morio Muscat, Cabernet Franc, Chardonnay, Baco Noir, Seyval Blanc, Vidal

Production: 10,500 cases

Average tonnage crushed: 140 tonnes

Grapes bought in: 20 tonnes

Winemaking philosophy: "Balance and harmony. I like to work with the fruit in a facilitative not a dominative way to bring out the best that particular year has to offer. Although I have very clear views on the general direction that I want to head the wine in, I still give it a broad path in which it can find its own way. We like to produce wines which are truly unique and distinctive whether in style or variety."

LCBO wines: Estate Blanc

Own store: *white*—Export Blanc, Chardonnay, Barrel-fermented Chardonnay, Reserve Chardonnay★, Morio Muscat, Riesling Icewine, Vidal Icewine★

red—Baco Noir, Cabernet Sauvignon, Merlot, Pinot Noir

sparkling—Blanc de Noir

STONEY RIDGE CELLARS

1468 Highway 8
(at Fifty Road)
Winona, Ontario
L0R 2L0

phone: (416) 643-4508
fax: (416) 643-0933

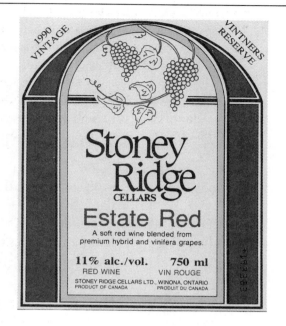

Jim Warren was a gifted and highly successful amateur winemaker (and high school teacher) before he took the commercial plunge in 1985 with two partners. The original winery was located at Vinemount on the Escarpment in a tin shed the size of a bungalow. In 1990, he went into partnership with Murray Puddicombe, a grower at the base of the Escarpment in Winona. A spanking new facility was built, housing the store, a fruit market and a second storey balcony restaurant.

Jim has a unique winemaking style that produces opulent, aromatic, sometimes exotic wines with ripe fruit flavours. He believes in small-lot crushing and cold-settling his juice. He uses French and American small oak. A testimony to his skills is the number of medals his wines have won, especially his single vineyard Chardonnays in competition with leading labels from France, California and Australia. His reds are some of the best in Canada. For such a small winery he makes an amazing range of products, including the specialty port-style Passion and Jasmine.

Jim also makes small batches of experimental wines. In the 1991 vintage he made 35 different wines from 26 varieties!

Winemaker: Jim Warren

Acreage: 200

Varieties: Seyval Blanc, Vidal, Chardonnay, Riesling, Gewürztraminer, Morio Muscat, French Colombard, SV 23-512; De Chaunac, Gamay, Pinot Noir, Merlot, Cabernet Franc

Production: 13,000 cases

Average tonnage crushed: 140 tons

Grapes bought in: approximately 60%

Winemaking philosophy: "I like to produce wines with abundant flavour and bouquet—wines that are top quality yet very appealing, well-balanced and honest to the grape variety. In a word, well-balanced, varietal character, good fruit."

LCBO wines: *white*—Seyval Blanc★, Premium Dry Vidal★, Chardonnay Estate (Puddicombe Vineyard)★, Riesling (French Oak Vineyard)★★

rosé—Romance★

red—Estate Red★

Own store: *white*—Estate White★, Premiere, Riesling-Musqué, Riesling (Plekan Vineyard), Riesling Dry, Noblesse, Morio Muscat★, Gewürztraminer★, Chardonnay (Eastman Vineyard)★★, Chardonnay (Eastman Vineyard)★, Chardonnay (Lenko Vineyard)★★, Chardonnay Reserve (Eastman Vineyard)★, French Colombard★★

specialty wines—Late Harvest Riesling★★, Jasmine, Passion, Vidal Icewine★, Gewürztraminer Icewine

rosé—Grenache

red—Pinot Noir★, Cabernet (Buis Vineyard)★, Cabernet Franc★★, Zinfandel★(70% Sonoma fruit), Cabernet Winemaker's Reserve★(70% Sonoma mountain fruit)★, Merlot Reserve★★

Store on premises: Daily 10 am – 5 pm

Public tastings: 11 am – 2 pm

Tours: by appointment

VINELAND
ESTATES WINES

R.R. # 1
3620 Moyer Road
Vineland, Ontario
L0R 2C0

phone: (416) 562-7088

Winemaker Allan Schmidt is now a partner in the winery whose reputation he helped to build. In 1992, with John Howard, a former board member of the Japanese Canon company, he purchased the winery from Herman Weis. Herman Weis's family owns a winery in the Mosel called St. Urban as well as Germany's largest private grape vine nursery. In 1979, in order to crack the Canadian market for his virus-free vines, he bought with other partners, two 50-acre vineyards in Vineland, subsequently called St. Urban and St. Hilarius. Their first commercial crop of Riesling was vinified by Barnes in 1982. Two years later winemaker Dieter Guttler opened his own winery, named Vineland Estates, using grapes from these vineyards. Ownership of the winery passed to Herman Weis in 1987, who took on as his partner a dynamic, young British Columbia winemaker Allan Schmidt. (Allan's grape-grower father Lloyd had been a partner in British Columbia's Sumac Ridge winery.)

Set on the Bench of the Niagara Escarpment, Vineland Estates is the most picturesquely situated winery in Ontario with its 1845 farmhouse (now the tasting room, small restaurant and store) and small bed-and-breakfast cottage on the edge of the vineyard.

The emphasis here is on Riesling, although much care is given to the barrel-femented or barrel-aged Chardonnays (50% new Allier and Nevers and American oak) and Icewine.

Winemaker: Allan Schmidt

Acreage: 50

Soil: Gently sloping vineyard, clay loam soil, well drained; rolling hills.

Varieties: Riesling, Chardonnay, Pinot Noir, Seyval Blanc, Vidal

Production: 10,000 cases

Average tonnage crushed: 150

Grapes bought in: 15 to 18 tons

Winemaking philosophy: "Riesling not over-ripe. Cool fermentations giving slightly higher acidity than normal. Chardonnay—no malolactic fermentation. Prefer crisper, fresher style."

LCBO wines: Vintners Select Dry, Riesling Dry★★, Riesling Semi Dry★, Chardonnay

Own store: Late Harvest Riesling★, Vidal Icewine★★, Riesling Icewine★★, Pinot Noir

Shop on premises: 10 am – 5 pm, seven days a week

Public tasting: as per shop hours

Tours: daily 11 am, 1 pm, 3 pm

VINOTECA INC.

61 Caster Avenue
Woodbridge, Ontario
L4L 5Z2

phone: (416) 856-5700
fax: (416) 856-8208

Giovanni (Johnny) Follegot and his wife Rosanna began by importing grape juice for the Italian community to make their own wine. In 1989, they set up a fermenting operation in a Woodbridge industrial park, using Ontario grapes trucked in from the Niagara Peninsula.

Twenty French and American oak barrels are used and the winery began making small batches of Icewine in 1990 from Vidal. In 1992, an Italian-style sparkling wine was produced using the Classico method.

Vinoteca wines are only available at the winery. The labels can be confusing, especially since three different styled 1989 Chardonnays bear identical labels. Vinoteca owns an 18-acre farm in Beamsville for future VQA wines.

Winemaker: Giovanni Follegot

Production: 3,000 cases

Average tonnage crushed (bought in): 50 tonnes

Winemaking philosophy: "Our total dedication and hard work has enabled us to produce valid wines that are well accepted by consumers, whose use is mainly to complement their meals. With confidence we are able to progress and improve our wines to reach the highest standards."

Wines: Own store only. Albino (white blend), Gaio (red blend), Pinot Chardonnay, Riesling, Pinot Noir, Cabernet Sauvignon; White Table Wine and Red Table Wine (returnable 18 litre containers)

Reserve wines: Pinot Chardonnay, Prosecco Chardonnay, Ice Wine; Cabernet Sauvignon

Store hours: 9 am – 6 pm

Tours: yes

Public tastings: during store hours

British Columbia

*I*n general terms, British Columbia differs from Ontario in climate, soil and grape varieties. Ontario's industry is much older than that of BC and is based on North American varieties. The BC industry, having been developed comparatively recently, established itself on French hybrids. Not only are the grape varieties of the two provinces different, but the flavours of the same varieties vary dramatically because of the vast differences in growing conditions. Ontario never experiences the intense heat, low humidity and cool nights of the desert summer; and the Okanagan, situated as it is on a latitude roughly equivalent to Timmins, enjoys significantly more hours of sunshine during summer days. While Ontario is moving slowly to *vinifera* vines, the BC industry started with *vinifera* and is now expanding with the next generation of new hybrids. British Columbia wines, as a result, tend to be highly flavoured, fruity and full-bodied with good acidity, especially the whites which resemble those of the Rhine rather than the softer Californian style.

The wine industry in BC did not really start until the 1930s. While the combined insanity of Prohibition and the Depression

WINE REGIONS OF BRITISH COLUMBIA

1. Okanagan
2. Similkameen
3. Fraser Valley
4. Vancouver Island

almost destroyed the Ontario wineries, ironically it provided the impetus for the birth of BC commercial winemaking in the Okanagan and Similkameen River valleys when *labrusca* varieties such as Campbell, Concord, Diamond, Patricia, Sheridan, Bath and Delaware were first planted.

The story goes back to the 1860s when the Oblate Fathers built a mission seven miles south of Kelowna and Father Charles Pandosy planted a few vines at the mission. But the farmers who followed were more interested in fruit crops such as apples, peaches and apricots than in grapes. The first commercial vineyard in the province was planted by W.J. Wilcox some 55 miles north of Kelowna, at Salmon Arm. This three-quarter acre plot yielded such Ontario varieties as Concord, Niagara, Delaware and Agawam for the table trade. Six years later Jim Creighton planted a small vineyard in Penticton, an area which would ultimately prove to be one of the best sites for grape growing along the shore of Okanagan.

The narrow, serpentine lake, carved out by prehistoric glaciers, stretches north for over 100 kilometres and the land rises steeply from the water on either side. Technically, the area is a desert since there is little rainfall (the southern end of the lake around Oliver gets no more than six inches of precipitation a year). In terms of latitude the Okanagan Valley is in the same belt as the Champagne region of France and the Rheingau of Germany — a fact which seduced many pioneers into believing that they could produce wines to rival the great Rieslings and sparkling Chardonnays — but the climate is very different from Europe. During the summer day the Okanagan vines experience tremendous heat and at night the temperature dips dramatically. Intense sunlight builds up the grape sugars and the freezing nights do not allow the acids to metabolize, so the berries have very high acid readings. Because of the lack of rainfall the vineyards have to be irrigated during the growing season.

The Okanagan experiences long, mild autumns, as does northern Germany, but by mid-October the temperature has fallen to a point where the grapes will no longer mature and they have to be harvested. On the plus side, British Columbian summers, like those in California, are consistent and predictable which ensures an even quality of grape from year to year. In spite of fluctuating temperatures, there are pockets along the valley's southern slopes that protect the vines from the killing frost that rolls down the lake from October on and the body of water ameliorates the air temperature on the coldest nights. Many of these microclimates have been identified by infrared aerial photography, through a program conducted by the Summerland Research Station in conjunction with the provincial government.

Without the advantage of such technology the early grape growers could only plant their vines, sit back and pray.

The first wines in British Columbia were not made from grapes at all but from loganberries which flourished in southern Victoria Island on the Saanich Peninsula. They rejoiced in such names as Slinger's Logan and Logana. But a few inspired souls turned their attentions to wine grapes. Peter Casoroa of Kelowna was a grape-growing pioneer in the 1920s. And in 1926 a farmer by the name of Jesse Willard Hughes, encouraged by the Hungarian oenologist Dr. Eugene Rittich, bought a 45-acre vineyard in Kelowna near the Oblate Fathers' mission and planted vines that had been locally propogated. He also purchased a 20-acre site on Black Mountain. The larger vineyard near Kelowna prospered to such an extent that four years later wines made from these grapes were vinified at the Growers' Wine Company in Victoria. Encouraged by his success, Hughes was to expand his vineyard to 300 acres. But the experiment at Black Mountain proved a disaster since the vines were wiped out by winter kill.

Rittich, however, was convinced that grapes could be grown on Black Mountain. It was just a question of finding the right variety and employing the correct viticultural practices to prevent winter kill. As the first champion of *vinifera* grapes in the province, he experimented with forty-four varieties on this site and one in the barren Oliver region. In 1930, he is said to have imported from Hungary a winter-hardy vine which would revolutionize the BC wine industry and provide the basis for its future development—a grape that became known as the Okanagan Riesling.*

In the same year Rittich was hired as the winemaker for the Growers' Wine Company, which had previously specialized in loganberry wine. A freak of nature was to give the fledgling industry the boost it needed. Successive abundant harvests of apples

---

* There is some controversy over the provenance of Okanagan Riesling. There are those who suggest that it is a Seyve Villard hybrid variety or a clone of Sauvignon Blanc. Lloyd Schmidt, a long-time grower in BC and now a consultant to vineyards in Ontario and Nova Scotia, traced the variety to a Hungarian grower named Teleki who had a grape breeding program near Oliver in the 1930s.

caused a glut on the market and many farmers were forced to tear up their orchards and plant grapes instead. Growers' Wine Company was paying $100 a ton for grapes (compared to $65 a ton in Ontario) while apples were left rotting under the trees. "A cent a pound or on the ground" was the farmers' anguished cry. "A dollar a box or on the rocks."

At the height of the Depression in 1932, an immigrant Italian winemaker named Guiseppe Ghezzi came to Kelowna with the idea of creating a winery to use the worthless apple crop. The idea had also occurred to a local hardware store owner, William Andrew Cecil Bennett who had discussed just such a possibility with his neighbour on Kelowna's main street, an Italian grocer, Pasquale "Cap" Capozzi. Both men were teetotallers but they joined with Ghezzi to form a company called Domestic Wines and By-Products. The company would manufacture not only wines but a whole gamut of products including "apple cider...brandy, alcohol, spirits of all kinds, fruit juices, soft drinks, fruit concentrates, jelly, jams, pickles, vinegar, tomato paste, tomato catsup, tomato juice and by products of every kind." The debonair Guiseppe Ghezzi stayed long enough to set up the winery before emigrating to California where he established a champagne plant.

Bennett and Capozzi set about raising money to finance their new operation. At a time when soup kitchens meant more to the public than wineries, they began selling $1 shares in the company; they raised $4,500 and although they were undercapitalized, they bought fermenting tanks and other equipment to begin this multi-faceted business. In September 1932, they took up residence in an old rented building on Kelowna's Smith Avenue. The following year they hired Guiseppe Ghezzi's son Carlo as winemaker to complete their staff of eight employees. Their initial production included four apple-based wines—Okay Red, Okay Clear, Okay Port and Okay Champagne. But the products were far from "okay." Even the company's official history records that the wines "were a bitter disappointment. Many bottles refermented on liquor store shelves and had to be thrown out. Liquor stores were reluctant to stock the ill-famed domestic wines and people were reluctant to buy them." Sales in the company's first full year of operation were a disaster, amounting to a mere few thousand dollars.

After three years of ineffectual competition against the genuine wines of the Growers' Company, Bennett and Capozzi realized that BC consumers just did not want apple wines. They switched to grapes which they bought in California and soon Growers' and the Victoria Wineries on Vancouver Island did likewise, perpetuating the fiction of making domestic wines by using what local grapes as were available.

With the change of style the former apple winery needed a change of name, and in 1936 the directors chose a phonetic spelling of the Indian place name where the company was born: Calona Wines Limited. Okay Clear apple wine became Calona Clear grape "wine" — a white semi-sweet product whose label read ominously, "When Fully Mature: About 28% Proof Spirit."

In 1940, W.A.C. Bennett left Calona to pursue a career in politics. One year later he was elected to the BC parliament and he sold his shares to Capozzi. When he became premier of the province in 1952, he took a serious look at the wine industry he had helped to create. If the wineries were to sell their products through the government-controlled liquor stores then they should do their part in promoting the grape-growing sector, he argued. In 1960, the BC government passed a law stating that wines vinified in the province had to contain a minimum percentage of locally grown grapes. Since there were only 585 acres under vines in the Okanagan Valley that figure was set at 25%. To encourage the planting of new vineyards, the Liquor Board stated that the quota would rise to 50% in 1962 and 65% by 1965.

Farmers in the Okanagan began planting French and American hybrids (Okanagan Riesling, De Chaunac, Maréchal Foch, Verdelet, Rougeon, Chelois and Baco Noir) with a vengeance and within four years the total acreage had risen by 400%.

In 1961, Andrew Peller built himself Andrés' spanking new winery at Port Moody; six years later a company called Southern Okanagan Wines of Penticton opened for business but soon changed its name to Casabello. At the same time the beautifully situated Mission Hill Winery was built on a ridge overlooking Okanagan Lake at Westbank. This facility was acquired in 1969 by the ebullient construction king and brewer, Ben Ginter, who promptly renamed it with characteristic flamboyance (if little understanding of consumer sophistication) Uncle Ben's Gourmet Winery. He also put a portrait of himself on his labels. Among the products Ginter was to market were such crass items as Fuddle Duck and Hot Goose.

In 1973, the Growers' Wines Cooperative, which had merged with Victoria Wineries and changed its name to Castle Wines, was acquired from Imperial Tobacco by Carling O'Keefe. Another corporate name change was in store. Castle Wines became Ste-Michelle Wines—a subsidiary of Jordan and Ste-Michelle Cellars Ltd.—in 1974. The company had long outgrown its facility in Victoria and looked to the mainland to build a modern winery to service the growing demand in the province for table wines. Four years later they began building at Surrey just south of Vancouver and opened operations in April 1978.

From 1974 to 1979 growers turned their attentions to grape varieties imported from California and Washington. Experimental plantings of Cabernet Sauvignon, Merlot, Chenin Blanc, Gewürztraminer, White and Grey Riesling, Semillon and Chardonnay were evaluated at 18 sites throughout the Okanagan. In 1975, George Heiss brought in Auxerrois, Pinot Gris and Gewürztraminer from France to plant in his Okanagan Centre vineyard.

In March 1977, the BC Ministry of Consumer and Corporate Affairs, responding to a strong lobby from the wineries and grape growers, announced a new liquor policy "to recognize the health and social costs caused by the abuse of alcohol on the one hand and consumer demand for better products, better prices and better premises in which to have a drink, on the other." The thrust of the new legislation was to encourage the consumption of wine, both imported and domestic, at the expense of hard liquor and beer.

To help the provincially based wineries compete with low-cost imports, the government lowered the mark-up on table wines from 66% to 46% (at the same time reducing imports from 117% to 100% mark-up).* To give their products a sales boost, BC wineries were allowed to open a retail store on their premises and under the aegis of the federal and provincial Ministries of Agriculture a five-year grape-growing program was introduced at a cost of $133,000 to upgrade the quality of the grapes they had to use. The program was directed by world-famous viticulturalist, the late Dr. Helmut Becker, then head of the Research Institute of Grape Breeding and Grape Propogation at Geisenheim in Germany. At the invitation of Andrés Wines, Dr. Becker selected twenty-seven European varieties for testing in BC soil.

---

*As a further incentive to the wineries the government relented over its ban on TV advertising and on October 1, 1992, the companies were allowed to promote their products on the air.

Two three-acre plots were chosen for the experiment — a southern site on light, sandy soil near Oliver, and a northern site in the heavier soil at Okanagan Mission. The first wines made from these grapes were vinified by the Summerland Research Station in 1980. The most promising varietals turned out to be Auxerrois, Ehrenfelser, Pinot Blanc, Bacchus, Gewürztraminer, Müller-Thurgau, Schonburger and Scheurebe.

Looking south to the Napa and Sonoma Valleys of California, the BC government realized that there was great tourist potential for a thriving wine industry in the beautiful Okanagan Valley setting.

After years of bureaucratic foot-shuffling they finally agreed to the creation of cottage or estate wineries; the first in the field was Claremont. In 1979, Bob Claremont took over a facility built by Marion John who had planted vineyards on a steep slope just north of Peachland nineteen years earlier. John's first wines were made and bottled at Mission Hill Winery, but Claremont, who had worked as a winemaker at Calona as well as at Jordan's Ontario plant, set up a crusher, fermentation tanks and a bottling line, and began to vinify BC's first estate bottle wines in 1979.

The BC Liquor Control and Licencing Branch, not knowing how to deal with the novel enterprise, hastily introduced regulations which both encouraged and inhibited the new winery. To be an estate winery the company had to cultivate 20 acres of vines and could only make a maximum of 30,000 gallons. (This is now 40,000 gallons for the domestic market and the estate wineries can exceed this figure if they export the product.) All the grapes used in the wine had to be grown in the province and 50% of these had to come from Claremont's own vineyards. The winery was allowed to open a retail store on its premises and could sell directly to licencees without having to pay the government mark-up. Claremont could sell two products through the specialty liquor stores only, but these would only carry the then mark-up of 15%.

Within the next three years Bob Claremont was joined by four other small producers in the Okanagan—Sumac Ridge, Vinitera (which subsequently went into receivership in 1982), Uniacke Cellars (now CedarCreek), Gray Monk, and in the spring of 1983, Divino Wines in Oliver. In those early days, there was a feeling of camaraderie among the operators of these small wineries and they helped each other out when they could by sharing facilities and equipment, such as hand-labelling machines, or storing one another's wines. They are the pioneers of a new phase of BC's growing wine industry. While the estate wineries still co-operate among themselves, most are well established enough to have their own equipment.

Meanwhile, Uncle Ben's Gourmet Wines, suffering the consequences of marketing dubious wines, fell foul of the banks and re-emerged briefly under the name of Golden Valley Wines. However, its reincarnation did not help its balance sheet; thanks to union animosity following troubles at Ginter's Red Deer Brewery, Ginter was forced to sell and the company was bought in 1981 by Anthony Von Mandl's Mark Anthony group, a successful Vancouver-based firm of wine importers, who immediately gave it back its original name of Mission Hill and began a massive reorganization.

The newest commercial winery to open in BC belonged to Brights. On land leased from the Osoyoos Indians south of Oliver near the American border, the company built a spectacular modern winery in 1981 to ferment grapes grown by Indian growers on the Inkameep vineyards. The building alone cost $2 million funded by development money from the provincial and federal governments. Brights has invested $3.5 million in equipment for the new facility.

In total there are currently twenty-two wineries operating in British Columbia. Six so-called "majors" (they don't like the term "commercial") — Andrés, Brights, Calona, Cartier, Mission Hill and Okanagan Vineyards; twelve estate wineries — CedarCreek, Chateau St. Claire, Divino, Domaine de Chaberton, Gerhinger Bros., Gray Monk, Hainle, LeComte, Quails' Gate, St. Laszlo, Sumac Ridge and Summerhill Estates; and four farmgate operations — A & H Vineyards, Hillside Cellars, Lang and Wild Goose. A fifth farm winery has just opened in Kelowna, called St. Hubertus Vineyard and in the fall two new operations on Vancouver Island await licence approval and two more are likely to open next year. In 1993, three farmgate operations are projected for the Naramata area and another estate winery may open in the Oliver area.

While the estate and farm wineries have to use locally grown grapes, the large commercial concerns can get the raw material where they please. Technically, they are obligated to use 80% of BC-grown grapes and under an agreement with the province's Grape Marketing Board the entire commercial production is contracted to the wineries. They must buy them in the corresponding percentage to their market share whether they need them or not. However, the grape crop in BC represents a mere 65% of the total grapes used for wine in the province. The balance comes from California, Washington or Oregon, giving BC wines a taste profile somewhat different from Ontario-made products, particularly when the wine can contain 100% Californian grapes and still have a BC label.

Until 1988, BC boasted 200 vineyards covering 3,400 acres in the Okanagan, Similkameen and Osoyoos areas. Under the free trade and GATT agreements the BC industry was forced to downsize. (Liquor boards across Canada were forced to get rid of tariffs on imported wines.) Two-thirds of the vineyards were pulled out. At the time of writing there are 115 vineyard sites in four growing areas recognized by the VQA: Okanagan, Similkameen, Fraser Valley and Vancouver Island. Total acreage is now about 1,500, mostly *vinifera*. The top ten varieties at the last grape census in 1991 were:

Riesling—161 acres
Chardonnay—127 acres
Pinot Blanc—111 acres
Gewürztraminer—87 acres
Pinot Noir—83 acres
Bacchus—83 acres
Auxerrois—44 acres
Chasselas—37 acres
Merlot—31 acres

Other specialty plantings of *vinifera* include:

Müller-Thurgau—27 acres
Optima—18 acres
Chenin Blanc—15 acres
Scheurebe—14 acres
Pinot Gris—13 acres
Siegfried Rebe—13 acres

Premium hybrids include:

Vedelet—122 acres
Vidal—50 acres
Seyval Blanc—35 acres
Maréchal Foch—34 acres

Chancellor—24 acres
Baco Noir—21 acres
Pearl of Zala—22 acres

BRITISH COLUMBIA WINERIES

LEGEND

** Gold Medal winning wine in competition
* Silver or Bronze medal winning wine
Note: wines listed at LDB (Liquor Distribution Branch) will also be found in the winery stores

The type and/or size of each winery is indicated by the symbol accompanying the winery's profile.

A & H VINEYARDS

R.R. #2
Trepanier Bench Road
S-27 C-16
Peachland
British Columbia
VOH 1X0

phone: (604) 767-9250

Founded in July 1991, A & H became the fifth farm winery in BC. The letters stand for the first names of the owners, Ann and Henry Moeller. Henry learned his winemaking from Bob Claremont who operated the first estate winery in the province (created by Marion John in 1978). He furthered his experience with three visits to the Mosel. The winery consists of a garage housing the bottling line and a tin-roofed, underground cistern which acts as a cellar.

Winemaker: Henry Moeller

Acreage: 8

Soil: Well-ventilated south-east slope, sandy loam.

Varieties: Johannisberg Riesling (5 acres), Kerner (3 acres)

Production: 700 cases

Average tonnage crushed: 10 tons

Grapes bought in: 4 tons

Winemaking philosophy: "Old European (German) ways of making wine."

Wines: Johannisberg Riesling Dry and Medium Dry

Store on premises: Summer hours: 9 am – 6 pm Tuesday to Sunday
Winter hours: 1 pm – 6 pm Thursday to Sunday or by appointment.

Tours: yes

Public tastings: yes

ANDRÉS
WINES (BC) LTD.

2120 Vintner Street
Port Moody
British Columbia
V3H 1W8

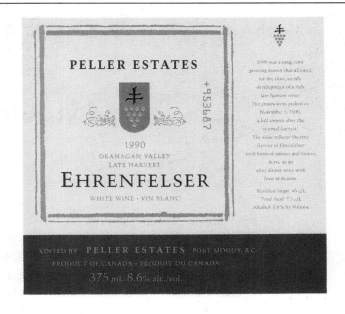

Andrés Wines began operating in Vancouver's western suburb of Port Moody in 1961 and opened wineries within a year in Nova Scotia and Alberta, followed quickly by Quebec, Manitoba and Ontario. Although the commercial heart has now shifted to the Winona plant in Ontario, Port Moody is the historic soul of the company. This facility on Vintner Street was purpose-built when Andrew Peller could not acquire a going concern at the price he wanted. The original winemaker Wallace Pohl, like the equipment, came from California. Early bottlings used California grapes which increased their price in the marketplace against wines of other BC houses. The public equated the expense with higher quality and bought Andrés' products to such a degree that Andrew Peller expanded quickly into other provinces. The growth took its toll on the founder's health and his son, Dr. Joe Peller, gave up his medical practice to run the company. In the 1970s, Andrés developed 300 acres of French hybrid and *vinifera* vines on Indian land near Oliver, called Inkameep Vineyards.

The company markets a variety of wines under different labels corresponding to the grape source: Franciscan California, Gold Coast (Australia), Domaine D'Or Cuvée Blanc and Dumons Cuvée Blanc (France) and Peller Estates for its VQA varietal wines.

The Domaine D'Or Chardonnay is a blend of several wine regions: Australia, California and Chile.

Winemaker: Ron Taylor

Acreage: 350 contracted

Production: 500,000 cases

Average tonnage crushed: 950 tonnes

Winemaking philosophy: "Andrés Wines produces good quality for good value, without compromise. Our quality assurance system guarantees this philosophy."

LDB wines: *white*—Cellar Reserve Superior, Cellar Reserve Dry, Cellar Reserve White, Clos Du Lac, Domaine D'Or, Domaine D'Or Chardonnay, Domaine D'Or Supérieur, Edna-Star, Ehrenfelser Late Harvest★, Grand Chablis, Hochtaler, Hochtaler Dry, Hochtaler Gold Riesling, Hochtaler Light, Nordique Blanc, Similkameen, Similkameen Ehrenfelser, Similkameen Chablis, Similkameen Pinot Blanc,

Similkameen Superior, Souvenance Blanc de Blanc, Stone's Green Ginger (under licence)

red—Cellar Reserve Dry, Domaine D'Or, Kellys, Similkameen Superior

Winery store: *Franciscan California label*—Chablis, Chardonnay; *Gold Coast label*—Chardonnay; Domaine D'Or Cuvée Blanc, Dumons Cuvée Blanc
Peller Estates label—Ehrenfelser Late Harvest★, Pinot Blanc, Seyval Blanc; Andrés Nordique Blanc★

red—Domaine D'Or Supérieur Dry, Franciscan California Burgundy, Peller Estates Maréchal Foch

Sparkling: Baby Duck, Baby Champagne, Dry Champagne, Kurhauser Trocken Sekt, Richelieu Deluxe Brut, Sparkling Hochtaler

Sherries: Almond Cream, Golden Cream, Medium Dry

Winery store hours: Wednesday 10 am – 6 pm
Thursday & Friday 12 pm – 8 pm
Saturday & Sunday 11 am – 4:30 pm

Tours: Saturday and Sunday 2 pm or by appointment

Public tastings: yes

BLUE MOUNTAIN VINEYARD AND CELLARS

R.R. #1, S-3, C-4
Okanagan Falls
British Columbia
VOH 1R0

phone: (604) 497-8244

We at Blue Mountain are proud to introduce our estate grown 1991 Pinot Gris — a wine of distinction.

This elegant wine opens with aromas of tropical fruit and anise. The mid-palate is filled with crisp fruit flavours and subtle undertones of French oak. The long rich finish is consistent with the wine-making style of Blue Mountain.

BLUE MOUNTAIN

PINOT GRIS
OKANAGAN VALLEY

BOTTLED BY
BLUE MOUNTAIN
VINEYARD AND CELLARS LTD.
Okanagan Falls, British Columbia
Canada VOH 1R0
(604) 497-8244

750ml   WHITE WINE / VIN BLANC   12.8% alc./vol.
ESTATE BOTTLED
Product of British Columbia, Canada / Produit du Columbie Britannique, Canada

At the time of writing Ian Mavety's Blue Mountain Vineyard and Cellars is not officially open but they released their first wines in the summer of 1992—a barrel-fermented Pinot Blanc and a blended barrel-and-tank fermented Pinot Gris. In 1993, they plan to release a Pinot Noir 1991 and a *méthode champenoise* sparkler. By 1994, they hope to add a Chardonnay to their list.

"Our excitement over the 1991 vintate and hence our decision to go to market with these wines," writes Ian, "is due to a culmination of events; firstly, an excellent growing season; secondly, the information gained over the last four years; and thirdly, in no small part our involvement with a consultant, Raphael Brisbois, currently the winemaker at Iron Horse Vineyards in Sonoma, California."

BRIGHTS
WINES (BC) LTD.

Box 1650
Oliver
British Columbia
V0H 1T0

phone: (604) 498-4981
fax: (604) 498-6505

Brights' contemporary-rustic 45,000 square foot building stands in splendid solitude in a wilderness of pine-clad granite mountains and arid plains in southern British Columbia. On the wall by the entrance hangs a framed photograph showing the Chief of the Osoyoos Indian Band, Sam Baptiste, shaking hands with the Managing Director of Brights, Ed Arnold. It is dated May 14, 1982, the official opening date of the winery (although the company had 1981 wines on the market, produced at the winery before the roof was on).

The Indian band farms the Inkameep vineyard adjacent to the winery. This vineyard is the largest in the Okanagan, 200 acres of which are contracted to Brights. Lynn Bremmer, BC's first woman winemaker, has presided over the winemaking since the facility opened. Her best wines, all varietals, appear under the Vaseaux Cellars label.

As in Ontario, Brights has been in the forefront of experimentation and grape research, the fruits of which appear as limited edition wines under the Brights label. A limited amount of Vidal Icewine is made.

Under its Ste-Michelle label the company bottles wines made from imported American grapes.

Brights' BC plant is also the largest cider producer in Canada.

Winemaker: Lynn Bremmer

Acreage: 200 acres contracted

Soil: ranging from sandy to clay

Production: 492,000 cases

Average tonnage crushed: 900

Grapes bought in: 2,000 tons from California and Washington

Winemaking philosophy: "The Okanagan Valley in the south-central BC area of Canada has unique geographical and climatological variations making it well-suited to the production of premium grape vines. To produce a great wine, vines must be grown near the northern limit of their cultural adaptability. Brights realizes that they are in a global market. We purchase wines from around the world for our marketplace—unique to Canada in that we bring in the raw material to Canada and process it here to keep jobs here."

LDB wines: *white*—Cuvée du Berceau, Entre Lacs, Entre-Lacs Classic Chardonnay, Dry House White, Liebesheim, Classic White, Manor St. David Medium Dry, Toscano Bianco, Sawmill Creek Fume Blanc

Vaseaux Cellars label—Chardonnay★, Okanagan Vintage Select, Pinot Blanc★★, Optima★, Vidal★, Vintage Select, Gewürztraminer★, Kerner★

red—Vaseaux Cellars Baco Noir★★, Vaseaux Cellars Pinot Noir, Cuvée du Berceau, Entre Lacs

sparkling—VC OK Champagne

sherries—Pale Dry Select, '67 Sherry, '74 Sherry, '74 Port

Winery store: Optima★, Ste-Michelle Bacchus, California House Red & White

Vaseaux Cellars label—Kerner★, Ehrenfelser, Rkatsiteli, Matsvani, Perle of Csaba, Bacchus, Gewürztraminer, Müller Thurgau, Schonburger, Sereksia Chornaya

Ste-Michelle label: Monta Rosa Chablis, Monta Rosa Burgundy, Ste-Michelle Johannisberg Riesling★★, Le Villageois, Spumante, B.S. Rich Red, Toscano Bianco, Toscano Rosso

Store hours: 8 am – 4 pm, Monday to Friday, September to April

8 am – 5 pm, Monday through Sunday, May through August

Tours: summer months only (May to August)

Public tastings: May to September, 9 am – 5 pm, daily

CALONA WINES

1125 Richter Street
Kelowna
British Columbia
V1Y 2K6

phone: (604) 762-3332
　　　1-800-663-5086
fax: (604) 762-2999

In 1932 when the original company was formed, apples were the raw material for their products. Later, other fruits were introduced under the Jack line (Cherry Jack is still in Calona's portfolio). Since its founding during the Depression, the winery has been associated with the Capozzi family who make no bones about the fact that they modelled their products and sales strategies on those of Ernest & Julio Gallo, the world's largest winery. In fact, in 1969 there was talk about an amalgamation of the two wineries. Calona's continuing prosperity has historically been based on its blended products, including such popular labels as Schloss Laderheim, Sommet Blanc and Sommet Rouge. The winery also bottles Almaden, Inglenook and Buena Vista wines from California and Hogue Cellars under the Washington Vineyards label.

The wines generally have a sweetness of flavour due to back-blending of 20% or more of fresh juice after fermentation.

Experiments with Okanagan-grown Chardonnay fermented and aged in both American and French oak are released under the Artists Reserve label.

Winemaker: Howard Soon

Production: 1,000,000 cases

Grapes bought in: 400 tons

Varieties: Johannisberg Riesling, Chardonnay, Rougeon, Chelois, Souvereign Opal

Winemaking philosophy: "Everything we do has a marketing emphasis. We find out what people like, what they're looking for. We look worldwide to see what's happening."

LDB wines: *white*—Mountain Sauterne, Pinot Blanc, Reserve Johannisberg Riesling, Reserve Sovereign Opal, Reserve Gewürztraminer★, Royal White, Schloss Laderheim (also Light and Dry versions), Sommet Blanc★, Sommet Supérieur, Spring Hill Chablis, White Dry

red—Chelois, Dry Red, Royal Red, Beaupre Royal Red, San Pietro, Sommet Rouge, Sommet Supérieur, Rougeon★

Own store: Pinot Noir★★

sparkling—La Scala Spumante, Pastel Peach

fortified—Cream Sherry, Cocktail, Royal French Vermouth white and red, Okanagan Valley Port

Own store: LBV Port

Store hours: 10 am – 6 pm

Tours: yes

Public tastings: yes

CARTIER WINES & BEVERAGES

2210 Main Street
Penticton
British Columbia

phone: (604) 492-0621
fax: (604) 492-6990

In 1966, a new company called Southern Okanagan Wines crushed their first grapes in Penticton. One year later they changed their name to Casabello. Located on the town's Main Street they became a major tourist attraction. The company was bought by Labatts in 1973 and became the BC arm of Ridout Wines which included Ontario's Chateau-Gai operation. Now it is owned by the management team who ran both wineries (see Cartier Wines & Beverages in Ontario).

In addition to its locally made wines, Cartier offers import selections.

Winemaker: Bruce Nicholson

Production: 500,000 cases

Average tonnage crushed: 300 tons BC grapes (American fruit bought in as required)

Winemaking philosophy: "Quality wines require commitment and involvement. Our grape growers, processing and bottling employees work together to achieve the highest standards possible."

LDB wines: *white*—Adagio, Alpenweiss, Capistro, Capistro Dry, Capistro Light, Chenin Blanc, Gala Dry, Gala Medium, Gewürztraminer★, L'Ambiance, White Riesling★

Casabello label—Chablis Blanc, Gala Dry, Gala Medium, L'Escapade, Osoyoos Select Dry, San Gabriel, Summerland Riesling

red—Chancellor★, Gala Medium Dry, L'Ambiance

Cassabello label—Burgon Rouge, Gala Italian, Gala (Dry, Medium, Rich), Osoyoos Select Dry, Regal

Fortified: Bounty, Private Stock Sherry★, Hallmark Cream Sherry

Imported: *French*—Chantonné white and red, Cuvée Sélectionne white and red; *Germany*—Weinkeller; *California*—San Gabriel California Chablis

Store hours: 10 am – 6 pm daily

Tours: yes

Public tastings: during store hours

CEDARCREEK ESTATE WINERY

5445 Lakeshore Road
Kelowna
British Columbia
V1Y 7R3

phone: (604) 764-886
fax: (604) 764-2603

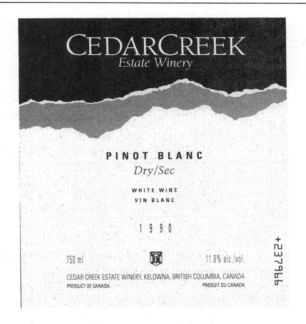

In 1986, David Ross Fitzpatrick of Kelowna bought Uniacke winery and vineyards (founded by grower David Mitchell in 1980). The contemporary Mediterranean-style winery built above the cellar was designed by a Uniacke partner, David Newman-Bennett. The winemaker then was the youthful Weinsberg-trained oenologist Tilman Hainle who went on to create his own winery with his grape grower father, Walter, in 1985.

CedarCreek is situated south of Kelowna near Okanagan Mission at an elevation of 300 metres. Fitzpatrick originally hired as winemaker Vienna-born Helmut Dotti who had worked at Ste-Michelle facilities across the country and for Mission Hill. Ann Sperling now makes CedarCreek wines. Extensive use of French oak in barrel fermenting and aging. Chardonnay is a combination of barrel fermentation, barrel aging and stainless steel. Their first Icewine was produced from Riesling grapes in 1991 (1500 half bottles).

Winemaker: Ann Sperling

Acreage: 30

Soil: Well-drained sandy loam that ranges from light to heavy from top to bottom of the steep southwest facing slope. Moderately saline and calcareous.

Varieties: Riesling, Chardonnay, Gewürztraminer, Auxerrois, Pinot Noir, Merlot

Production: 20,000 cases

Average tonnage crushed: 285 tons

Grapes bought in: 50%

Winemaking philosophy: "Fine wine is made in the vineyard. We have been working at planting the right varieties/clones to suit our conditions, then harvesting at optimum maturity to give full flavour development for that variety. We use traditional wine-making techniques to produce wines with a Pacific Northwest flavour and style to match our lifestyle and food style."

LDB wines: Proprietor's White★, Red★ & Blush★, Riesling Blanc, Pinot Blanc★, Johannisberg Riesling★, Reserve Auxerrois, Pinot Auxerrois★, Gewürztraminer★, Chancellor

Winery store: Johannisberg Riesling Dry★, Semillon, Chardonnay, Merlot Reserve★, Pinot Noir★

Store on premises: Hours: 9:30 am – 5 pm November to March
9:30 am – 5:30 pm April to October

Tours: May to October

Tastings: as per store hours

DIVINO ESTATE WINERY

Road 8, Box 866
Oliver
British Columbia
V0H 1T0

phone: (604) 498-2784
fax: (604) 498-6518

Joseph Busnardo is something of a maverick in the BC wine industry, choosing not to be part of the BC Wine Institute. He has been growing grapes for twenty-four years, experimenting with over 100 varieties most of which came from his native Italy. Currently he is making wine from the eight most successful *vinifera* varietals in his Oliver vineyard. His winery was founded in 1982 and is now the largest of the BC estate wineries. His winemaking technique is defiantly Italian and Veneto in particular. He uses only stainless steel for his Chardonnay. Joseph is planning to have a bistro facility at the winery.

Winemaker: Joseph Busnardo

Acres: 70.8

Soil: Rocky, gravelly, high pH factor. ("However, it is probably the best soil in the Okanagan Valley for *Vitis vinifera*.")

Varieties: Merlot, Cabernet France, Chardonnay, Trebbiano, Tocai, Pinot Bianco, Pinot Grigio, Malvasia, Perle of Csaba

Production: 17,000 cases

Average tonnage crushed: 200 to 250 tonnes

Grapes bought in: none

Winemaking philosophy: "My style of winemaking could be classed as *primitivo* and 'earthy'. I am attempting to produce

109

wines indicative of the Okanagan Valley. In order to have a good wine you must have good grapes. My philosophy is that if the wine is good enough for me, then it is good enough for the general public!"

LDB wines: *white*—Chardonnay* (vintage), Chardonnay (non-vintage), Malvasia*, Pinot Bianco*, Pinot Chardonnay*, Pinot de Pinot, Tocai, Trebbiano*

red—Merlot/Cabernet

Winery stores: *white*—Bacaro, Bianco di Giuseppe, Chardonnay Classico, Tesoro

dry rosé—Pinot Grigio

red—Bacaro, Cabernet, Merlot*, Rosso di Giuseppe

Dessert: Amarone Bianco, Amarone Rosso, Perle of Csaba, Tocai Late Harvest*

Stores:

Vancouver: Corks 'n Candles, 1610 Robson St.

New
Westminster: Divino's Quayside Cellar, 810 Quayside

DOMAINE DE
CHABERTON

1064 – 216th Street
Langley
British Columbia
V3A 7R2

phone: (604) 530-1736
              530-5398
fax: (604) 533-9687

In July 1991, Claude Violet opened his winery named after the farm he owned in southern France. A Parisian by birth, Claude comes from a French Catalan family that can trace itself back nine generations of winemakers over 350 years to Manaut Violet, cooper and grape grower. When Claude came to Canada in 1981 he brought his winegrowing experience that encompassed dealings in France, Switzerland and Spain. Instead of choosing the Okanagan, he bought a 55-acre farm in South Langley and converted it into vineyards, becoming the first commercial grape grower in the Fraser Valley. His winery is the most southerly on the BC mainland.

Winemakers: Elias Phiniotis and Claude Violet

Acreage: 27

Soil: "Top quality soil. Much less rain than Vancouver."

Varieties: Bacchus, Madeleine Angevine, Madeleine Sylvaner, Ortega, Chardonnay, Chasselas Doré

Average tonnage crushed: 52 tonnes

Winemaking philosophy: "In winemaking there must be love. I grew up in the atmosphere of wine so it is so natural, so normal. For me, it's quality before quantity."

Own store: *white*—Madeleine Angevine, Madeleine Sylvaner, Bacchus, Ortega★

Store hours: 10 am – 6 pm, Monday – Saturday
Noon – 5 pm, Sundays

Tours: yes

Public tastings: store hours

GEHRINGER
BROTHERS ESTATE
WINERY

R.R. #1
Site 23, Comp.4
Oliver
British Columbia
VOH 1T0

phone: (604) 498-3537
fax: (604) 498-3510

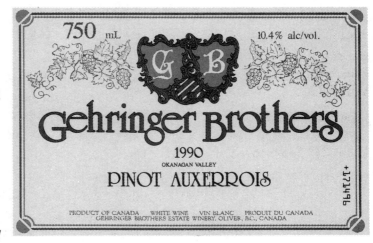

Walter and Gordon Gehringer made their first wine 1985, but not before both had acquired sound experience in oenology and viticulture at Germany's famed schools Geisenheim and Weinsberg, respectively. During their summer vacations, the brothers brought back winemaking equipment as well as techniques they had learned for application to the grapes grown by their father Helmut and his brother Karl. Slowly, they evolved the style which has become the benchmark for the company's white wines: fermentation to dryness and then back-blending with 10% fresh juice just before bottling.

In 1981, the Gehringers selected their vineyard site eight kilometres north of Osoyoos, north of Mount Kobau, and one year later Gordon returned to manage it. All white varieties were planted. In 1984, Walter, who had spent five years as winemaker for Andrés both in Ontario and BC, joined the enterprise. The following year they began construction of the winery.

No oak is used in the winemaking process. In 1991, the brothers produced their first Icewine. A consistent gold medal winner.

Winemakers: Walter and Gordon Gehringer

Acreage: 25

Soil: Located on a narrow upper bench of the valley above the frost zone at the southern end of the Okanagan. South-facing slope offers good exposure and air drainage.

Varieties: Johannisberg Riesling, Verdelet, Pinot Auxerrois, Ehrenfelser, Schonburger

Production: 15,000 cases

Average tonnage crushed: 220

Grapes bought in: 110 tons

Winemaking philosophy: "In the Fall the grapes are pressed and a portion of the juice is stored fresh and unfermented. Before bottling in the Spring, we blend the unfermented juice, which has retained its rich flavour, back into the dry wine. This results in the varietal fruit flavour components being combined with the developed wine, yielding a complex, full-bodied wine. All our wines have a pleasant, harmonious taste, bringing out the subtle, yet distinctive flavours of each grape variety."

LDB wines: *white*—Ehrenfelser★★, Johannisberg Riesling Dry (vintage★★ and non-vintage), Johannisberg Riesling★★, Müller Thurgau★★, Pinot Auxerrois★★, Verdelet★

red—Cuvée Noire (Baco Noir, Rougeon, Rosette, Chancellor)

Winery store: Schonburger★, Ehrenfelser Icewine★, Chancellor Icewine★

red—Johannisberg Riesling Icewine

Store hours: July to August 10 am – 5 pm
September to June: Monday – Friday 10 am – 5 pm
Saturday 10 am – 1 pm

Tours: by appointment only "for larger groups"

Public tastings: during store hours

**GRAY MONK
CELLARS**

Box 63
Okanagan Centre
British Columbia
J0H 1P0

phone: (604) 766-3168
        1-800-663-4205
fax: (604) 766-3390

The vineyards sweep down the eastern slope from the winery which commands a spectacular view Okanagan Lake. It is the most northerly estate winery on the continent. George Heiss, born and raised in Vienna, started building his classically simple farm-house style winery in January 1982, ten years after he had torn out acres of aged orchard and planted his first European vines. The winery name is a translation of what the Austrians call the Pinot Gris grape—Gray Monk. The caricature of a chubby tonsured monk appeared on the Gothic-scripted label (surely the worst in the country!). But it's what is in the bottle that counts and George, his wife Trudy and German-trained son, George Jr., make some of the best white wines in BC as evidenced by the number of medals the winery has won in provincial, national and international competitions.

The style as you would expect is Germanic, but remarkably delicate.

All the wines are made in stainless steel and some are exported to Japan.

Winemaker: George Heiss, Jr.

Acreage: 25

Varieties: Auxerrois, Pinot Gris, Ehrenfelser, Bacchus, Kerner, Rotberger, Seigerrebe, Gewürztraminer

Production: 15,000 – 18,000 cases

Average tonnage crushed: 240 tons

Grapes bought in: 100 tons

Winemaking philosophy: "We take pride in producing 100% varietals and showing the marketplace what can be done in the Okanagan."

LDB wines: *white*—Bacchus★, Ehrenfelser (Auslese★, Spätlese★★), Gewürztraminer Kabinett, Gewürztraminer Reserve★, Johannisberg Riesling★★, Kerner (Auslese★★, Spätlese★, Dry), Müller-Thurgau, Pinot Auxerrois★★, Pinot Blanc★★, Pinot Chardonnay★★, Pinot Gris★, Siegerrebe★★

red—Pinot Noir★, Rotberger Rosé★★

Own store: Latitude Fifty

Store hours: May 1 to October 31: 10 am – 5 pm every day
November 1 to April 30: Tuesday to Friday 1 pm – 5 pm
Saturday 11am – 5 pm
Sunday 12 pm – 4 pm until Christmas

Tours: yes (large tours by appointment)

Public tastings: during store hours

HAINLE
VINEYARDS

Trepanier Bench Road
R.R. #2, S27A, C6
Peachland
British Columbia
V0H 1X0

phone/fax:
(604) 767-2525

The Hainle family has been making wine in the Okanagan for over twenty-two years — and before that for 10 generations in Germany. Father Walter made Canada's first Icewine from Okanagan Riesling in 1973 for the benefit of family and friends. His son Tilman became winemaker at Uniacke Cellars at the tender age of twenty-one. He left when the winery was sold (to become CedarCreek) and joined his father across the lake near Peachland to create Hainle Vineyards in 1985.

Father and son built up an inventory of wines until they had sufficient to receive an estate winery licence in 1987. The winery is a 3,000 square foot block-construction building which will eventually allow for the 40,000 gallon annual production limit for estate wineries.

In 1991, Tilman began making champagne method sparkling wine (60% Pinot Noir, 30% Chardonnay, 10% Pinot Meunier). He adds sulphur dioxide only after fermentation to preserve the wine, believing that some oxidation of the fresh juice helps to clarify the wine so that little or no fining and filtering is necessary (which can rob the wine of varietal character).

Winemaker: Tilman Hainle

Acreage: 18.5 (No insecticides or herbicides used. Yields are kept low to make plants more resistant to disease and pests.)

Soil: Very light sandy soils, pH 6.5 – 6.8. High gravel content; glacio-fluvial slopes with south to south southeast exposure. Very good air circulation.

Varieties: Riesling, Traminer, Chardonnay, Chasselas, Pinot Noir and small plantings of Merlot, Pinot Meunier, Perle of Csaba, Trollinger, Lemberger

Production: 5,000 cases

Average tonnage crushed: 60 tons

Grapes bought in: 20 to 25 tons (Inkameep Vineyards, Hans Fischer, Southview Vineyards, Elisabeth Harbeck)

Winemaking philosophy: "To make wines in as natural a way as possible, to ferment them dry, avoid use of sulphites where possible, make wines to match with foods rather than as stand-alone beverages. Increase character of matured wine and aging notes in place of fruity primary aromas."

LDB Liquor stores wines: White Riesling Dry★, White Riesling, Riesling Dry Estate, Traminer Dry Estate★, Traminer Dry, Chasselas, Pinot Blanc, Riesling Icewine★★

Winery store: Trolling with Lemberger, Pinot Noir, Baco Noir★, Pinot Blanc Dry★, Okanagan Riesling Icewine

Winery store on premises: November to April, 1 pm – 5 pm May to October, Tuesday – Sunday, 10 am – 5 pm

Tours: by appointment

Public tastings: during shop hours

FARM

HILLSIDE CELLARS

1350 Naramata Road
Penticton
British Columbia
V2A 6J6

phone/fax:
(604) 493-4424

HILLSIDE CELLARS

Red Wine 1990 Vin Rouge

GAMAY

GROWN AND PRODUCED
by HILLSIDE CELLARS, PENTICTON, B.C.

750 ml 10.1% alc./vol.

PRODUCT of BRITISH COLUMBIA, CANADA PRODUIT DE LA COLOMBIE BRITANNIQUE, CANADA

Vera and Bohumir Klockocka came to Canada in 1968 when Soviet tanks rolled into Czechoslovakia. They settled in Kelowna and eventually bought a house and orchard in Naramata in the mid-1970s and began growing grapes. Vera taught herself winemaking and in 1990 she applied for a farmgate winery licence. She uses stainless steel tanks. In 1991 she made her first 25 cases of Cabernet Sauvignon (with 25% Merlot).

Winemaker: Vera Klockocka

Acreage: 5.6

Soil: Mostly stoney, sloping vineyard overlooking Naramata Road and Lake Okanagan.

Varieties: Johannisberg Riesling, Pinot Auxerrois, Muscat d'Alsace (Clevner), Gamay Beaujolais, some Cabernet Sauvignon

Production: 1,000 to 1,200 cases

Average tonnage crushed: 10 to 14 tons

Grapes bought in: 25%

Winemaking philosophy: "We produce the varietal wines dry fermented, 100% grape juice, no additives except sulphites. We try to stay as close to Nature as we can."

Wines: Johannisberg Riesling (no sweet reserve added), Pinot Auxerrois★, Muscat (Clevner), Gamay

Store on premises: Summer 10 am – 6 pm

Tours: on request

Tastings: as per store hours

LANG VINEYARDS

R.R. 1, S11, C55
2493 Common Road
Naramata
British Columbia
VOH 1N0

phone: (604) 496-5987
fax: (604) 496-5706

Guenther Lang has the distinction of being the first farm winery in Canada. In 1980, he gave up a lucrative executive position with Mercedes-Benz in Stuttgart and settled in the Okanagan Valley. The house he and his wife Kristina bought in Naramata had a nine-acre vineyard. What started as a hobby for the Langs turned into a business. In 1985, Guenther approached the BC government and asked if he could sell the wines he made. After some years of lobbying, a proffered bottle to then Premier Bill Van der Zalm seemed to oil the wheels of government because in 1990 the legislation was passed to set up farm wineries.

Guenther Lang sells some of his fruit to Mission Hill Vineyards. He makes his wines in stainless steel.

Winemaker: Guenther Lang

Acres: 9

Soil: West-facing slope, sandy-stone/clay soil.

Varieties: Gewürztraminer, Johannisberg Riesling, Pinot Noir, Pinot Meunier, Maréchal Foch

Production: 1,400 cases

Average tonnage crushed: 15 tons

Bought in grapes: 3 tons

Winemaking philosophy: "We strive for the highest quality grapes possible by controlling every step of viticulture, especially thinning to have a lighter crop. We harvest as late as possible to have a high degree of ripeness. We only make wine from healthy, truly ripe grapes using only *Vitis vinifera* varietals."

Wines: Own store only. Gewürztraminer★, Johannisberg Riesling Dry, Johannisberg Riesling Vintner's Reserve (medium sweet)★, Johannisberg Riesling Late Harvest★★, Maréchal Foch★★, Pinot Noir★★, Pinot Meunier

Store: May 15 – September 30, 10 am – 6pm daily
October – May by appointment

Tours: by arrangement

Public tastings: during store hours

LECOMTE ESTATE
WINERY

Box 498
Okanagan Falls
British Columbia
V0H 1R0

phone: (604) 497-8267
fax: (604) 497-8073

Albert LeComte founded his winery in 1983 between Skaha Lake and Vaseaux Lake, south of Okanagan Falls.

Winemaker: Albert LeComte

Soil: light sandy loam, hillside slopes

Acreage: 50

Varieties: Bacchus, Seyval Blanc, Müller-Thurgau, Ehrenfelser, Chardonnay, Pinot Blanc, Chelois, Maréchal Foch, Muscat Ottonel, Gewürztraminer, Pinot Noir, Riesling, Gamay Beaujolais

Production: 5,000 cases

Average tonnage crushed: 100

Grapes bought in: 40 tonnes

Winemaking philosophy: "To produce quality wines."

LDB wines: *white*—Bacchus, Chardonnay, Chenin Blanc, Gewürztraminer, Gewürztraminer Late Harvest★★, Johannisberg Riesling, Müller-Thurgau, Okanagan Riesling, Pinot Blanc★, Pinot Gris

red—Chelois, Chelois Private Reserve★, Maréchal Foch, Pinot Noir

Own store: Blanc de Noir, Spice Wine

Store hours: May and June, 10:30 am – 5 pm (Wednesday through Sunday)
July to April, 10:30 am – 5 pm daily

Tours: July to October, 12 pm, 2 pm, 4 pm daily (off season phone ahead)

Public tastings: during store hours

MAJOR

MISSION HILL VINEYARDS

Box 610
Westbank
British Columbia
VOH 2A0

phone: (604) 768-5125
fax: (604) 768-2044

MISSION HILL
1989
Private Reserve

BOTRYTIS AFFECTED
OPTIMA

The name is something of a misnomer since Mission Hill, one BC's most beautifully sited wineries, no longer owns vineyards but buys in its grape needs from over 200 contracted growers. This is a large enterprise that thinks like a sophisticated California estate winery and consistently produces award-winning wines. It takes its style from its flamboyant owner, Anthony von Mandl, president of The Mark Anthony Group, a wine, beer, spirit and cider conglomerate which also owns beverage alcohol stores.

Founded in 1966 by a consortium of Okanagan businessmen under chemist R.P. "Tiny" Walrod, Mission Hill has undergone several changes of ownership and name. It was taken over by Ben Ginter in 1970 who called it Uncle Ben's Gourmet Wines and then Golden Valley Wines. His larger-than-life activities in the brewing industry brought the winery close to bankrupcy. Ultimately, he was forced to sell to von Mandl who with Nick Clark, subsequently the first Director of BC's Wine Istitute, began to create a new image of quality for the winery. The winemaker is Daniel Lagnaz, who studied oenology in his native Switzerland and worked for one of Europe's largest wine companies, Schenck, in their Spain operation and for Lindeman in Australia.

Currently, Mission Hill has 400 French and American oak barrels with 200 more coming. In 1992, they released their first champagne-method sparkling wines: Cuvée Chardonnay and Cuvée Chenin Blanc.

The winery offers three labels, corresponding to three levels of quality: Mission Hill Private Reserve, Mission Hill Vintner's Series and Mission Ridge. They also carry some throwbacks to earlier days under the Golden Valley label, Caves Chauvignon and Cabaret Wines.

Winemaker: Daniel Lagnaz

Production: over 200,000 cases

Average tonnage crushed: over 1,700

Winemaking philosophy: "At Mission we have been inspired by the vision Robert Mondavi brought to the Napa Valley. In this spirit, our focus has been on quality and innovation. As the Okanagan Valley is a relatively young wine producing district, we felt it was important to experiment with a wide variety of *vinifera* varietals, allowing us over time to focus on those wines we believe have the greatest potential. Our focus is principally on dry wines, both white and red, and where we see exceptional potential to produce strictly limited quantities of specialty wines (Botryis Affected, Late Harvest, Méthode Champenoise, Vintage Port)...1989 was the vintage where we introduced the concept of aging white wines (Chardonnay, Semillon, Sauvignon Blanc) in new oak barrels. We are currently researching which type of toasting levels suit our wines and styles best. Our primary objective is to produce wines that show true varietal character and have excellent aging potential."

LDB wines: *Mission Hill Private Reserve label:*
white—Chardonnay, Reserve Chasselas, Chenin Blanc*, Gewürztraminer**, Johannisberg Riesling*, Pinot Blanc, Sauvignon Blanc*, Semillon* (stainless steel and oak-aged), Traminer Riesling*; red—Cabernet Sauvignon**, Merlot*, Pinot Noir, Vin Nouveau*; dessert—Botrytis Affected Optima**, Late Harvest Johannisberg Riesling**, Muscat of Alexandria

Mission Hill Vinter's Series: white—Chablis, Chenin Blanc, Dry White, Harvest Riesling, Riesling Dry, Semillon/ Sauvignon, Traminer/Riesling; red—Burgundy, Dry Red, Caravel Ruby, Maréchal Foch, Kuhlmann/Cabernet*

Mission Ridge Cellars: white—Premium Dry White, Premium Light White, Dry Chenin Blanc, Classic Riesling Dry, Traditional Harvest Riesling★, Semillon/Chardonnay★★, Verdelet/Riesling (Organic); *red*—Maréchal Foch★★ (Organic), Premium Dry Red, Premium Dry Rosé.

Winery stores: Bacchus, Chardonnay Bin 33 (barrel-fermented), Bin 77 (barrel-aged), Optima Botrytis Affected Dry, Cabernet Sauvignon/Merlot★

Fortified: Reserve Sherry★, Port★

Stores (in addition to winery boutique):

Vancouver: Granville Island Brewing Company, 1441 Cartwright St.

North Shore Wine Cellars, Lonsdale Quay Market, 159-123 Carrie Cates Court, North Vancouver

Marquis Wine Cellars, 1034 Davie St.

Broadway International Wine Shop, 2752 West Broadway

Richmond: Mark Anthony's Winemart, 8040 Ciook Rd.

Coquitlam: Charlie's Wine Cellar, #940 Sunwood Square, 3025 Lougheed Highway

White Rock: Mark Anthony's Winemart, Royal Centre, 15220 North Bluff Rd.

Burnaby: Charlie's Wine Cellar, 1120C-4700 Kingsway, Eaton Centre, Metrotown

Sechlet: Sunshine Coast Brewers Ltd., 1298 Wharf St.

Saanich: Mark Anthony's Winemart, 2560-A Sinclair Rd.

Tours & public tastings: daily 10 am – 4 pm, "later in summer."

OKANAGAN VINEYARDS/ OLIVER CELLARS

11 Road
Oliver
British Columbia
V0H 1T0

phone: (416) 498-6411
fax: (416) 498-4566

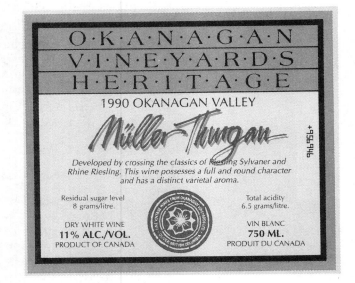

O·K·A·N·A·G·A·N
V·I·N·E·Y·A·R·D·S
H·E·R·I·T·A·G·E

1990 OKANAGAN VALLEY

Müller Thurgau

Developed by crossing the classics of Riesling Sylvaner and
Rhine Riesling. This wine possesses a full and round character
and has a distinct varietal aroma.

Residual sugar level
8 grams/litre.

Total acidity
6.5 grams/litre.

DRY WHITE WINE
11% ALC./VOL.
PRODUCT OF CANADA

VIN BLANC
750 ML.
PRODUIT DU CANADA

Mike Daley runs this winery founded in 1984 with its Spanish-style building. The investment comes from an English company, Bimadex Ltd. Recently planted are serious amounts of *vinifera* vines. The first vintage of Cabernet Sauvingon, Merlot and Chardonnay will be in 1993. VQA wines are bottled under the Okanagan Vineyards Heritage label. Imported California and Washington State wines are sold under the Ocean Crest and Cascades Estates labels.

Winemaker: Sandor Mayer

Acreage: 22

Soil: Partially stoney soil with light loam, sloping gradually with southern exposure. The vineyard is located a few kilometres from Canada's only desert.

Varieties: Cabernet Sauvignon, Merlot, Chardonnay, Johannisberg Riesling, Pinot Noir, Gewürztraminer

Production: 22,000 cases

Average tonnage crushed: 100 tons

Grapes bought in: 100 tonnes

Winemaking philosophy: "To develop distinct personality for the winery and provide style continuity through the production of high quality wines."

LDB wines: *white*—Gewürztraminer, Johannisberg Riesling, Bacchus, Premium White, Heritage Cayuga, Heritage Oberlin Foster, Hidden Valley Mountain Chablis, Müller-Thurgau★, Okanagan Riesling, Perle of Csaba★

Oliver Cellars label: white—Dry White, Medium Dry White, Chablis, Mountain chablis, Medium white

Oliver Cellars label: red—Classic Premium, Heritage Maréchal Foch★, Premium Red

Winery store: Late Harvest Riesling, Verdelet; Pinot Noir★

Store hours: 10 am – 4 pm daily (seasonal)

Tours: May to October

Public tastings: during store hours

PYRAMID CELLARS

R.R. #4, S-1, C-22
4870 Chute Lake Road
Kelowna
British Columbia
V1Y 7R3

phone: (604) 764-4345
fax: (604) 764-2598

Stephen and Wendy Cipes founded their sparkling wine operation in 1991.

Pyramid Cellars also makes a limited amount of Icewine.

Winemaker: Eric von Krosiek

Acreage: 60

Soil: A cross-section of light to heavy sandy loam.

Varieties: Riesling, Chardonnay, Pinot Meunier, Pinot Noir, Cabernet Franc, Gewürztraminer, Bacchus, Ehrenfelser

Production: 10,000 cases

Average tonnage crushed: 200 tonnes

Grapes bought in: 100 tonnes

Winemaking philosophy: "Our wines are made solely from BC grapes which are minimally processed to allow the full natural varietal character to come through. Special oak aging allows for full and mature wines to be made into traditional style *méthode champenoise*."

Store hours: 10 am – 6 pm (restaurant pending approval)

Tours: yes

Public tastings: during store hours

QUAILS' GATE
ESTATE WINERY

3303 Boucherie Road
Site 14, R.R. #1
Westbank, British Columbia
V0H 2A0

phone: (604) 769-4451
fax: (604) 769-3451

One of Okanagan's newest wineries is situated on one of the region's oldest settlements. The Stewart family first planted the 70-acre vineyard in 1961 on a site on the west side of Lake Okanagan first chosen by the original pioneers, John and Susan Allison, in 1873. Their original log cabin homestead has been restored for use as the company's wine shop. When Ben and Ruth Stewart decided to make the leap from grape growers to a farm winery they hired oenologist Elias Phiniotis as their winemaker. Hungarian-trained Elias, who made wine in his native Cyprus before coming to Canada in 1976, worked for many years at Casabello.

The winery has 30 French oak barrels.

Winemaker: Elias Phiniotis

Acreage: 70 (total estate 115 acres)

Soil: South sloping exposure with soils varying from clay to sand.

Varieties: Riesling, Chasselas, Chardonnay, Pinot Noir, Optima, Chenin Blanc, Gewürztraminer

Production: 11,000 cases

Average tonnage crushed: 150 tonnes

Grapes bought in: 15 tonnes

Winemaking philosophy: "To pursue excellence through quality control from grapes to bottle. To provide the means and take the time to offer the market above average to excellent quality wines, packaged in their own personality labels and appearance. To combine wine with heritage and contemporary life style."

LDB wines: Riesling, Riesling Dry*, Chasselas, De Chaunac-Rougeon*

Own store: Chardonnay*, Pinot Noir, Botrytis Optima

Shop on premises: Monday through Sunday, 10 am – 5 pm

Tours: yes

Public tastings: during store hours

ST. HUBERTUS VINEYARD

R.R. # 4
5225 Lakeshore Road
Kelowna
British Columbia
V1Y 7R3

phone/fax:
(604) 764-7888

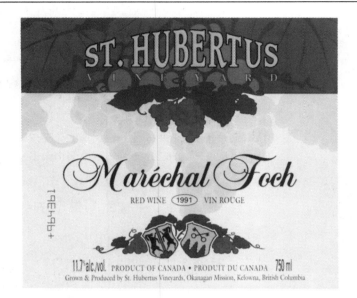

St. Hubertus, one of BC's newest farm winery, is named after Leo Gebert's family lodge in Switzerland. The vineyard, established in 1948, was purchased in 1984 and the winery licence issued in 1992. With his wife Barbara, Leo brings to the Okanagan years of experience in grape growing from his native country.

Winemaker: Leo Gebert

Acreage: 25 planted (5 vacant)

Soil: sandy, close to Lake Okanagan

Varieties: Johannisberg Riesling, Bacchus, Maréchal Foch, Pinot Blanc, Verdelet, Gamay, Chasselas, Pinot Meunier

Production: 2,500 cases

Average tonnage crushed: 60 tons ("25 tons for our own use")

Grapes bought in: 5 tons

Winemaking philosophy: "The Okanagan has an excellent and unique microclimate for growing grapes. We don't have to compete with other wine regions, we simply have to promote our own distinct taste. Since we operate a small cottage winery we know and understand the needs of our customer and are able to give them the wine which matches the wine-lover's taste."

Wines: At winery store only. *white*—Johannisberg Riesling, Verdelet, Pinot Blanc

red—Maréchal Foch

Store hours: 10 am – 5:30 pm daily until September 30

Tours: by arrangement only

Public tastings: yes

ST. LASZLO VINEYARDS

R.R. #1, Site 95, Lot 8
Keremeos, British Columbia
V0X 1N0

phone: (604) 499-6663

Joe Ritlop and his family made the first crush at St. Laszlo in 1978 (Joe named the winery after his birthplace in Yugoslavia). They had already planted vineyards in the early 1970s south of Keremeos on slopes above the Similkameen River, experimenting with a range of hybrid and *vinifera* vines. Joe is considered something of a maverick in the BC industry and has followed an independent path from the beginning. He makes his wine organically, using no chemicals in the vineyard and no sulphites, sorbates or preservatives in the cellar. The grapes are fermented on their own yeasts. The St. Laszlo style is full-bodied. Joe's late harvest wines such as Tokay Aszu and Golden Nectar are well worth trying, though costly. He has made Icewine since 1982.

Winemaker: Joe Ritlop

Varieties: Tokay, Riesling, Perle of Csaba, Pinot Auxerrois, Chardonnay, Semillon, Sovereign Royal, Verdelet, Maréchal Foch, Rougeon, De Chaunac, Cabernet Franc.

Winemaking philosophy: "I will create my wine in my own fashion. I cannot do anything else. We can make as good or better white wines here than any of the European countries."

SUMAC RIDGE
ESTATE WINERY

17403 Highway 97
P.O. Box 307
Summerland
British Columbia
V0H 1Z0

phone: (604) 494-0451
fax: (604) 3456

Harry McWatters has run Sumac Ridge since it foundation in 1980. Originally, grower Lloyd Schmidt was a partner (his son Allan made wine there before moving east to Vineland Estates). Now Bob Wareham has joined the operation. The ample and bearded Harry, who was instrumental in getting Ontario's VQA regulations accepted in BC, is a leading force in BC's industry. Sumac Ridge is the only winery in the world to have a nine-hole public golf course on the property. Players can sample the wines in the club house restaurant as well as wines of competitors.

The winery uses French oak tanks of Limousin and Nevers and is the largest BC producer of barrel-fermented Chardonnay. Sumac Ridge was the first BC proucer to make a *méthode champenoise* sparkling wine. The Pinot Noir goes into the sparkling wines and Cabernet Franc and Merlot are currently planted.

Winemaker: Harold Bates

Acreage: 20

Varieties: Pinot Noir, Gewürztraminer, Riesling

Average tonnage crushed: 275

Grapes bought in: long-term agreement for Guy Wilson's 13-acre vineyard in Naramata

Production: 17,000 cases

Winemaking philosophy: "We have attempted to be leaders and innovators with: 1. such grapes as Chancellor; 2. new products such as our *méthode champenoise*. We are dedicated to the marriage of food and wine. We produce distinctive wines to complement distinctive food flavours."

LDB wines: *white*—Bacchus Irvine Vineyard, Chardonnay, Cuvée Maison, Gewurtzling Po Toe, Gewürztraminer Private Reserve★★, Gewürztraminer★, Johannisberg Riesling Late Harvest, Johannisberg Riesling, Okanagan Riesling, Okanagan Blanc, Perle of Csaba★, Pinot Blanc★, Summer, Verdelet

red—Chancellor★, Chancellor Private Reserve★, Cuvée Maison, Summerland Rosé

Own store: Okanagan Blush, Stag Horn Cuvée white and red

Sparkling: Stellar's Jay Cuvée, Blanc de Blanc★, Blanc de Noir

Fortified: Chancellor Port

Store hours: Winter: Monday to Friday, 9 am – 5 pm
Summer: Daily 9 am – 6 pm

Tours: Summer, between 9 am and 5 pm

Public tastings: 9 am – 6 pm

WILD GOOSE
VINEYARDS

S-3, C-ll, R.R. #1
Okanagan Falls
British Columbia
V0H 1R0

phone: (604) 497-8919
fax: (604) 497-8400

Along with Guenther Lang and the Klockockas, Adolf Kruger was one of the pioneers of the farm winery concept in BC. A consulting engineer and talented amateur winemaker formerly from Kehrberg in East Germany, Adolf was forced to make his hobby a profession when a downturn in the economy left him without work in electrical engineering. With his sons, Roland and Hagen, he opened Wild Goose Vineyards in June 1990, days after Lang Vineyards started up as the first farm winery in Canada. Adolph had realized his dream of turning his vineyard (planted in 1984) into a winery to take advantage of free trade possibilities. He represents the farm wineries on the BC Wine Institute board.

The winery has twelve French oak barrels.

Winemaker: Adolf Kruger

Acreage: 10

Soil: Riesling has a southern exposure on rocky soil which absorbs a lot of heat during the day and releases it in the evening. Gewürztraminer is planted in clay-like soil with scattered stones. Very hot summers.

Varieties: Riesling, Gewürztraminer

Production: 1,100 cases

Average tonnage crushed: 15 tons

Grapes bought in: 3 tons

Winemaking philosophy: "As a small family winery we take much pride in the wines we vint. Minimal filtration is used and all production is done by the family unit. Trying to produce the best wines possible, no wine will be bottled or sold before it passes our strict tasting standards. People visiting our winery are given personal treatment and always are met by one of the smiling family members."

Wines: Johannisberg Riesling Dry and Semi-Dry, Gewürztraminer, Pinot Blanc, Maréchal Foch

Store on premises: 10 am – 5 pm

Tasting: during store hours

Tours: by appointment

VIGNETI ZANATTA

5039 Marshall Road
Glenora
Duncan
British Columbia

phone: (604) 748-2338

Loretta and Dennis Zanatta planted five acres of Ortega and Cayuga on Vancouver Island—BC's newest wine region—in 1986. Loretta crushed and fermented 4,500 litres in 1991 for the opening of their farmgate winery in the summer of '92. A further ten acres of Pinot Auxerrois have been planted with experimental plots of Pinot Noir, Pinot Gris and Ehrenfelser.

Wines (own store): Dry Ortega, Cayuga (from 1993)

QUEBEC

When you think of Canadian wine, images of Ontario's Niagara Peninsula or British Columbia's Okanagan Valley may spring to mind. With a little imagination perhaps you might conjure up Nova Scotia's Annapolis Valley or the Northumberland Strait. But wine made from grapes in Dunham, Quebec?

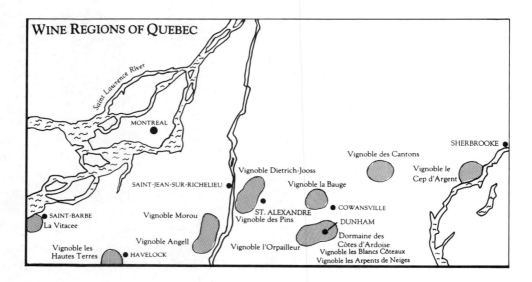

The idea that they actually grow wine in the Eastern Townships 80 kilometres south of Montreal is not only a revelation to most Canadians but an on-going source of amazement to virtually all the 3,108 inhabitants of this old loyalist village. "Even our neighbours don't understand what we're doing," confesses Jacques Breault, one of the partners in Vignoble Les Arpents de Neige. "They can't understand why people would drive here to taste our wines."

Dunham is to Quebec what Bordeaux is to France, in micro-
cosm: the epicentre of the province's wine industry, accounting
for nearly half of all bottles bearing Quebecois labels. Since 1985,
15 licenced cottage wineries have mushroomed along the Ver-
mont-New York State border from Sainte-Barbe to Sherbrooke.
These heroic pioneers, with the vision to turn this rolling landscape of farms and orchards into vineyards, produce some 250,000
bottles a year, roughly the annual output of Château Mouton-
Rothschild in the Médoc. Quebec makes 90% white wine, mostly
from the hybrid Seyval Blanc grape, and its vignerons accomplish
the feat against horrendous odds. Not the least of which is the
bureaucratic indifference of the provincial liquor board, but more
about that later.

The winemakers themselves speak lovingly yet defensively about
their magnificent obsession. The terms "artisanal" and "marginal"
are often used when they refer to the wines and the *terroir* that
provides them; there is something Quixotic about the compul-
sion to make wine in Quebec, a place of snow and polar temperatures where winter's only harvest used to be maple syrup. But soon
its harvest may be Icewine if the dreams of Jacques Breault and
his highly motivated colleagues are realized. Icewine, says Christian Barthomeuf, the co-owner of Domaine des Côtes d'Ardoise,
could be the saviour of the Quebec wine industry which currently
exists from vintage to vintage on its novelty value rather than the
quality and price of its products. Nine dollars and fifty cents or
more for a fresh, young wine similar in style to a Muscadet is a
hefty charge for a domestic Seyval, especially when a Sauvignon
Blanc or Chardonnay from Chile costs only $7.85 at the local
SAQ (La Societé des Alcools du Québec) store. But Montrealers
are showing the flag by taking the bridge south for a day in the
country and bringing back a few bottles as souvenirs.

Winemaking in Quebec is not a twentieth century phenomenon. In 1535 when Jacques Cartier sailed down the St. Lawrence
on his second voyage to New France, he anchored off "a great
island." Here Cartier found masses of wild *labrusca* grape vines
growing up the trees. He named the place Ile de Bacchus but on
reflection—thinking that this might seem too frivolous for his
masters in Paris—renamed it Ile d'Orléans after the duc d'Orléans,
son of his monarch, Francis I.

The Jesuit missionaries who followed in Cartier's footsteps
brought barrels of sacramental wine with them and when they
ran out they tried their hand at winemaking using the native wild

grape. They recorded that the grapes were plentiful but the wine they produced was only sufficiently tolerable to be sipped at Mass, not quaffed back in quantities capable of warming the hearts of the settlers during the long Quebec winters.

Various attempts at establishing a wine industry in Lower Canada were tried during the eighteenth and nineteenth centuries but these were abandoned because of the severity of the climate. Ice can split the trunk of a vine stock and even the hardiest *labrusca* plants are susceptible to winter kill. A vine will only grow in temperatures of 10 degrees Celsius or higher and it requires a certain number of sunshine hours during the growing season to ripen the fruit. The average Quebec sunshine hours during this season are approximately 930; but in Dunham and Magog the figure rises to 1150 (in Bordeaux the average sunshine hours are 2069). Dunham's secret—with the other growing regions in Quebec—is that it is a microclimate, possessing highly localized topographical features that create warm spots and allow a vine to thrive. Such features could be a body of water near a vineyard that stores up heat during the summer and acts like a hot water bottle during the winter as well as reflecting the sun's rays onto the vines, or a warm wind that blows down the valley from Montreal or a well-protected south-facing slope.

However, there is still the problem of winter and frozen vines. The most radical measure to safeguard the plants is burial: to cut them back after the harvest and cover them with earth until the spring. The operation is called "hilling," banking earth over the roots by back-ploughing between the rows of vines, an exercise that costs the grower four cents a plant to cover and another four cents to uncover.

The concept of hilling was brought to Quebec by an oenologist from the south of France, Hervé Durand, who had learned of it in Russia and China. In 1980, he purchased a farm in Dunham and two years later planted a vineyard. His neighbour Frank Furtado was so intrigued that he bought into the dream and with winemaker Charles-Henri de Coussergues (and later Pierre Rodrigue) founded what has become Quebec's most successful winery. The enterprise owes it name to the province's renowned singer-poet, Gilles Vigneault, who told Durand, "To make wine in Quebec is like panning for gold." *L'Orpailleur* is the French term for a man who searches for gold by panning, an apt metaphor for the time, patience and skill it takes to extract wine from the soil of *la belle province*.

Three years later when the vines produced their first commercial crop, Vignoble de l'Orpailleur made 15,000 bottles of Seyval. In 1990, the figure was up to 85,000 but because of a fierce frost last year (1991) the total dropped to 70,000. Such is the partners' confidence in their future that they are building a new cellar. Currently they produce a Seyval fermented in stainless steel, one fermented and aged for nine months in French and American oak and an aperitif called l'Apérid'Or in Pineau des Charentes style (pure alcohol is added to the fresh grape juice making a sweet, appley drink with good acidity). L'Orpailleur is also experimenting with a champagne-method sparkling wine and a rosé made from Cabernet Sauvignon and Gamay grapes. The glamour grape, Chardonnay, is also planted and next year they will know if it's possible to produce wine from this much sought-after variety.

The ebullient Frank Furtado, known more for his theatrical firework displays, also talks of creating a nursery to sell vines to other Quebec wineries.

Jacques Breault, who studied agriculture in Ste. Hyacinthe, worked for three years at L'Orpailleur. His family bought a farm a few kilometres down the highway from L'Orpailleur in 1988 to create Vignoble Les Arpents de Neige, a name that resonates with French history ("a few acres of snow" were not worth fighting about, according to French King Louis XIV's advisors). In addition to the ubiquitous Seyval, Breault has planted Vidal, Pollux, Ortega, a Geisenheim clone, the red Chancellor and "a bucket and a half of Cabernet Sauvignon. We don't expect much from *vinifera* vines like Cabernet or Pinot Noir," he says. "Hybrids are more versatile. *Vinifera* we find grows too much."

Les Arpents de Neige, which has its own restaurant ("cheese plate: $8.50, paté and cheese: $12.50, pot au feu: $15.95") and gift shop to augment the income from the sale of wines, produces Seyval, a Seyval and Vidal blend, a new wine called Premier Neige, a rosé from Chancellor and an aperitif called Apérot.

Near neighbours are Pierre Genesse and his wife Marie-Claude who own Les Blancs Coteaux, a bijou winery with a production of 6,000 bottles. Twenty-two-year-old Pierre, another Ste. Hyacinthe graduate, learned his winemaking in Burgundy while picking grapes in the Mâconnais. All his products are hand labelled, including the vinegar, jams and jellies, dried flowers and herbs he and his wife sell from their beautiful old farmhouse. The couple have their grapes crushed at Les Arpents de Neige, a testimony to the concern that Quebec's winemakers have for their mutual survival. "There are complicated feelings," explains Jacques Breault. "We're competitors in one way but if I attract a customer the others know he'll visit their wineries too. If I need a tractor, they'll loan it to me. If they need bottles, I'll do the same for them. But we're always watching what the others are doing."

Further east on Route 202 towards the town of Dunham is Domaines de Côtes d'Ardoise, a name that speaks to the slatey soil in the eight hectare vineyard, shaped like an amphitheatre. This unique landscape configuration Christian Barthomeuf will assure you gives him 184 frost-free days a year which means an extra three weeks of growing season over his competitors.

Barthomeuf, from Arles in southern France, used to be a film producer. He came to Quebec on sabbatical in 1974 and stayed. He bought his farm in 1977 and planted his vineyard two years later, having read every book on viticulture he could find. He began with Seyval, Maréchal Foch and De Chaunac, and in 1983 he tried his first *vinifera* vines, Pinot Noir, Gamay, Chardonnay and Riesling. His current newsletter, *La Feuille de Vigne*, asks the provocative question: Can you produce good red wines in Quebec? His answer is at Côtes d'Ardoise and is a resounding yes! Reds such as Maréchal Foch and Gamay Nouveau, if not the holy grail of the world's winemakers, Pinot Noir are produced.

Barthomeuf and his Dijon-trained winemaker Patrick Barrelet produce Seyval, a Pinot Noir/Gamay blend, a blend of Maréchal Foch and De Chaunac called Haute Combe, an Aurore/Seval blend under the La Maredoise label, a blend of all the red hybrids called Cinq Messidor and a *vin doux naturel* in port style called Estafette at 17% alcohol.

In the vineyard that rises up from the old barn that serves as the winery is a sign inscribed with a quote from Voltaire: "The only thing on earth I know that is serious is the culture of the vine."

What makes the wineries of Dunham and their *confrères* in other parts of Quebec "marginal" are the regulations under which they are forced to operate. While most sell all the wines they can produce, they have to rely on the passing tourist traffic and the sale of sweatshirts and other souvenirs to stay in business. (Vignoble de la Bauge in Brigham offers homemade wild boar pâté!) The only place they can sell what they produce is at the winery, which means their customers have to come to them. The provincial liquor board is not interested in carrying the products and restaurants are frightened off by the monstrously high handling charge the SAQ insists upon to supply the local wines to the hospitality industry. Yet for all the difficulties presented by God and man, the winemakers of Quebec are buoyant about their future. Dunham may never be the Napa Valley or even Niagara-on-the-Lake — unless global warming accelerates to a point where the region of Estrie enjoys as many sunshine hours as Bordeaux — but it will continue to provide a cottage industry of growing confidence and quality. The wines are fresh and well made and they speak to the soil and the climate in which they are produced. The dedicated men and women who work the tractors and the presses come from a variety of backgrounds: Vignoble Dietrich-Jooss in Iberville is owned by Victor and Christiane Dietrich-Jooss, who learned their winemaking in their native Alsace; La Vitacée was created by two University of Montréal biochemists, Robert Cedergen and Roger Morazain; Domenico Agarla came from Piedmont in Italy to start Vignoble St-Alexandre; and Vignoble Angell in St-Bernard de Lacolle is owned by Guy Angell who runs a string of martial arts schools across Canada.

QUEBEC WINERIES

DOMAINES DES CÔTES D'ARDOISE

879, Route 202 -
C.P. 189
Dunham, Quebec
J0E 1M0

phone: (514) 295-2020

Ardoise means slate which speaks to the soil of Christian Bartomeuf and Dr. Jacques Papillon's horseshoe-shaped vineyard behind the weathered old barn that acts as winery and tasting room. Bartomeuf, a film producer from Arles, came to Quebec in 1974 on sabbatical and stayed. He bought the farm in 1977 and planted the vineyard two years later. Jacques is a Montreal plastic surgeon.

Hybrids were first planted, but Jacques was convinced that his particular microclimate can support the noble European varieties, so in 1983 he put in Riesling, Chardonnay, Gamay and Pinot Noir. The winery offers an unusually large number of products for a Quebec enterprise of this nature. The winemaker, Patrick Barrelet, was trained in Dijon and worked in Puligny Montrachet.

His red wines are aged in Limousin oak. Christian Bartomeuf publishes a newsletter with a 25,000 copy distribution.

Winemaker: Patrick Barrelet

Acreage: 20

Soil: Slatey, south-facing slope in a natural amphitheatre.

Varieties: Aurore, Seyval Blanc, Chelois, De Chaunac, Maréchal Foch, Riesling, Chardonnay, Gamay, Pinot Noir

Production: approximately 1,600 cases

Winemaking philosophy: In the vineyard is a printed sign quoting Voltaire: "The only thing on earth that I know is serious is the culture of the vine."

Wines: *white* — La Maredoise (Aurore with 10% Chardonnay), Carte d'Or Seyval (oak-aged)★, Chardonnay, Estafette (fortified *vin doux naturel*)

red — Haute Combe (Maréchal Foch/De Chaunac), Côte d'Ardoise (Pinot Noir/Gamay oak-aged), Cinq Messidor (a blend of red hybrids and Gamay), Primardoise (Maréchal Foch nouveau), Estafette (fortified *vin doux naturel*)

Shop: yes (restaurant open June to September)

Tours: Group reservations (20 or more) from May 15 to October 15; wine and cheese visit ($10.20); tours with meals etc., by reservation.

Public tastings: yes ($3.20)

LA VITACÉE

816 Chemin de l'Eglise
Sainte-Barbe, Quebec
VOS 1P0

phone: (514) 373-8429

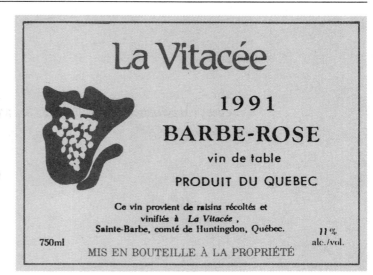

La Vitacée

1991

BARBE-ROSE

vin de table

PRODUIT DU QUEBEC

Ce vin provient de raisins récoltés et
vinifiés à *La Vitacée* ,
Sainte-Barbe, comté de Huntingdon, Québec.

750ml

11%
alc./vol.

MIS EN BOUTEILLE À LA PROPRIÉTÉ

141

Two biochemists from the University of Montreal, Robert Cedergren and Roger Morazain, created this bijou operation in 1979 when they planted their original vineyard. In spite of the size of their winery they have done much to increase the knowledge of what varieties will thrive in Quebec's difficult growing conditions with their experimental plantings of esoteric hybrids.

As befits their calling, the partners spend much time in vineyard research as well as into the right yeasts to use.

The red wines are aged in Missouri oak.

Winemaker: Roger Morazain

Acreage: 10

Microclimate: Situated near Lac Saint-François in the warmest region of Quebec.

Varieties: De Chaunac, Maréchal Foch, Kay Gray, Saint-Pépin, Lacrosse

Production: 500 cases (150 red)

Winemaking philosophy: "Since its foundation, our principal acitivity has been to concentrate on evaluating new hybrid varieties that don't need winter protection and have the potential to produce good wines. While continuing to evaluate these new varieties we have begun planting larger quantities of those grapes we have kept and production ought to increase in the coming years."

Wines: Barbe-Rouge, Barbe-Blanc, Barbe-Rosé

Store hours: April to December, 12 am – 5 pm, Tuesday to Sunday

Tours: yes

Tastings: during store hours

LE VIGNOBLE ANGILE

267, 2e. Rang Ouest
(Route 218)
Saint-Michel-de-
Bellechasse
Quebec
G0R 3S0

phone: (418) 884-2583
fax: (418) 884-2327

BOISSON ALCOOLIQUE DE FRAISE ET DE FRAMBOISE

Produit du Québec

Aromatisée au sirop d'érable pur

14 % alc./vol.

Ambroisia

Mis en bouteille par:
André Lefebvre,
2e Rang ouest (route 218)
Saint-Michel-de-Bellechasse

750 ml

Since 1985 André Lefebvre has made fruit wines from his twenty acres of strawberries and raspberries as well as blended table wines from three esoteric hybrids, including two Russian varieties, the *riparia* Eona and Mitchurinetz, which Roger Dial introduced to his Grand Pré vineyard in Nova Scotia's Annapolis Valley. The winery is a thirty-five minute drive east of Quebec City.

All the wines are made in stainless steel.

Winemaker: André Lefebvre

Acreage: 5.5 (vines); 20 (soft fruit)

Soil: Gravelly with a south-facing slope.

Varieties: Eona, Minnesota, Mitchurninetz

Production: 500 cases

Average tonnage crushed: 3

Winemaking philosophy: "My objective is to produce 15,000 bottles a year."

Wines: Cuvée d'Angile Blanc (Sec), Cuvée d'Angile Rouge (Sec)

Fruit wines: Picoline (14% alcohol, strawberry), Ambrosia (14% alcohol, strawberry and raspberry with maple syrup), Grand Frisson (14% alcohol, raspberry)

Store hours: Saturday & Sunday, 9 am to 6 pm (open seven days a week except during festival period

Tours: by reservation

Public tastings: during store hours

VIGNOBLE
LA BAUGE

155 des Erables
Brigham, Quebec
J0E 1J0

phone: (514) 263-2149

The boar eating grapes on the label of Alcide Naud's *vin blanc* gives the game away. Alcide had been a dairy farmer for forty years in Brigham before he bought a herd of wild boar, deer, wild sheep and stags. He began growing wine in 1987, and now rears his game menagerie for terrine. He also offers a 45-minute tour of the woods to see the wild boar in their natural habitat. You can also taste the terrine with a glass of wine for $4.

Winemaker: Alcide Naud

Acreage: 5

Soil: gravelly

Varieties: Seyval Blanc, Chancellor (400 vines)

Average tonnage crushed: 5 to 6 tonnes

Production: 335 cases

Winemaking philosophy: "I hope that one of my five sons will follow in my footsteps because it's a fascinating pursuit."

Wines: Seyval Blanc

Shop: yes

Tours: yes (picnic tables available)

Public tastings: yes

VIGNOBLE DE L'ORPAILLEUR

1086 Route 202
Dunham, Quebec
J0E 1M0

phone: (514) 295-2763
fax: (514) 295-3112

Hervé Durand, a winemaker from Avignon who studied in Dijon and taught oenology in Argentina, bought the Dunham farm in 1980 and planted his vineyard two years later. His neighbour, Frank Furtado, an impressario who puts on firework displays, was so intrigued by the notion that he became a partner. Later, publisher Pierre Rodrigue bought in and with French winemaker Charles-Henri de Coussergues the winery has become the commercial leader in the province. Gilles Vigneault inadvertently named the enterprise when he told Hervé, "making wine in Quebec is like panning for gold." L'Orpailleur is a man who does just that.

A white woodframe farmhouse stands in front of a modern cedar-built winery with a magnificent terrace where you can dine on summer days. The store sells sweatshirts and other winery memorabilia. French and American oak barrels are used. A new cellar is planned.

Winemaker: Charles-Henri de Coussergues

Acreage: 24

Soil: Sand and gravel. The soil is very dry and warm with gentle slopes.

145

Variety: Seyval Blanc

Production: 6,500 cases

Average tonnage crushed: 85

Winemaking philosophy: "Our wine is made exclusively from grapes grown in Quebec. We will continue to do research to discover the best varieties to plant in our soil."

Wines: L'Orpailleur Vin Blanc★, L'Orpailleur Elevé en fût de Chéne, Apérid'Or, Vin Nouveau, Méthode Champenoise (sparkling wine)

Store hours: January 1 to April 30, Saturday & Sunday 10 am – 12 pm, 1 pm – 5 pm (the rest of the week by appointment) May 1 to December 31, every day 9 am – 5 pm

Tours & tastings: May 15 to October 15 (restaurant facilities)

VIGNOBLE DES PINS

136 Grand Sabrevois
Sabrevois, Quebec
J0J 2G0

phone: (514) 347-2794

One of the newest of the Quebec wineries is Gilles Benoit's Vignoble des Pins which opened in May 1990. Situated in the plains, there was no topographical feature of note to name his winery after so he called it after the stands of red and white pines around the property. His soil has more clay than the hillier region around Dunham which gives more body to his red wines. Currently a red and white are produced and a champagne-method sparkler is about to be released.

Winemaker: Gilles Benoit

Soil: clay-loam

Varieties: Seyval, Aurore, Maréchal Foch, De Chaunac. Experimental plantings of Bacchus, Chardonel, Cayuga White, Seyve-Villard

Production: 250 cases

Wines: Vin Blanc (90% Seyval, 10% Aurore), Vin Rouge (Maréchal Foch and some De Chaunac)

Sparkling: same blend as Vin Blanc

VIGNOBLE
DIETRICH-JOOSS

407 Grande-Ligne
Iberville, Quebec
J2X 4J2

phone: (514) 347-6857

Husband and wife Victor Dietrich and Christiane Jooss come from the Alsace village of Ingersheim where their respective families had been immersed in viticulture and winemaking for generations. The couple founded their company in 1986 and the following year planted the vineyard in the Richelieu Valley, east of Iberville. In order to find the best varieties for their microclimate they have some thirty-six different plants in the ground, primarily white. An experimental plot includes vines from South Africa, Australia, United States, South America and the noble varieties of Europe, including several Geisenheim clones which, says Victor, appear promising. These grapes go into his wines neck-labelled Cuvée Spéciale.

Their label bears a replica of the coat of arms that appeared on the bottles Victor made in his native Alsace. He believes that Chasselas, Gamay and certain Pinot varieties could do well in Quebec. Much of the equipment comes from Alsace. American oak is used.

Winemaker: Victor Dietrich

Acreage: 11

Soil: Silty-sand, lightly pebbled; vineyard benefits from the proximity of two bodies of water, the Richelieu River and Lake Champlain.

Varieties: French hybrids, including Seyval, Cayuga, Vidal and Vineland 50201, several Geisenheim clones. Reds include Maréchal Foch, De Chaunac, Chancellor and Villard Noir. Some *vinifera* is planted, including Chardonnay and Riesling.

Production: 1,250 cases (350 cases red)

Winemaking philosophy: "As winemaker from Alsace in Quebec I want to use traditional Alsatian winemaking techniques to create that particular style in the wines we make here. My experiments in the vineyard are aimed at finding wines that resemble Riesling in character."

Wines: Vin Blanc, Vin Rosé★, Vin Rouge★, Vin Blanc Cuvée Spéciale, Storikengold (a wine made for fish and sea food)

Wine store: open all year

Tours: yes

Public tastings: yes (group reservations necessary)

VIGNOBLE
LE CEP D'ARGENT

1257 Chemin de
la Rivière
Magog, Quebec
J1X 3W5

phone and fax:
(819) 864-4441

Le Cep d'Argent is Estrie's most eastern winery, situated between Magog and Sherbrooke. From three grape varieties winemaker François Scieur makes eight different products to attract consumers to this small facility across the railway tracks from the banks of Petit Lac Magog. François and his brother Jean Paul are orginally from the Champagne region, which accounts for the presence of champagne-method sparkling wine, kir and ratafia on their product list. In fact, they were the first to produce sparkling wine from grapes grown in the province. The winery was founded in 1985 after research to find the right site for the vineyard was undertaken by Jacques Daniel and his son Marc. The other partner in the enterprise is Denis Drouin. The champagne cellar with its A-frames set up for riddling is well worth seeing.

The recently built brick reception hall accommodating 150 people resembles a medieval armoury.

Winemaker: François Scieur

Acreage: 25

Soil: Silty sandy-clay; south-southeast slope.

Varieties: Seyval, Maréchal Foch, De Chaunac

Production: 2,600 cases

Average tonnage crushed: 36

Winemaking philosophy: "Our philosophy is to ignore the ideas of people who say that the vine can't produce wines of quality in Quebec."

Wines: Le Cep D'Argent Vin Blanc, Délice du Chais Vin Rouge, Fleur de Lys (Kir), Fleuret (Pineau des Charentes style aperitif), Mistral (Ratafia-style aperitif), L'Archer (digestif made from red wine, cognac and maple syrup), Sélection des Mousquetaires (*Méthode champenoise blanc de blanc*), Sélection des Mousquetaires Rosé

Store hours: all year 9 am – 5 pm

Tours: Hour-long bilingual tours with tasting $3.75 per person (children 12 and under free). Restaurant facilities.

VIGNOBLE LES ARPENTS DE NEIGE

4042 rue Principale
Dunham, Quebec
J0E 1M0

phone: (514) 295-3383

Jacques Breault and his brother Alain bought the old farm with its historic farmhouse at Christmas in 1988 although the vineyard had been planted since 1986. The name refers to a pejorative reference to New France as "acres of snow" that were considered not worth fighting for by French King Louis XIV's advisors.

Jacques studied agriculture in Ste. Hyacinthe and worked for three years at L'Orpailleur before starting his own winery. His experience in selling and operating farm machinery stood him in good stead for Quebec viticulture because he became expert at "hilling," the covering of vines in winter and uncovering them in the spring.

The winery has a large reception hall which acts as a function room and weekend restaurant and a gift shop. Along with a flock of geese, a tame sheep named Helmut graces the garden to the delight of children.

The winery uses four American oak barrels and a Vidal Icewine is in the works.

Winemaker: Alain Bélanger (trained in Alsace)

Acreage: 19

Soil: Deep gravelly soil. Wind from the St. Lawrence Valley and turbulence caused by an escarpment to the southeast create a favourable microclimate.

Varieties: Seyval, Vidal, Vineland 50201, Geisenheim clones, Pollux, Ortega, Cayuga, Chancellor and "a bucket and half of Cabernet Sauvignon" (35,000 vines)

Production: 2,000 cases

Average tonnage crushed: 25 tonnes

Grapes bought in: 3 – 4 tonnes

Wines: Seyval Blanc, Cuvée Sélectionné (Seyval with some Vidal), Premiere Neige (Seyval nouveau), Vin Rouge (Chancellor with a little 10% Cabernet), Rosé de Printemps (Chancellor rosé), Apéro (Seyval aperitif wine); occasionally, some Vidal Late Harvest is released.

Store hours: 9 am – 9 pm daily

Tours: yes (restaurant)

Public tastings: yes

VIGNOBLE LES BLANCS COTEAUX

1046 Route 202
Dunham, Quebec
J0E 1M0

phone: (514) 295-3503

The youthful Pierre Genesse and his wife Marie-Claude founded their tiny winery in 1989. Pierre learned his winemaking in Burgundy while picking grapes in the Mâconnias. He also studied agriculture in Sherbrooke. The beautiful old brick farmhouse which doubles as the cellar and the couple's home also has a shop where you can buy homemade vinegars, jams, jellies, dried flowers and herbs. Bottling and labelling are done by hand and the crush is done nearby at Les Arpents de Neige.

Pierre removes leaves to expose the grape clusters to the sun. He vinifies in stainless steel to maintain the perfume of the fruit although he does have six French and American oak (barriques) and is currently experimenting with Cabernet Sauvignon. He also makes a cider by the champagne method.

Winemaker: Pierre Genesse in collaboration with oenologist Alain Bélanger

Acreage: 5

Soil: Rocky loam on slate above clay. Warm air currents off Lake Champlain avoid spring frost. Situated at the foot of a hill; good drying wind and heat during the day.

Variety: Seyval Blanc

Production: 600 cases

Average tonnage crushed: 5

Winemaking philosophy: "To maintain very high quality standards without becoming a large commercial producer."

Wine: Seyval Blanc La Taste

Store hours: Thursday to Sunday, 9 am – 5 pm (small restaurant during the summer)

Tastings: during store hours

VIGNOBLE MOROU

238 Route 221
Napierville, Quebec
J0J 1L0

phone: (514) 245-7569

Etienne Héroux and Monique Morin founded Vignoble Morou in 1987 (just north of Vignoble Angell), planting a range of hybrids to see what was best for their particular microclimate which they assert is "the best in Quebec" (the same claim is laid by every vineyardist in the province!). They use Kentucky oak barrels to age their higher priced red wine.

Winemaker: Etienne Héroux

Acreage: 8

Soil: Sandy soil, rapid drainage; vineyard influenced by Lake Champlain.

Varieties: Seyval, Vidal, Geisenheim clones; Maréchal Foch, Gamay, Chancellor and some Cabernet Sauvignon

Production: 1,000 cases

Winemaking philosophy: "Small family vineyard, wines of superior quality and a warm welcome for visitors."

Wines: Morou vin Rouge, Morou vin blanc, Cuvée Spéciale blanc, Cuvée Spéciale rouge

Shop: 10 am – 6 pm, seven days

Tours: yes

Public tastings: yes ($1 per variety)

VIGNOBLE ST-ALEXANDRE

364 Grande Ligne
St-Alexandre, Quebec
J0J 1S0

phone: (514) 347-2794

This winery, owned by Dominico Agarla, was formerly known as La Farm Abrutrezzi.

VIGNOBLE DES CANTONS

1457 Cemin Bromont
Waterloo, Quebec

phone: (514) 539-2799

VIGNOBLE LES HAUTES TERRES

360 Chemin Covey Hill
Havelock, Quebec
J0S 1E0

phone: (514) 826-0132
         (514) 827-2603

Nova Scotia

*L*ief Ericsson may have discovered wild grapes in New-foundland at the beginning of this millenium, but there is harder evidence to support Nova Scotia's claim to be a wine-growing province at least as far back as the beginning of the seventeenth century. In 1611, Louis Hébert, de Mont's apothecary, loaded his canoe with vines he brought with him from

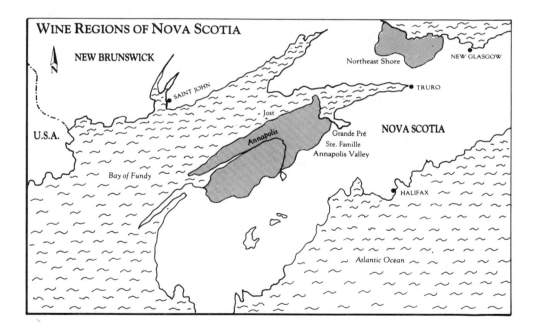

France and paddled up the Bear River between Annapolis and Digby Counties to plant himself a vineyard.

Serious attempts to turn the province into a wine-growing region had to wait until this century. As early as 1913, the Agriculture Canada research station at Kentville had been planting experimental plots to see what varieties might flourish in the province's short, cool growing season (to date they have evaluated over 175 cultivars). After several decades of trial and error they suggested in a departmental publication in 1971 that only table varieties seemed viable (even the hardy Concord did not ripen sufficiently). But a decade later they would be proved mistaken.

Nova Scotia is situated midway between the equator and the north pole and the time between the last spring frost and the first fall frost is much shorter than that in Ontario or British Columbia. The average daily temperature during the growing season is also lower than the other two grape-growing provinces.

But, happily, there are always those healthy skeptics who challenge accepted wisdom and more often than not are proved correct. Roger Dial, a Californian born in 1942, can justifiably claim to be the father of the Nova Scotia wine industry. Although Andrés had a bottling plant in Truro, there were no wine grapes grown on a commercial scale in the province until the late 1970s. Andrés opened its winery in Truro's Industrial park in 1965 and purchased Chipman Wines in 1983, an enterprise founded in 1941 that produced fruit wines from apples, cherries, elderberries, blueberries and cranberries.

A political scientist by training, Roger Dial came to lecture at Dalhousie in 1969. During his university days in California he had worked his way through school as a wine sales representative and had been a partner in the small Davis Bynum winery in Healdsburg. At Dalhousie he met an economist, Norman Morse, who had planted some table grapes on his property at Grand Pré. Roger convinced him to plant wine grapes that he had purchased for his own home winemaking production. In 1978, the two men put in a further three acres of vines — no *vinifera* since they had been advised against these tender plants, but two hardy Russian varieties from the Amur Valley on the Chinese border, Michurinetz and Severnyi. (This had a certain resonance for Roger Dial since his Ph.D was in Chinese politics.) The vines had been imported to Canada as a result of a barter deal with the Soviets: Nova Scotian raspberries for Russian vines. The stocks had originally been propogated at the Summerland research station in British Columbia and another barter deal landed them in Kentville. This time the commodity was Nova Scotia blueberries. (The planting of vines must have a domesticating effect because in 1981 Roger purchased the vineyard and his colleague's house — a splendid

1819 Georgian woodframe building — with the intention of creating a cottage winery.)

Emboldened by the success of the Russian varieties in his basement winemaking activities, Roger Dial convinced Morse to plant more vines and to extend to *vinifera* varieties as well. In 1979, Chardonnay and Gewürztraminer were put into the ground — the first in eastern Canada — but the weather during the following year was so bad that it nearly killed the entire vineyard. Yet 1980 was not without its triumphs. That vintage of Cuvée d'Amur, a Michurninetz-based wine, won a gold medal in New York at the International Wine and Spirit Competition and a silver in Bristol, England. Subsequent harvests proved that wine grapes could flourish in Nova Scotia if they were placed in suitable microclimates. In 1982, Cuvée d'Amur was voted by wine writers as the best Canadian red at a Department of External Affairs tasting to select wines for Canadian embassies and high commissions around the world. It just may have been coincidence but that was the year when the Wine Growers' Association of Nova Scotia was founded with Roger Dial as Chairman and as Vice Chairman Hans Jost, a grape farmer in Malagash, Cumberland County, who would start Nova Scotia's second cottage winery two years later. In 1983, Roger Dial had planted a 22-acre vineyard 15 miles from his winery at Lakeville and was busy contracting the produce of other local growers to satisfy the demand for his wines at provincial liquor stores. It was not until 1986 that the Nova Scotia government passed the Farm Winery Act enabling him to sell wines at the winery directly to licencees and the visiting public. By 1988, he had 200 acres of vineyards that were either owned outright, bought as joint ventures or contracted in, and had annual sales of $1.2 million. Grand Pré had a healthy 6% of the provincial wine market. Unfortunately, the combined pressures of the October 1987 stock market crash and the Free Trade Agreement eventually took their toll and forced Roger Dial's winery into receivership. After a couple of years of restructuring Jim Landry and Karen Avery took over the operation, bringing in Bob Claremont as consulting winemaker and wine buyer.

The Farm Winery Act, though long in coming, helped to consolidate Nova Scotia's nascent wine industry. Under its provisions a winery could sell 350 cases of wine at the farmgate for every acre under vine (minimum ten), even if those newly planted vines had yet to produce a crop. Nor did the wines sold have to be from grapes grown in the province. In order to give incentive to farm wineries to plant grapes the government allowed them to bottle imported wines, either blended into locally grown grapes or as 100% imports. These are usually sold through the Nova Scotia Liquor Commission (NSLC) and the estate-bottled wines are available at the wineries.

At this time there are three estate farm wineries in Nova Scotia whose grapes are augmented by 38 growers managing 150 acres of vines in seven counties. Production is close to 200 tons. Suitable grape varieties for winemaking in Nova Scotia are more limited than Ontario and British Columbia. The most widely planted varieties are reds — Michurinetz, Maréchal Foch; whites — Seyval Blanc, New York Muscat, V-53261 (L'Acadie Blanc) and a Geisenheim clone, GM.

NOVA SCOTIA WINERIES

GRAND PRÉ
ESTATE WINERY

P.O. Box 18
Kings County
Nova Scotia
B0P 1M0

phone: (902) 542-1470
fax: (902) 542-1471

Grand Pré in the Annapolis Valley was founded in 1980 by the visionary Roger Dial. In 1988, the winery went into receivership, but Roger's drive and energy had ensured that Nova Scotia would become a winemaking province. Grand Pré was taken over by Jim Landry and Karen Avery. They employed Bob Claremont (who used to have his own estate winery in BC and now works for Culotta) as consulting winemaker and wine buyer.

Roger Dial had planted the Russian variety Michurinetz in his vineyard and created a wine called Cuvée d'Amur (a pun on the name Amur Valley between Russia and China where the grape was propagated and *amour*) which is still on the list. The winery has now expanded into barrel-fermented and aged Chardonnay

159

and produces a "sherry," a "port" and a wine-based liqueur. French, American and Slovanian oak is used.

There is no formal restaurant as such on the premises, but a lobster and steak buffet is served in the wine cellar.

Winemaker: Bob Claremont

Acreage: 32.5 (17 acres at the winery)

Soil: Sandy-loam on southern slopes. The main vineyard is located near the Bay of Fundy.

Varieties: Michurinetz, Severnyi, Maréchal Foch, Baco Noir; Seyval, L'Acadie Blanc, Chardonnay

Production: 24,000 cases

Average tonnage crushed: 60

Grapes bought in: 30 tons

Winemaking philosophy: "At Grand Pré we are more concerned with quality than quantity. This starts in early March with special pruning techniques. The harvest is hand-picked and only selected grapes go into the making of our wines. The white wine is permitted to age for a period of at least one year before bottling. The red wine is permitted to sit for 18 to 24 months in oak. With the complexity of the new wines this is just enough time for the proper marrying of wine with oak to produce that special taste."

Winery store only: *white* — Village Blanc, Chablis Superior, Avon Blanc, Cuvée Evangeline, L'Acadie Blanc, Seyval Blanc, Chardonnay, Vidal

red — Village Rouge, Avon Rouge, Cuvée Evangeline Rouge, Cuvée d'Amur, Pinot Noir, Vin Table Spéciale, Vin Nouveau

Store hours: Monday to Saturday, 10 am – 5 pm

Tours: yes (self-guided walking tour)

Public tastings: daily 10 am – 5 pm

JOST VINEYARDS

Malagash, Nova Scotia
B0K 1E0

phone: (902) 257-2636
fax: (902) 257-2248

Hans Christian Jost took over the winemaking and management duties of the family business when his father, Hans, died in 1988. The older Jost, who had owned a winery in the Rhine Valley before emigrating to Canada in 1970, was a grape farmer who started Nova Scotia's second cottage winery in 1984. He sent his son to study winemaking at Geisenheim.

Jost Vineyards, located on the Northumberland Strait along what is called "The Sunshine Coast of Nova Scotia" is one of three such enterprises in the province. The winery is in the basement of a small log cabin crammed with stainless steel tanks. Hans Christian buys in grapes from Ontario and Washington state to augment his needs. He still holds the record for Canada's most expensive wine: St. Nicholas Icewine 1985 from Riseling, Kerner and Bacchus grapes. It sold for $60.25 for a half bottle.

Winemaker: Hans Christian Jost

Acreage: 21

Soil: Clay loam — loam clay with a reddish hue due to iron content.

Varieties: Maréchal Foch, De Chaunac, Seyval Blanc, and Geisenheim clone 6493-4

Production: 25,000 cases

161

Grapes bought in: 200 tons

Winemaking philosophy: "Our goal is to produce crisp, clean wines. The flavour of the wine should come from the fermentation of clean grapes and juice. There should be no outside influences such as stems or oak."

NSLC wines: *white* — Amore, Chablis, Christian Maria Gewürtzraminer, Christinenhof Cabinett, Comtessa, Kellermeister Veevant, Riesling/Vidal, Sonnenhof Vidal

red — Comtessa, Maréchal Foch

rosé — Blush

Winery store: Chablis House, Rhine House, Cuvée Blanc, Riseling Gold, Habitant Blanc, Beaver Creek Geisenheim, R.P. Geisenheim, Sweet Muscat of Alexandria, St. Nicholas Icewine

red — Grand Cru Rouge, Maréchal Foch

rosé — Pink Chablis

Winery store hours: Monday to Saturday, 10 am – 5 pm Summer, 10 am – 6 pm

Tours: summer 3 pm

Public tasting: during store hours

SAINTE FAMILLE WINES

Falmouth, Nova Scotia
B0P 1L0

phone: (902) 798-8311/
1-800-565-0993
fax: (902) 798-9418

In 1989, Suzanne and Doug Corkum opened their tiny winery next to their vineyard on an old Acadian village site known as "La Paroisse Sainte Famille de Pisquit," a community settled in the 1680s. Today it's known as Falmouth, the gateway to the Annapolis Valley. The square wood building that acts as a winery and gift shop has a California feel about it. Suzanne learned winemaking from her father in Oregon's Willamette Valley. After twelve years of grape growing the Corkum family decided to make the leap to a small winery based on Suzanne's considerable experience as a home winemaker.

Nevers, Limousin and Allier oak are used in the winemaking. Two champage-method sparklers are currently maturing on the lees. A restaurant on the premises is planned. Eventually all 35 acres will be under vine.

Winemaker: Suzanne Corkum (consultant Nick Opdam)

Acreage: 17

Microclimate: South-facing slope protected by the Avon River from extremes of temperature during winter months.

Varieties: Chardonnay, Riseling, Seyval Blanc, Ortega, Auxerrois, German hybrids; Michurinetz, Maréchal Foch

Production: 3,000 cases (aiming at 6,000 maximum)

Average tonnage crushed: 35

Grapes bought in: 15 – 20 tonnes

Winemaking philosophy: "We are committed to producing premium wines from Nova Scotia grapes with a majority of the wines being from estate-grown grapes. We are not into the 'bag and box market.' We promote our wines through up-scale restaurants, our gift baskets or box presentations and our winery gift shop store. We will shortly have a small restaurant where we will promote a limited menu of items that are selected specially for our wines."

NSLC wines: Johannisberg Riesling, Chardonnay

Own store: *white* — Dry Riesling, Gold Bell(semi-sweet), Chablis
red — Maréchal Foch★, Michurinetz★★, La Paroisse Rouge (a blend of Maréchal Foch and Michurinetz)

Store hours: Monday to Saturday, 10 am – 6 pm
Sunday, 12 pm – 5 pm

Tours: yes

Public tastings: during store hours

ICEWINE

The best-kept secret in the wine world is Canadian Icewine. Ontario is the most prolific source of this gift of winter to the wine lover. Twenty wineries in the province produce the honeyed nectar on an annual basis. Inniskillin gave this fact global recognition at Vinexpo 1991 in Bordeaux when they won a gold award for their Vidal Icewine 1989 — one of only 19 such medals out of 4,100 entries.

Canada is, in fact, the world's largest producer of this vinous rarity. In the 1991 vintage over 80,000 half bottles were produced in Ontario alone (small amounts are made in British Columbia and Nova Scotia).

Icewine, or *Eiswein* as the Germans call it, is the product of frozen grapes. A small portion of the vineyard is left unpicked during the September/October harvest and the bunches of grapes are allowed to hang on the vine until the mercury drops to at least minus 7 Celsius. At this frigid temperature the sugar-rich juice begins to freeze. If the grapes are picked in their frozen state and pressed while they are as hard as marbles, the small amount of juice recovered will be intensely sweet and high in acidity. The wine made from this juice will be an ambrosia fit for Dionysus himself.

Like most gastronomic breakthroughs the discovery of Icewine was accidental. Producers in Franconia in 1794 made virtue of necessity by pressing juice from frozen grapes. They were amazed by the abnormally high concentration of sugars and acids which hitherto they had achieved only by allowing the grapes to desiccate on straw mats before pressing or by the effects of *Botrytis Cinerea*. (This disease is known as "noble rot"; it afflicts grapes in autumn usually in regions where there is early morning fog and humid, sunny afternoons. A mushroom-like fungus attaches itself to the berries, puncturing their skins and allowing the juice to evaporate. The world's great dessert wines such as Sauternes, Riesling Trockenbeerenauslese and Tokay Aszu Essencia are made from grapes afflicted by this benign disease.)

It was not until the middle of the last century in the Rheingau that German wine growers made conscious efforts to produce Icewine on a consistent basis. But they found they could not make it every year since the sub-zero cold spell has to last for several days to ensure that the berries remain frozen solid during picking and the lengthy pressing process which can take up to three days or longer. Grapes are 80% water. When this water is frozen, it is driven off under pressure as shards of ice and the resulting juice is miraculously sweet. If there is a sudden thaw, the ice will melt, diluting the sugar in each berry.

This means that temperatures for Icewine are critical. In Germany the pickers must be out well before dawn to harvest the grapes before the sun comes up. Some German producers even go so far as to rig an outdoor thermostat to their alarm clocks so as not to miss a really cold morning. But in Ontario there is no need for such dramatics. The winemakers can get a good night's sleep secure in the knowledge that sometime between November and February our climate will afford them a stretch of polar temperatures. As a result, Ontario Icewine is an annual event and as predictable as the leaves turning on the maple trees. Sometimes the cold comes early, as it did in 1991. On October 29th in British Columbia, Hainle Vineyards, CedarCreek and Gehringer Brothers were able to pick frozen grapes for Icewine when temperatures plunged to minus 13 Celsius.

Not all grapes can make Icewine. Only the thick-skinned, late-maturing varieties such as Riesling and Vidal can hang in there for the duration against such predators as gray rot, powdery mildew, unseasonal warmth, wind, rain, sugar-crazed starlings — and the occasional Ontario bureaucrat. The very first attempts at producing Icewine in Canada on a commercial basis were sabotaged by bird and man. In 1983, Inniskillin lost its entire crop to birds the day before picking was scheduled. Walter Strehn at Pelee Island Vineyards had taken the precaution of netting his vines to protect them from the feathered frenzy. Some persistent blue jays, however, managed to break through his nets and were trapped in the mesh. A passing bird-fancier reported this to the Ministry of Natural Resources whose officials descended upon the vineyard and tore off the netting. Strehn not only lost $25,000 worth of Riesling grapes to the rapacious flock but, to add insult to injury, he was charged with trapping birds out of season, using dried grapes as bait! Happily, the case was dropped and with the grapes that were left Strehn managed to make a small amount of Riesling Icewine 1983.

Since those days, more and more Ontario wineries have jumped on the Icewine bandwagon. Their wines literally sell out the moment they reach the stores. To avoid disappointment, customers have been encouraged to reserve their bottles while the grapes are still hanging on the vine.

Whenever you leave grapes on the vine after they have ripened you are taking an enormous gamble. If birds and animals don't get them, mildew and rot or a sudden storm might. So growers reserve only a small portion of their Vidal or Riesling grapes for Icewine, a couple of acres at most. A vineyard left for Icewine is really a very sorry sight. The mesh-covered vines are completely denuded of leaves and the grapes are brown and shrivelled, hanging like so many bats from the frozen canes. The wrinkled berries are ugly, but taste wonderfully sweet like frozen raisins. Usually there is snow and a high wind which makes picking an experience similar to Scott's trek to Antarctica. The stems that attach the bunches to the vine are dried out and brittle. A strong wind or an ice storm could easily knock them to the ground. A twist of the wrist is all that is needed to pick them. But when the wind howls through the vineyard, driving the snow before it, the wind-chill factor can make a temperature of minus 10 Celsius seem like minus 40. Harvesting Icewine grapes is a torturous business. Pickers, fortified with tea and brandy, brave the elements for two hours at a time before rushing back to the winery to warm up.

And when the tractor delivers the precious boxes of grapes to the winery the hard work begins. Since the berries must remain frozen, the pressing is done *al fresco* or the winery doors are left open. The presses have to be worked slowly otherwise the bunches will turn to a solid block of ice yielding nothing. Some producers throw rice husks into the press which pierce the skins of the berries and create channels for the juice to flow through the mass of ice. Sometimes it takes two or three hours before the first drop of juice appears. And this will be the sweetest since grape sugars have a lower freezing point than water.

Roughly speaking, one kilogram of grapes will produce sufficient juice to ferment into one bottle of wine. The juice from a kilogram of Icewine grapes will produce one-fifth of that amount and less depending on the degree of dehydration caused by wind and winter sunshine. The longer the grapes hang on the vine the less juice there will be. So a cold snap in December will yield more Icewine than a harvest date in February.

Once the oily juice is extracted from the marble-hard berries, it is allowed to settle for three or four days and then it is clarified of dust and debris by racking from one tank to another. The colourless liquid is too cold to start fermenting and a special yeast has to be added to activate that process in stainless steel tanks. Because of the very high sugar levels, the fermentation is very slow and can take months. But when the amber wine is finally in bottle it has the capacity to age for a decade or more.

While Germany may be recognized by the world as the home of Icewine, ironically they cannot make it every year. Canadian winemakers can. Klaus Reif, the winemaker at Reif Winery, has produced Icewine in both countries. While studying oenology at the Geisenheim Institute in Germany, he worked at a government winery in Neustadt in the Rheinpfalz. In 1983, he made his first Icewine there from Riesling grapes. Four years later he made Icewine from Vidal grapes grown in his uncle's vineyard at Niagara-on-the-Lake. "The juice comes out like honey here," says Reif. "In Germany it drops like ordinary wine." Robert Mielzynski of Hillebrand Estates, who also studied winemaking in Germany, agrees: "A lot of the Icewines I tried in Germany were less viscous and more acidic that ours. We get higher sugar levels."

Neustadt is around the 50th latitude; Niagara near the 43rd. Although our winters are more formidable than those of Germany we enjoy a growing season with more sunshine hours, resembling that of Burgundy. Our continental climate in southern Ontario gives us high peaking temperatures in July, the vine's most active growing month. This means that grapes planted in the Niagara Peninsula can attain higher sugar readings than in Germany — especially late-picked varieties because of dramatic fluctuations of temperature in the fall season. "From September on," says Karl Kaiser, winemaker and co-owner of Inniskillin, "the weather can turn cold and then suddenly warm up again. This warming-freezing effect makes the grapes dehydrate. Loss of water builds up the sugars. In January we have very windy weather that further desiccates the grapes so that when we harvest the Icewine we have very concentrated flavours."

So when the thermometer takes that first plunge of winter think of the grape pickers down on the Niagara Peninsula, bundling up to harvest the grapes of frost. Bat-brown and shrivelled like the old men of the mountains, those bunches hanging precariously from the vine may look unappetizing, but the lusciously sweet wine they produce is worth all the numb fingers and raw cheeks. At least the vintners have machines to press the juice from the frozen berries. They don't have go through the procedure in their bare feet.

The credit for the first Canadian Icewine must go to Walter Hainle in British Columbia who began making it from Okanagan Riesling in 1973 for family and friends. Tilman Hainle confesses that the family has one bottle of the 1974 vintage left ("in a glamorous Lowenbräu bottle with matching cap and homemade label"). "We have made Icewine every year since then, except in 1977. It is possible to make Icewine every year in BC, although the picking dates and quantities vary widely. Usually we have to wait until November or December for the appropriate temperatures."

Up until 1983 the Hainles used Oakangan Riesling to make their Icewine, but since then they have used a number of varieties including Traminer, Pinot Noir and Riesling. "We felt that Riesling is the most successful variety for our Icewine," says Tilman. Over the years their sugar levels have varied from 33 Brix to 57.5 Brix. A range of 35 to 40 Brix is typical at a temperature of minus 9 degrees Celsius to minus 12 degrees Celsius.

The quanity of juice the Hainles got from their frozen grapes ranged from as little as 20 litres in 1990 to as much as 580 litres in 1987. "The maximum quantity for us is limited by our mechanical capability: one press will yield from 150 to 300 litres of juice, and we don't have the crop or the time to do more than one press." Tilman Hainle is also reluctant to produce large quantities of Icewine. The wine, he contends, is a curiosity which garners a lot of publicity chiefly because of its rarity and it is not sufficiently cost efficient to warrant making it a large part of their portfolio.

Hainle Vineyards Icewine Production Method

We start with 1/5 acre of healthy, high sugar Riesling grapes. Yield is very low due to a number of factors — we keep our yields at 2 to 3 tons per acre but we also lose a lot of grapes to birds, coyotes and the occasional bear. There is no *Botrytis* due to the dry climate.

We pick the grapes in mid-November/early December, starting at 5:30 am at temperatures of at least minus 8 Celsius with a crew of 10 pickers. We finish before sunrise and transport the grapes to the winery. We crush the grapes in a 1,000 litre Willmes pneumatic press that has been sitting outside overnight to cool. The pressing (done outdoors) is slow and gentle — as the grape material becomes a solid block of ice — and then we repeat the process. The pressing is finished by 11:00 am during which time the pickers are supplied with mulled wine and warm brioches.

The juice is allowed to warm to room temperature and champagne yeast is added to start the fermentation as quickly as possible.

Fermentation lasts from one to four months depending on the vintage (we don't stop the fermentation). The Icewine is left on the lees in glass or plastic carboys to self-clarify for 12 to 36 months and then is racked. Use of sulphites at the racking stage is minimal.

The wine receives one relatively coarse clarifying filtration (with filter pads) just prior to bottling. The typical free sulphite level at bottling is approximately 20 ppm.

The alcohol level at bottling depends on how completely the yeast has fermented the sugar. It ranges from 9% (1978) to 17.5% (1983). Residual sugar similarly ranges from 3.5% (1983) to 25% (1978). Acidity at bottling ranges from 8 to 14 grams per litre.

We bottle the wine as early as three years after the vintage or as late as 13 years. We will hold the wine for at least three months after bottling before we release it.

Icewine is typically oxidative rather than reductive in style with caramel and vinous aromas dominating over fruity notes. Some of our older vintages were not sulphited and have a dark amber colour. In some years the wine takes on a character very similar to a sherry, with nutty aromas.

Cooking with Icewine is rather like cooking with champagne. The idea of using an expensive product causes most people to throw up their hands in horror. But the particular sweetness and high acidity of Icewine can make for some remarkable taste sensations. Toronto chef Michael Statlander uses Icewine like truffles, to add a festive touch to a dish. He will sprinkle a tablespoonful over fresh summer fruits or use it in aspic or as a salad dressing (combined with hazelnut oil and served over a warm salad of crab with green and white asparagus).

Icewine added at the last minute to sauces, says Statlander, provide a wonderful flavour for poultry. (Use a reduction of the stock in which you cook the bird and then add Icewine and finish with unsalted butter.)

Michael Statlander's Foie Gras sauce: combine in a food processor, butter, reduced stock, Foie Gras and Icewine.

Michael Statlander's Apricot Icewine Mousse (serves 6)
1/4 litre 35% cream (whipped)
4 egg yolks
2 tablespoons sugar
1 cup apricot purée (fresh or preserved in light syrup)
1/2 cup Icewine
3 sheets leaf gelatin

Method:
1. Make a sabayon from egg yolks, Icewine, sugar and apricot purée. (To make a sabayon, combine ingredients in a stainless steel bowl over boiling water and whip vigorously until it has the consistency of hollandaise sauce. Be careful not to use an overly high heat or you may wind up with sweet and expensive scrambled eggs.)
2. Add gelatin leaf that has been soaked in cold water.
3. After the mixture has cooled to lukewarm, fold in the whipped cream.
4. Place in individual serving bowls or glasses and chill two hours before serving.

CANADIAN WINE & FOOD

REDS

Dish	Game	Beef Lamb Duck	Ham Pork Hamburger	Chicken Veal
Wine Style	Rich, full- bodied reds	Full-bodied to medium- bodied reds	Medium to light-bodied reds	Medium to light- bodied reds or dry rosés
	Baco Noir Chancellor Cabernet Sauvignon Cabernet Franc Merlot Michurinetz	Maréchal Foch Pinot Noir Chambourcin Leon Millot Cabernet Blends	Gamay Zweigeltrebe Chelois De Chaunac Villard Noir	- or - Dry Riesling Barrel-fermented Chardonnay Pinot Gris/Pinot Grigio

WHITES

Dish	Salmon Lobster Crab	White Fish	Shrimps Scallops Oysters Mussels	Fish in Cream Sauce	Canadian Cheeses
Wine Style	Dry full- bodied whites	Medium- bodied white wines	Medium to light-bodied white wines	Medium-bodied aromatic whites	*Mild —* Chardonnay dry Vidal Pinot Blanc
	Oak-aged Chardonnay Gamay Blanc Pinot Blanc Dry Riesling Sauvignon Blanc Dry sparkling	Chardonnay (non-oaked) Chenin Blanc Chasselas Seyval Blanc Dry sparkling	Auxerrois Aligoté Dry Vidal Grüener Veltliner Quebec Seyval Blanc	Ehrenfelser Bacchus Off-dry Riesling dry Optima Perle of Csaba	*Strong flavoured —* Pinot Noir Maréchal Foch Chelois

			Thai Mexican Cajun	Desserts
			Gewürztraminer Scheurebe Müller-Thurgau Optima Muscat	Late Harvest Riesling Late Harvest Optima Late Harvest Vidal Icewine off-dry and sweet sparkling

TASTING NOTES

The following tasting notes are my personal assessments of the wines at the time I sampled them. I have evaluated them on their colour, bouquet and taste and then I rated them using a zero to four star system.

Since wines mature in the bottle they may change their characteristics: with age a young red wine will lose the astringency as its tannins soften, and whites will develop more bouquet. But there is an underlying architecture to a fine wine that does not change. If a wine is well balanced — when its fruit, alcohol, acidity and tannins (and oak if barrel-aged or barrel-fermented) are all in harmony with no one element overpowering the rest — then its breeding will show at every stage of its development.

Unless otherwise noted, all wines were tasted from the standard 750 mL bottles at room temperature. Where I tasted a barrel sample — a wine that was still in the cask or tank and had not yet been bottled — I have noted the fact. I did not, for instance, put all the Ontario Chardonnays or BC Rieslings together and taste them in competition with each other. I judged each product on its merits as it presented itself in the glass, keeping in mind how the winemaker described it on the label. I have also noted alcohol strength, although this can vary by a degree.

Where no vintage date is given there was none on the label. Vintage-dated wines speak to the quality of the fruit that year, but the notes will give you an idea of the winemaker's individual style which will impress itself on the wine like a fingerprint. Where the information was available I have given the constituents of the blends.

In some cases I have given three stars to the least expensive wines when I deemed them to be well-made examples of what they are and have noted when I consider a wine to be of good value in terms of its price/quality ratio.

Rating System

No stars: an unacceptable wine

★ : a poorly made wine, chemical taste or has no character at all

★★ : an acceptable wine with not much to recommend it

★★★ : a good wine, clean and well made, true to its grape type

★★★★ : a fine wine, the best that Canada has to offer

I have also given half stars (½) when a wine falls between two categories. When I consider that the wine will be better with at least a year of bottle age I have used the following device: ★★★(>★★★★)

Descriptive Terms

Trying to convey a sense of smell and taste in words is not easy. Wines can smell and taste of fruits, flowers, vegetables, nuts, hay and grass, and more organic substances such as tobacco, earth, chalk, petrol, tea and chocolate. They can also smell of leather or rotting hay, like a barnyard or forest undergrowth (which is not necessarily unpleasant as any lover of red Burgundy will tell you). I have used certain terms repeatedly almost as short-hand, which I would like to expand on here.

Colour: White wines I see as varying shades of straw colour ranging to lemon and gold. If I say straw-lime, to me it means a basic straw colour with hints of lime green. For reds the range is cherry to purple-black with the majority falling in the ruby category. When reds begin to age they can take on a tawny hue with hints of browning in the ruby.

Appearance: For sparkling wine I have also assessed the quality of the bubbles (mousse) and have noted if it's is made by the Champagne method (secondary fermentation in the bottle) or by the Charmat process (secondary fermentation in steel tanks).

Bouquet: When the wines offers little in the way of bouquet I call it shy (others may say "dumb").

Aromatic: spicy, usually referring to the nose of Riesling, Muscat or Gewürztraminer

Austere: very dry, lean fruit

Citric: the fresh, acidic smell of citrus fruit

Commercial: a wine that is made to appeal to a wide range of palates, usually with some residual sugar

Complexity: a wine with more than one flavour, nuances in the bouquet and taste

Extract: the flavour of the grape, more concentrated when fully ripe and yields are small

Finish: the final taste, the taste that's left on the palate when you've swallowed the wine

Flat: a wine that lacks acidity

Flinty: the smell of struck flint

Good length: a lingering flavour carried along by the acidity

Herbaceous: grassy, leafy bouquet and flavour

Herby: the smell of dried herbs

Off-dry: a touch of sweetness balanced by acidity

Residual sugar: a winemaker will stop the fermentation to leave some sugar in the wine or will add concentrated fresh grape juice to give the wine a touch of sweetness

Soft: a smooth, glycerol feeling of the wine on the tongue, usually associated with wines that have some residual sugar

Structure: the shape of a wine, defined by its fruit, acidity and alcohol

Sulphur: the burnt match-head smell in a wine. Sulphur is used to clean barrels and sulphites are employed as anti-oxidants. If too much is used and gets bound into the wine it will be evident on the nose.

Tannin: the bitter-tasting compound in the skins, stalks and pits of grapes that gives young red wines a rasping, astringent finish. Tannins can also taste dusty in maturing wines.

Unctuous: an oiliness that coats the tongue, usually in sweet wines

Varietal character: a wine should smell and taste of the grape from which it is made

Volatile: the smell of acetone, balsamic vinegar or nail polish; a fault when too evident

Young vines: a green, immature taste in the wine

TASTE

If a wine reminds me of a well-known style then I have described it as such, that is, Chablis-like, Mâconnais-style. I have indicated whether the wine is dry, off-dry or sweet and when it is full-bodied I have drawn attention to the fact. The mark of a great wine is how long it lingers on the palate once you have swallowed it. This characteristic is evident in such descriptions as "good length."

ONTARIO WINES

ANDRÉS	WHITE

★½ DOMAINE D'OR VIN BLANC (11.5% ALC) Screwtop litre

(bottled under licence from the Burgundy shipper Dumons, with Ontario wine)

Colour: pale straw   **Bouquet:** undistinguished   **Taste:** appley, touch of residual sugar, long acidic finish. Astringent.

★★ DOMAINE D'OR SUPÉRIEUR (11.5% ALC)

(bottled under licence from the Burgundy shipper Dumons, with Ontario wine)

Colour: pale straw   **Bouquet:** citric   **Taste:** soft, appley, Burgundy-style. Some residual sugar. Slightly gluey on the finish.

★½ HOCHTALER DRY (11% ALC) Screwtop litre

Colour: pale straw   **Bouquet:** aromatic, peachy, lemony **Taste:** very dry, citrus flavour. Tart, cardboard-like finish.

★ HOCHTALER (11% ALC) Screwtop litre

Colour: pale straw   **Bouquet:** lemony, wet fur   **Taste:** off-dry, unctuous, not much grape character. Mealy finish.

★★½   HOCHTALER GOLD RIESLING (11.5% ALC) Screwtop 1.5 litre

Colour: straw-lemon   **Bouquet:** petrol   **Taste:** sweet, soft, sweet lime and apple flavour, full in the mouth. Commercial. Good value.

★★½   PELLER ESTATES CHARDONNAY 1990 (11.5% ALC)

Colour: pale straw   **Bouquet:** nutty, apple   **Taste:** soft, sweet apple and bitter almond flavour. Touch of cinnamon on the finish.

★★½   PELLER ESTATES CHARDONNAY 1991 (11.95% ALC)

Colour: straw   **Bouquet:** apple   **Taste:** straightforward apple flavour, soft on the palate, clean

---

★★½   PELLER ESTATES FRENCH CROSS (11.5% ALC)

Colour: straw   **Bouquet:** light, melon   **Taste:** soft, touch of residual sugar, dry caramel flavour. Good length. Good value.

★★★   PELLER ESTATES VIDAL 1989 (11.5% ALC)

Colour: pale straw   **Bouquet:** Chinese gooseberry
Taste: dry, with good middle fruit. Good length, well made.

★★½   PELLER ESTATES VIDAL 1990 (11.5% ALC)

Colour: pale straw   **Bouquet:** Chinese gooseberry   **Taste:** dry with good middle fruit. Hint of appley sweetness in the middle taste. Medium weight.

RED

★★½   DOMAINE D'OR ROUGE (11.5% ALC) Screwtop litre

(bottled under licence from the Burgundy shipper Dumons, with Ontario wine)

Colour: light tawny ruby   **Bouquet:** smoky, earthy, blackberry
Taste: dry, light, raspberry and orange peel. Touch of tannin for interest. Good value.

★★   DOMAIN D'OR ROUGE SUPÉRIEUR (11.5% ALC)

(bottled under licence from the Burgundy shipper Dumons, with Ontario wine)

Colour: tawny ruby   **Bouquet:** plummy, raspberry
Taste: sweeter, rounder than Domaine D'Or Rouge. Off-dry, raspberry flavour. Not as interesting, lacks structure.

★★½   PELLER ESTATES CABERNET (11.5% ALC)

Colour: tawny ruby   **Bouquet:** plum, spicy   **Taste:** soft, sweetish, light. Little tannin. Good value.

★★½   PELLER ESTATES CHAMBOURCIN 1988 (11.5% ALC)

Colour: ruby-plum   **Bouquet:** oaky, volatile   **Taste:** dry, perfumed raspberries

SPARKLING

★½   CANADIAN CHAMPAGNE DRY (11.5% ALC)

(Charmat process)

Appearance: sluggish mousse   **Colour:** pale straw   **Bouquet:** chalky, lemony   **Taste:** sweetish, bland, lacks acidity

---

★½   CANADIAN CHAMPAGNE BLUSH (11.5% ALC)

(Charmat process)

Appearance: active mousse   **Colour:** pink with bluish tints
Bouquet: candied raspberry   **Taste:** sweet, peppery, foamy. No structure.

BARNES WINES   WHITE

★½   HERITAGE ESTATES CANADIAN CHABLIS (11% ALC)

(a product of Cartier Wines)

Colour: palest straw   **Bouquet:** earthy   **Taste:** dry, hint of grapefruit peel, watery

Red

★★   HERITAGE ESTATES CANADIAN BURGUNDY (11% ALC)

Colour: ruby-plum   **Bouquet:** cooked cherries   **Taste:** dry, lean, light cherry flavour. Chillable.

BRIGHTS   White

★½   CHARDONNAY ZABECK VINEYARDS 1990 VINTAGE SELECTION (11% ALC)

Colour: pale straw   **Bouquet:** gluey nose   **Taste:** dry, not much flavour, lacks varietal character

★★   ESTATE CHARDONNAY 1991 (11% ALC) Barrel sample

Colour: pale straw   **Bouquet:** apple peel   **Taste:** lean, dull apple character. Astringent finish.

★★   ENTRE-LACS DRY WHITE (11% ALC) Screwtop litre

Colour: lemon-straw   **Bouquet:** almond, hay   **Taste:** dry, soft, peachy, commercial

★★½   GEWÜRZTRAMINER 1990 VINTAGE SELECTION (10.5% ALC)

Colour: pale straw   **Bouquet:** faint spicy, steely   **Taste:** soft, spicy apple, clean finish

★   HOUSE WINE DRY (11% ALC) Screwtop litre

Colour: pale straw   **Bouquet:** non-descript   **Taste:** dry, melon, inoffensive

★½   HOUSE WINE (11% ALC) Screwtop litre

Colour: pale straw   **Bouquet:** gooseberry   **Taste:** soft, fruity, commercial

½   MARIA CHRISTINA (10% ALC) Screwtop litre

Colour: straw   **Bouquet:** earthy, lemon peel   **Taste:** sweet, synthetic. Browning apple finish.

★★½   RIESLING 1989 VINTAGE SELECTION (10.5% ALC)

Colour: straw, hints of lime   **Bouquet:** lime, petrol
Taste: dry, crab apple and citrus flavour. Finishes rather flat.

★★½   VIDAL 1989 (11% ALC)

Colour: yellow straw   **Bouquet:** shy nose   **Taste:** green plum, fruity, dry lemony finish

---

★★½   VIDAL ICEWINE 1989 (11.5% ALC) Half bottle

Colour: coppery-gold   **Bouquet:** candied orange peel
Taste: Burnt orange peel; short, astringent finish

★   VIDAL EISWEIN 1986 (13% ALC)

Colour: pale straw   **Bouquet:** foxy, toffee   **Taste:** heavy, bitter. Tastes like a wine made in a laboratory.

RED

★★   BACO NOIR 1989 (12% ALC)

Colour: dense purple   **Bouquet:** plummy   **Taste:** dry, smoky plum, good acidity. Stewed plum flavours, but rather short with a tart, acidic finish.

★★★½   BACO NOIR LATE HARVEST 1988 (12% ALC)

Colour: blackish purple with browning edges   **Bouquet:** smoky plum   **Taste:** dry, blackberry. Not much complexity, rustic. An Ontario country wine.

★★★   BACO NOIR LATE HARVEST 1989 (12% ALC)

Colour: purple-ruby   **Bouquet:** smoky blackberry and plum
Taste: dry, less intense than '88. Simple, but lots of flavour.

★★★   ENTRE-LACS RED (12% ALC) Screwtop litre

Colour: light ruby   **Bouquet:** tobacco, oak   **Taste:** dry, medium weight, well balanced. Red berry flavour, well made. Touch of tannin on the finish. Good value.

★½   HOUSE WINE RED DRY (12% ALC) Screwtop litre

Colour: purple ruby   **Bouquet:** sappy   **Taste:** dry, plummy, hint of tannin

---

★★   HOUSE WINE RED (12% ALC) Screwtop litre

Colour: cherry   **Bouquet:** smoky strawberry   **Taste:** light, strawberry flavour, touch of residual sugar commercial

---

★½   MARIA CHRISTINA RED (11.5% ALC) Screwtop litre

Colour: purple   **Bouquet:** sour cherry   **Taste:** sweet, plummy, no structure

SPARKLING

★★   PRESIDENT GRANDE RESERVE CANADIAN CHAMPAGNE BRUT (12.5% ALC)

Appearance: large persistent bubbles   **Colour:** deep straw **Bouquet:** lime   **Taste:** dry, austere, tart metallic finish

---

★½   PRESIDENT GRANDE RESERVE CANADIAN CHAMPAGNE (12.5% ALC)

Appearance: not much activity   **Bouquet:** caramel toffee **Taste:** soft, off-dry, not much flavour, bitter finish

---

★★½   PRESIDENT GRANDE RESERVE CANADIAN CHAMPAGNE PINK (12.5% ALC)

Appearance: active mousse   **Colour:** deep pink-amber **Bouquet:** leafy, raspberry candy   **Taste:** off-dry, raspberry flavour. Clean finish.

★½   PRESIDENT PREMIUM CANADIAN PORT (19% ALC)

Colour: tawny cherry   **Bouquet:** volatile   **Taste:** sweet, alcoholic, heavy

---

★★★½   CLASSIC CREAM CANADIAN SHERRY (19% ALC)

Colour: amber-bronze   **Bouquet:** nutty   **Taste:** sweet, focused taste, good acidity, minty nutty flavour

---

★★★   PALE DRY SELECT CANADIAN SHERRY (19% ALC)

Colour: straw   **Bouquet:** salty, camomile   **Taste:** off-dry, baked nutty flavour. Good length.

★★★   PRESIDENT PREMIUM CANADIAN SHERRY (19% ALC)

Colour: deep copper   **Bouquet:** sweet, alcoholic
Taste: sweet, fruit cake, nutty finish

SAWMILL CREEK
LABEL   WHITE

The major constituent of these products is wine from new world growing regions.

★★   DRY RIESLING (11% ALC)

Colour: palest straw   **Bouquet:** not much varietal character
Taste: off-dry, citrus flavour. Good length.

★★   FUMÉ BLANC (11% ALC)

Colour: pale straw   **Bouquet:** papery, no Sauvignon Blanc character   **Taste:** soft, off-dry, herbaceous. Good length.

★★½   CHARDONNAY (11% ALC)

Colour: straw   **Bouquet:** appley   **Taste:** dry appley flavour. Light on the palate, good length.

SAWMILL CREEK
LABEL RED

★★½   ZINFANDEL GAMAY (11% ALC)

Colour: salmon pink   **Bouquet:** candied raspberry
Taste: sweetish, raspberry candy. Good acidity.

★★★   MERLOT-BACO (12% ALC)

Colour: ruby   **Bouquet:** black currant   **Taste:** dry, medium weight. Evident Merlot black currant taste, good smoky undertone from the Baco.

★★½   CABERNET-BACO (12% ALC)

Colour: ruby   **Bouquet:** faint Cabernet character   **Taste:** dry, medium weight. Thin Cabernet taste, little concentration of flavour.

CARTIER WHITE

ADAGIO (7% ALC) Screwtop litre

Colour: straw   **Bouquet:** lemon candy   **Taste:** thin, sweetish, little wine character, odd finish

---

★★   ALPENWEISS (10.5% ALC) Screwtop litre

Colour: palest straw   **Bouquet:** citrus   **Taste:** sweetish appley, almond. Short on the palate. Commercial.

CAPISTRO (7% ALC) Screwtop bottle

Colour: almost water white   **Bouquet:** cardboard, hybrid
Taste: sweet, watery, chalky finish

★½   CHANTONNÉ (11% ALC)

(a blend of French and Ontario wines)

Colour: straw   **Bouquet:** toasty, earthy   **Taste:** sweet lemon, not much character

★½   L'AMBIANCE WHITE (11% ALC)

Colour: pale straw   **Bouquet:** earthy, nutty   **Taste:** soft, off-dry, citrus, watery finish

---

★★   L'ESCAPADE (11% ALC) Screwtop litre

Colour: straw   **Bouquet:** toasty, earthy, citrus   **Taste:** soft, touch of residual sugar. Commercial. Good value.

★   VINTNER'S CHOICE WHITE WINE FRENCH SELECTION (10.5% ALC) One litre tetrapak

(French and Ontario wines)

Colour: pale straw   **Bouquet:** non-descript   **Taste:** off-dry, appley, acidic finish. Inoffensive. Heavy in the mouth.

★½   VINTNER'S CHOICE SEMI-DRY WHITE WINE GERMAN SELECTION (10.5% ALC) One litre tetrapak

(German and Ontario wines)

Colour: pale straw   **Bouquet:** earthy, lemon   **Taste:** soft, sweetish, hint of orange

RED

★★   L'AMBIANCE RED (11% ALC)

Colour: ruby, white at the rim   **Bouquet:** spicy, earthy
Taste: dry, medium-bodied, raspberry flavour. Slightly volatile, soft middle taste.

★★   MARÉCHAL FOCH 1990 (10.5% ALC)

Colour: ruby   **Bouquet:** acetone, volatile   **Taste:** dry, perfumed, floral, good length. Touch of tannin, green finish.

★½   ALPENWEISS SPARKLING (10.5% ALC)

Appearance: little mousse   **Colour:** pale straw   **Bouquet:** gummy   **Taste:** sweet, foamy, browning apple flavour

---

★½   IMPERIAL CANADIAN CHAMPAGNE BRUT (12% ALC)

(Charmat process)

Appearance: active mousse   **Colour:** palest straw **Bouquet:** shy, hint of licorice   **Taste:** off-dry, not much flavour, licorice taste. Lacks acidity.

★   IMPERIAL CANADIAN CHAMPAGNE DRY (12% ALC)

(Charmat process)

Appearance: active mousse   **Colour:** pale straw   **Bouquet:** lemon and licorice   **Taste:** round, sweetish, bitter finish

---

★★   IMPERIAL CANADIAN CHAMPAGNE PINK (12% ALC)

(Charmat process)

Appearance: active mousse   **Colour:** pink-amber **Bouquet:** raspberry   **Taste:** soft, sweetish. Commercial.

★½   SPUMANTE BIANCO (7% ALC)

Appearance: lazy mousse   **Colour:** almost water white **Bouquet:** synthetic nose **Taste:** sweet, foamy, sparkling grape juice character

---

★★★   SPUMANTE CLASSICO (7% ALC)

Appearance: light mousse   **Colour:** water white   **Bouquet:** lychee   **Taste:** sweet lychee flavour, good length. Good value.

FORTIFIED

★★½   PRIVATE STOCK CANADIAN SHERRY (18% ALC)

Colour: copper-bronze **Bouquet:** sweet, raisiny
Taste: sweet, nutty. Good length, spicy finish.

★★★   PRIVATE STOCK CANADIAN PORT (18% ALC)

Colour: tawny ruby **Bouquet:** alcohol, raisiny **Taste:** sweet,
raisiny. Good length.

CAVE SPRING
CELLARS   WHITE

★★½ (>★★★)   CHARDONNAY 1990 (12.5% ALC)

Colour: straw **Bouquet:** sweet butter **Taste:** apple butter,
good spine of acidity. Lacks middle fruit.

★★★   CHARDONNAY 1988 (12.6% ALC)

Colour: straw-lemon **Bouquet:** lemony, barnyard
Taste: lean, focused, somewhat austere Chablis style. Grassy,
citrus taste with a touch of oak. Hint of toffee on the finish, but
low in extract.

★★★½
(>★★★★)   BARREL-FERMENTED CHARDONNAY 1990 (12.5% ALC)

Colour: pale straw **Bouquet:** vanilla, fresh grapefruit
Taste: spicy, lean Chabliseque quality. Lemon and lime flavour.
Well balanced, clean, good length. Toasty finish.

★★★★   CHARDONNAY RESERVE 1990 (12.5% ALC)

Colour: straw **Bouquet:** vanilla, apple, hay **Taste:** dry,
buttery, rich flavour with good length and a lemony finish.
Evident oak. Excellent now, will improve.

★★★★ CHARDONNAY 1989 (12.5% ALC)

Colour: straw **Bouquet:** grapefruit, oak, touch of barnyard
Taste: full-bodied grapefruit flavour. Lots of extract, good
acidity. Chablis style.

★★★½ ESTATE CHARDONNAY 1991 (13% ALC) Barrel sample

(aged in old oak)

Colour: straw **Bouquet:** grapefruit **Taste:** good extract, rich
grapefruit flavour, spicy

★★★★ CHARDONNAY RESERVE 1991 (13.2% ALC) Barrel sample

(partially barrel-fermented and aged in oak)

Colour: straw **Bouquet:** spicy grapefruit **Taste:** lots of
extract and spice. Fine balancing acidity.

★★★★ CHARDONNAY RESERVE 1989 (12.5% ALC)

Colour: rich straw **Bouquet:** vanilla, buttery **Taste:** soft,
sweetish fruit with vanilla. Well balanced, great length with a
nutty finish. Meursault-style. Will cellar well.

★★★★ CHARDONNAY RESERVE 1988 (12.6% ALC)

Colour: yellow straw **Bouquet:** lemon, butter, spicy **Taste:**
rich, spicy, lemony flavour. Well integrated oak. Good length,
long acidic finish.

★★★(>★★★½) CHARDONNAY MUSQUÉ 1990 (12% ALC)

Colour: pale straw **Bouquet:** oaky, apple **Taste:** sweetish
apple, touch of spice, fresh flavour. Good acidity but still closed.

★★★½ CHARDONNAY MUSQUÉ 1991 (12.5% ALC)

(stainless steel aging)

Colour: pale straw **Bouquet:** floral-apple **Taste:** hint of
Muscat behind the apple. Good acidity.

★★ GEWÜRZTRAMINER 1990 (11.5% ALC)

Colour: pale straw **Bouquet:** lychee, apple blossom
Taste: nose suggests more fruit than the palate delivers. Short finish, acidic. Young vines?

★★★½ RIESLING DRY 1991 (11.5% ALC)
(>★★★★)

Colour: pale straw **Bouquet:** minty, grassy **Taste:** crisp, elegant lime and grapefruit flavour. Beautifully balanced.

★★★½ RIESLING DRY 1990 (11.5% ALC)

Colour: pale gold **Bouquet:** flinty, grapefruit **Taste:** very dry, grapefruit and lime. Great length and acidity.

★★★½ RIESLING RESERVE 1990 (11% ALC)

Colour: pale straw **Bouquet:** grapefruit peel **Taste:** very dry, fat middle fruit (grapefruit and lime), good length with a tart finish

★★★(>★★★½) RIESLING OFF-DRY 1991 (11% ALC)

Colour: straw **Bouquet:** earthy, grapefruit **Taste:** soft, sweet grapefruit, good length but lacking the structure of the Dry version

★★★ RIESLING OFF-DRY 1990 (10.5% ALC)

Colour: pale straw **Bouquet:** sweet grapefruit peel
Taste: soft, slightly soapy taste, grapefruit finish

★★★★ INDIAN SUMMER RIESLING 1990 (10% ALC) Half bottle

Colour: copper-gold **Bouquet:** touch of Botrytis, honeyed apricot **Taste:** medium sweet, intense fruit character, well balanced with lingering acidity

★★★ RIESLING FRENCH OAK VINEYARD 1990 BOTRYTIS AFFECTED (12.5% ALC) Half bottle

Colour: old gold   **Bouquet:** rich apricot and pineapple
Taste: unctuous, sweet tropical fruit flavours with good acidity, but the fruit dies before the acidity finishes

★★★★ RIESLING ICEWINE 1990 (11.5% ALC) Half bottle

Colour: old gold   **Bouquet:** oily grapegruit and apricot
Taste: lively sweet grapefruit, dried peach, apricot and tea. Well balanced, great length.

RED

★★★½ GAMAY NOIR 1990 (11.5% ALC)

Colour: purple-ruby   **Bouquet:** earthy, strawberry
Taste: sweet fruit, light blood orange flavour with vanilla overtones. Charming.

★★★ GAMAY ROSÉ 1990 (11.5% ALC)

Colour: deep rose   **Bouquet:** earthy, stewed strawberry
Taste: dry, crisp, wild strawberry and cranberry flavour. Well made. A good summer wine.

★★★ ROSÉ 1991 (12% ALC)

(blend of Gamay and Pinot Noir)

Colour: deep salmon   **Bouquet:** raspberry   **Taste:** fresh, very dry, unripe raspberries. Light Tavel style.

★★★½ MERLOT 1990

Colour: light ruby   **Bouquet:** spicy cinnamon and nutmeg
Taste: black raspberry flavour, oaky, light bodied

★★ (>★★½) Pinot Noir 1989 (11% alc)

Colour: ruby **Bouquet:** light raspberry **Taste:** dry, light raspberry and green apple flavours. Long, astringent, tannic finish. Not enough extract for the acid.

CENTRAL VALLEY WINES White

★★ White (11.5% alc)

Colour: straw **Bouquet:** piney, gingery **Taste:** soft, spicy with a hint of sweetness. Gingery finish. Great value in large format.

Red

★★½ Red (12.% alc)

Colour: light ruby **Bouquet:** cherry **Taste:** light, sweetish, peppery. Beaujolais style. Great value.

CHÂTEAU DES CHARMES White

★★★ Cour Blanc (11% alc) Screwtop litre

(60% Californian French Colombard, 40% Ontario Riesling and Vidal)

Colour: straw **Bouquet:** sweetish vanilla **Taste:** soft perfumed marshmallowy taste, sweetish, easy drinking, clean, well made. Good value.

★★★½ Aligoté 1990 (11.5% alc)

Colour: pale straw **Bouquet:** stoney, acidic nose **Taste:** crisp, clean, well balanced. Surprising sweetness of fruit in the middle taste. Good length with a dry honey finish.

★★★★   AUXERROIS 1990 (11.5% ALC)

Colour: pale straw   **Bouquet:** crisp, appley   **Taste:** sweetish middle fruit, almost vanilla custard. Well made, fine lingering flavour.

★★   RIESLING 1989 (11.5% ALC)

Colour: straw   **Bouquet:** licorice and lime   **Taste:** soft, fruity taste, round on the palate but ultimately short, bitter finish

★★★   SEYVAL BLANC 1989 (11.5% ALC)

Colour: straw   **Bouquet:** parsley   **Taste:** crisp, clean, pebbly taste. Very dry, herby taste. Good length, well made.

★★★½   GAMAY BLANC 1989 (11.5% ALC)

Colour: straw   **Bouquet:** herbs and leather   **Taste:** dry appley flavour, good extract. Good depth of grapefruit flavour, finishes well.

★★★½   SAUVIGNON BLANC 1991
(70% Chilean Sauvignon Blanc, 5%
Ontario Sauvignon Blanc, 25% Ontario Riesling)

Colour: straw   **Bouquet:** green fig   **Taste:** sweetish fruit, soft middle palate, slightly alcoholic, good length. Good value.

★★★½   PINOT BLANC DE NOIR 1988 (11.5% ALC)

Colour: straw   **Bouquet:** sweet vanilla and green plum
Taste: green plum with a crême caramel finish. Good length.

★★½   CHARDONNAY 1990 (12% ALC) White label

Colour: yellow straw   **Bouquet:** buttered popcorn nose
Taste: rich spicy apple, soft sweetish Australian style (Lindemans Bin 65). Hot, slightly bitter finish.

★★★½   CHARDONNAY 1990 ESTATE (12.5% ALC) Black label

Colour: yellow straw   **Bouquet:** nutty, vanilla   **Taste:** rich spicy fruit, soft caramel and apple flavour. Sweetish with a nutty finish. Drink soon.

★★½ (>★★★)   CHARDONNAY 1990 PAUL BOSC ESTATE (12.5% ALC)

Colour: straw, lime hints   **Bouquet:** oaky vanilla, apple and banana nose   **Taste:** soft, sweetish, good peachy fruit but short and somewhat green on the finish. Young vines. Next vintage should be better.

★★   GEWÜRZTRAMINER 1989 (11% ALC)

Colour: pale straw   **Bouquet:** delicate Muscat-like nose
Taste: lean, rather metallic. Not much varietal character. Bitter finish.

★★★½   RIESLING LATE HARVEST 1989 PAUL BOSC ESTATE (11% ALC) Half bottle

Colour: pale gold   **Bouquet:** petrol and honey   **Taste:** sweet, peachy. Unctuous and soft with good acidity.

★★★★   RIESLING LATE HARVEST 1990 PAUL BOSC ESTATE (11% ALC) Half bottle

Colour: pale gold   **Bouquet:** honeyed Botrytis nose   **Taste:** coats the tongue. Rich peach, apricot and honey flavours, sweet, wonderful length and good acidity. An elegant dessert wine.

RED

★★   COUR ROUGE (11% ALC) Screwtop litre

(70% California Cabernet Sauvignon, 30% Ontario Gamay)

Colour: plum   **Bouquet:** light, leathery with a floral overtone
Taste: blackberry fruit, sweetish with a peppery tannic finish. Good value.

★★   GAMAY NOIR 1989 (12% ALC)

Colour: ruby   **Bouquet:** discreet plummy nose   **Taste:** jammy fruit, soft with a lean, chalky finish

★★½   GAMAY/CABERNET 1989 (11.5% ALC)

(Ontario Gamay with Chilean Cabernet Sauvignon)

Colour: tawny plum   **Bouquet:** vanilla, earthy blackberry
Taste: sturdy mouthfeel; tannin, black currant, slightly green finish

★★½ (>★★★)   PINOT NOIR 1989 (11.5% ALC)

(small percentage of Chilean wine)

Colour: tawny ruby   **Taste:** raspberry jelly, good varietal character, soft on the palate. Touch of tannin and the bitterness of young vines on the finish.

★   PINOT NOIR 1988 (12% ALC)

Colour: tawny ruby   **Bouquet:** sweaty nose   **Taste:** cooked taste, bitter chocolate, tannic, evident oxidation

★★★½   ESTATE PINOT NOIR 1990 (12% ALC)

Colour: light ruby   **Bouquet:** sweet violet and raspberry nose
Taste: sweet red fruit, well made, soft mouthfeel, touch of tannin

★★½   CABERNET SAUVIGNON 1988

(wine from Chile)

Colour: purple ruby   **Bouquet:** earthy black currant leaf
Taste: good middle fruit, sweetish, jammy, tobacco flavours. Chocolate finish. Good value.

★★★   MERLOT 1990 PAUL BOSC ESTATE (12.5% ALC)

Colour: purple   **Bouquet:** good varietal character, plum and jasmine   **Taste:** sweet berry fruit, good length, soft tannins

★★★(>★★★½) CABERNET FRANC 1990 PAUL BOSC ESTATE (12.5% ALC)

Colour: purple   **Bouquet:** blackberry and leather, perfumey
Taste: pomegranate and violets, well balanced, good acidity

★★★(>★★★½) CABERNET SAUVIGNON 1990 PAUL BOSC ESTATE (12.5% ALC)

Colour: dense purple   **Bouquet:** leather, black currant, cedar
Taste: good black currant flavour, a little short, tannin that will soften with age

---

★★★½
(>★★★★)

CABERNET 1990 PAUL BOSC ESTATE (12.5% ALC)

(a blend of 50% Cabernet Sauvignon, 25% Cabernet Franc, 25% Merlot)

Colour: dense purple   **Bouquet:** sappy, oaky nose with hints of coconut flesh   **Taste:** spicy blackberry, dominated now by oak but will come through with bottle age. Good length, some tannin.

★★

CABERNET 1988 ESTATE (12% ALC)

Colour: plum   **Bouquet:** sweaty, leathery   **Taste:** sweet fruit but drying out. Not much extract, tannic.

SPARKLING

★★★

CANADIAN CHAMPAGNE BRUT

(50% Pinot Noir, 50% Chardonnay)

Colour: straw   **Appearance:** light mousse but persistent, small bubbles   **Bouquet:** hay-like nose   **Taste:** appley; surprisingly sweet for a Brut

---

★★

CANADIAN CHAMPAGNE SEC

(50% Chardonnay, 50% Riesling and Gamay)

Colour: pale gold   **Appearance:** good active mousse
Bouquet: honeyed apple   **Taste:** sweetish, foamy in the mouth. Vanilla flavour but short with a bitter finish.

★★★   HALLMARK DRY CANADIAN SHERRY (18% ALC)

(a Cartier Wines product)

Colour: golden bronze   **Bouquet:** winey   **Taste:** off-dry, toasty, nutty. Good length.

★★★   HALLMARK CREAM CANADIAN SHERRY (18% ALC)

(a Cartier Wines product)

Colour: amber-bronze   **Bouquet:** treacle toffee, orange peel
Taste: sweet, nutty, smooth. Good length.

COLIO   WHITE

★★★   EXTRA DRY (12% ALC) Screwtop litre

Colour: straw   **Bouquet:** sweetish, green plum   **Taste:** dry, appley, a good, clean blend. Finishes well. Good value.

★★½   BIANCO SECCO (12% ALC) Screwtop litre

Colour: straw   **Bouquet:** dusty, apple skin   **Taste:** sweetish, soft, off-dry, appley, fruity. Good value.

★   BIANCO SEMI-DRY (12% ALC) Screwtop litre

Colour: pale straw   **Bouquet:** sulphurous   **Taste:** sweet, candied. Low acidity, cloying finish.

★★★   RISERVA BIANCO 1990 (12% ALC)

Colour: straw   **Bouquet:** dry pineapple   **Taste:** dry, well balanced, good middle fruit, lingering finish. Great value.

★★   CASTLE CELLAR (12% ALC) Screwtop litre

Colour: pale straw   **Bouquet:** pear skin   **Taste:** sweetish, soft, very commercial. Well balanced, clean. Good value.

★★★   PINOT BLANC 1990 LE BLANC VINEYARD (12% ALC)

Colour: pale straw   **Bouquet:** soft peachy nose   **Taste:** good fruit, well balanced, clean, touch of sweetness. True to the variety.

★★½   CHARDONNAY 1990 (12% ALC)

Colour: straw   **Bouquet:** candy apple nose   **Taste:** sweet apple fruit, soft, easy drinking

---

★★½   PINOT BLANC (NV)

Colour: pale straw   **Bouquet:** sweetish, marshmallow nose **Taste:** sweet peachy flavour, good balance of fruit and acidity, medium bodied

---

★★   CARLO NEGRI CHARDONNAY 1989 (12% ALC)

Colour: straw   **Bouquet:** appley nose   **Taste:** aged appley flavour, acidic with some astringency on the finish

---

★★½   ICEWINE 1990 (11.5% ALC) Half bottle

Colour: gold   **Bouquet:** oaky, peachy   **Taste:** sweet pineapple, light fruit extract. Vanilla oak overrides the flavour. Mouthfilling but blunt finish.

★★½ (>★★★)   NOBILE VIN DU CURÉ 1989

Colour: old gold   **Bouquet:** ripe banana skin and caramel **Taste:** semi-dry flavour of dried fruits, lean and oaky, some tannin, astringent finish

---

★½   RIESLING 1989 (12% ALC)

Colour: straw with lime tints   **Bouquet:** dried dates **Taste:** lean, dry, woody. Not much varietal character.

Red

★★	**BLANC DE NOIR BLUSH 1990**

Colour: tawny pink   **Bouquet:** earthy, strawberry
Taste: sweet, candied raspberry, soft finish. Needs more acidity.

★½   **ROSSO SECCO (12% ALC) Screwtop litre**

Colour: cherry   **Bouquet:** sweet candied raspberry
Taste: sweetish cranberry flavour, bitter finish

★★★   **RISERVA ROSSO 1989 (12% ALC)**

Colour: ruby   **Bouquet:** smokey, flinty, blackberry
Taste: tarry, plum, soft tannins. Great value.

★★★½   **MARÉCHAL FOCH 1990 (12% ALC)**

Colour: ruby   **Bouquet:** perfumed raspberry   **Taste:** sweetish raspberry, delicate and well balanced. A pretty wine. Excellent value.

★★½   **CABERNET FRANC 1990 (12.5% ALC)**

Colour: ruby-plum   **Bouquet:** candied raspberry
Taste: raspberry, dry, medium weight. Fruity and straightforward with a touch of sweetness. Good value.

★½   **ROSSO SECCO (12% ALC) Screwtop litre**

Colour: cherry   **Bouquet:** sweet candied raspberry
Taste: sweetish cranberry flavour, bitter finish

Sparkling

★★   **CHATEAU D'OR CANADIAN CHAMPAGNE (12% ALC)**

(Charmat process)

Colour: straw   **Appearance:** foamy   **Bouquet:** candied nose
Taste: sweetish and frothy, a little short

★★½   SPUMANTE (7% ALC)

(Charmat process)

Colour: pale straw   **Appearance:** active mousse
Bouquet: candy floss   **Taste:** sweet and grapey. Acidic finish.
A good Asti Spumante substitute.

CULOTTA   WHITE

★★   CANADIAN CHABLIS (11% ALC)

Colour: pale straw   **Bouquet:** gummy, licorice   **Taste:** very
dry, herby. Italian-style white wine.

★½   CHARDONNAY 1990 (11.5% ALC)

Colour: pale straw   **Bouquet:** sulphur   **Taste:** dry, thin, little
varietal character. Crisp, bitter finish.

★★½   CHARDONNAY 1991 (11.4% ALC) Barrel sample

(aged in French oak)

Colour: straw   **Bouquet:** apple peel   **Taste:** light, appley, hint
of oxidation

★★★½   GEWÜRZTRAMINER 1989 (12.4% ALC)

Colour: pale straw   **Bouquet:** smoky, lychee   **Taste:** soft, dry,
aromatic. Flavours of rose, red peppers, lychees. Good length.

★   RIESLING (11.5% ALC)

Colour: pale straw   **Bouquet:** spicy baked apple
Taste: heavy, cloyingly sweet. Lacks balancing acidity.

★½   SEYVAL BLANC (11% ALC)

Colour: pale straw   **Bouquet:** dusty, little character
Taste: dry, soapy apple and lemon flavour. Acidic, hot finish.

★★   MARÉCHAL FOCH 1989 (12% ALC)

Colour: ruby   **Bouquet:** cooked beets   **Taste:** dry, sour cherry flavour. Medium weight, touch of tannin on the finish.

★★   PETITE SIRAH/FOCH/DE CHAUNAC (11% ALC)

(the Petite Sirah is imported)

Colour: ruby   **Bouquet:** sappy, peppery   **Taste:** light, dry, unripe blackberries. Not much fruit extract. Tannic finish.

★½   CABERNET SAUVIGNON 1988 (11.5% ALC)

Colour: ruby   **Bouquet:** woody   **Taste:** very dry, lean, woody. Little extract. Astringent, bitter tannic finish.

SPARKLING

★   PREMIUM CANADIAN CHAMPAGNE DRY (12.5% ALC)

(Charmat process)

Appearance: lazy mousse   **Colour:** straw   **Bouquet:** oily, sweet, foxy   **Taste:** foxy, grapey flavour. Foamy, sweet, soapy.

D'ANGELO   WHITE

★★★   VIDAL 1989 (12% ALC)

Colour: straw   **Bouquet:** shy nose   **Taste:** good fruit, dry herby gooseberry flavour, banana-like finish. Good acidity.

★★★½   LATE HARVEST (10% ALC) Half bottle

Colour: pale straw   **Bouquet:** delicate, lilac and honey **Taste:** medium-sweet, light, peachy. Good length. Auslese quality.

★★★½   VIDAL ICEWINE (13.1% ALC) Half bottle

Colour: deep gold   **Bouquet:** intense; spicy orange
Taste: heavy apricot, intensely sweet, honeyed and velvety.
Good acidity.

RED

★★★   CABERNET-MERLOT 1990 (11% ALC)

(50% Cabernet Sauvignon, 50% Merlot; 10 months in American oak)

Colour: ruby-purple   **Bouquet:** oaky, plummy, black currant
leaf   **Taste:** light-bodied, blackberry and vanilla flavour. Spicy,
cinnamon finish. Evident acidity.

★½   FOCH 1990 (10.5% ALC)

Colour: purple   **Bouquet:** fruitcake nose with floral overtones
Taste: light, lean, thin on the palate. High acid. Unripe pomegranate taste.

DE SOUSA   WHITE

★★½   DOIS AMIGOS SEMI DRY WHITE (10.5% ALC)

Colour: pale straw   **Bouquet:** sweet pear   **Taste:** soft, off-dry,
easy drinking. Heavier than the stated alcohol suggests.

★★★   DOIS AMIGOS RIESLING LIMITED EDITION 1989 (12% ALC)

Colour: pale straw   **Bouquet:** citrus, biscuity   **Taste:** melon,
medium-bodied, fresh orangey finish

RED

★★★   DOIS AMIGOS VIN ROUGE (12% ALC)

(De Chaunac, Maréchal Foch, Pinot Noir)

Colour: ruby   **Bouquet:** smoky, cherry   **Taste:** dry, medium-
bodied, earthy Baco Noir, touch of residual sugar. Good value.

WHITE

★★★   CHARDONNAY 1991 (13.1% ALC)

Colour: straw   **Bouquet:** yeasty, grapefruit   **Taste:** crisp, good intensity, good length. Clean, full in the mouth.

★★★   CHARDONNAY 1990 (12.4% ALC)

Colour: straw   **Bouquet:** vanilla, grapefruit, hint of barnyard **Taste:** dry, lean, appley flavour. Evident acidity. Good length. Chablis style.

★★★(>★★★½) BARREL-FERMENTED CHARDONNAY 1991 (12.9% ALC) Barrel sample

Colour: straw   **Bouquet:** smoky, flinty, grapefruit   **Taste:** soft, melon-like fruit character

---

★★★   BARREL-FERMENTED CHARDONNAY 1990

Colour: straw   **Bouquet:** sweet, vanilla, cloves   **Taste:** dry pineapple and cinnamon flavours, good length. Lactic note on the finish.

★★★★   PROPRIETOR'S RESERVE CHARDONNAY 1991 (13.2% ALC) Barrel sample

Colour: straw   **Bouquet:** spicy   **Taste:** full-bodied, lively lemon and pear flavours

---

★★★★   PROPRIETOR'S RESERVE CHARDONNAY 1990 (12.6% ALC)

Colour: straw   **Bouquet:** spicy vanilla   **Taste:** clean, well balanced, spicy apple. Elegant, great length, grapefruit peel finish.

★★½   VIDAL 1990 (11.1% ALC)

Colour: pale straw   **Bouquet:** sweet, leathery   **Taste:** soft, off-dry green plum flavour, well balanced

★★★ RIESLING 1990 (10.9% ALC)

Colour: straw-lemon **Bouquet:** minerally, barnyard
Taste: dry, lime and grapefruit. Full in the mouth, flinty. Well structured with a touch of residual sugar. Good length.

★★½(>★★★½) RIESLING PROPRIETOR'S RESERVE 1990 (12% ALC)

Colour: deep straw **Bouquet:** apricot, peach **Taste:** soft, off-dry, lime and peach flavour. Crisp finish. Elements are not together yet.

★★★ GEWÜRZTRAMINER 1990 (12% ALC)

Colour: yellow straw **Bouquet:** jasmin, hint of lychees
Taste: spicy but without concentration of fruit. Well balanced.

★★★★ RIESLING ICEWINE 1990 (11% ALC) Half bottle

Colour: old gold **Bouquet:** spicy tropical fruit and lychee
Taste: honeyed orange and toffee; rich unctuous mouthfeel, well balanced, good acidity and lingering barley sugar taste

★★★ LATE HARVEST SEYVAL BLANC 1991 (12.5% ALC) Half bottle

Colour: straw **Bouquet:** sweaty, green pea **Taste:** sweet, soft middle, nutty flavour with a citric finish. Good acidity.

★★ SEYVAL BLANC 1989 (12.1% ALC) VQA

Colour: Straw **Bouquet:** earthy, spicy nose, pear, lime and nuts **Taste:** tart, medium weight. Very acidic.

RED

★★½ GAMAY NOIR 1990 (12% ALC)

Colour: light ruby **Bouquet:** plum **Taste:** dry, acidic, lean. Sour cherry flavour. Good length.

★★★   MERLOT 1990 (12.7% ALC)

Colour: ruby   **Bouquet:** vanilla, flint, dill   **Taste:** dry, spicy blackberry, medium weight. Not a lot of extract. Cinnamon and peppery tannins on the finish.

HERNDER
ESTATE   WHITE

★★   VIDAL 1991 (11.8% ALC)

Colour: pale straw   **Bouquet:** yeasty, banana   **Taste:** dry, lean fruit, austere acidic finish

RED

★★   VIDAL SEMI DRY 1991 (11.5% ALC)

Colour: pale straw   **Bouquet:** sweaty   **Taste:** off-dry, banana flavour, high acidity

HILLEBRAND
ESTATES   WHITE

★★½   LE BARON BLANC (11% ALC)

Colour: pale straw   **Bouquet:** dry apple skin   **Taste:** appley, good fruit, good acidity. Bordeaux-blanc style. Good value.

★½   BRULÉ BLANC VIDAL (11% ALC)

Colour: pale straw   **Bouquet:** shy nose   **Taste:** sweetish, soft, not much character. Sweet finish.

★★½   SCHLOSS HILLEBRAND (11% ALC)

Colour: straw   **Bouquet:** grapey, Muscat nose   **Taste:** sweet Muscat flavour, soft, lingering spicy-sweet finish. Good value.

★★½   CHARDONNAY HARVEST 1989 (12.5% ALC)

Colour: straw   **Bouquet:** lemon, biscuity   **Taste:** soft, sweetish apple fruit with a touch of spice. Good length, but marred by a hot finish.

★★★   CHARDONNAY 1989 HEUBEL VINEYARD (12.8% ALC)

Colour: straw   **Bouquet:** oaky, lemon   **Taste:** apple, touch of caramel and mint. A little bitter on the finish.

★★★½   COLLECTORS' CHOICE CHARDONNAY 1989 (12.8% ALC)

Colour: straw   **Bouquet:** sweet caramel nose   **Taste:** rich caramel and vanilla flavour. Toffee-like finish. Well balanced.

★★★½   CHARDONNAY 1990 (11.9% ALC)

(barrel aged — selected vineyards)

Colour: straw   **Bouquet:** vanilla, buttery, spicy
Taste: clovey, full-bodied, good acidity

★★★(>★★★½) TRIUS CHARDONNAY 1991 GLENLAKE VINEYARD (12.7% ALC)

Colour: straw   **Bouquet:** vanilla, apple   **Taste:** apple and pear flavours, fine acidity. Full-bodied and well balanced.

★★★½   TRIUS CHARDONNAY GLENLAKE VINEYARD 1990 (12.7% ALC)

(barrel fermented)

Colour: straw   **Bouquet:** lemon, grapefruit, vanilla
Taste: soft mouthfeel, lemony fruit, a little light on extract, high alcohol

★★★½   TRIUS CHARDONNAY HUEBEL VINEYARD 1991 (12% ALC)

Colour: straw   **Bouquet:** vanilla, lemon   **Taste:** good fruit, soft middle palate, zesty acidic finish. Elegant.

★★★½　TRIUS CHARDONNAY HEUBEL VINEYARD 1990 (12% ALC)
(>★★★★)

(barrel fermented)

Colour: straw-lemon　**Bouquet:** oak, apple, olives　**Taste:** spicy, buttery, good fruit, well balanced, lingering lemony finish

---

★★★(>★★★½) TRIUS SHOEMAKER VINEYARD CHARDONNAY 1991 (12.5% ALC)

Colour: straw　**Bouquet:** hint of barnyard, apples
Taste: crisp, appley flavour. Lean, Chablis character.

★★★★　TRIUS CHARDONNAY SHOEMAKER VINEYARD 1990 (12.7% ALC)

(barrel fermented)

Colour: straw　**Bouquet:** caramel, vanilla　**Taste:** oaky, apple, spicy, well balanced, good length

---

★★　CUVÉE 1812 CANADIAN CHABLIS (12.5% ALC)

Colour: straw　**Bouquet:** leafy, citrus　**Taste:** soft, citrus and melon flavours, slightly sweet. Easy drinking.

★★½　GAMAY BLANC HARVEST 1990 (11.5% ALC)

(>★★★★)　**Colour:** pale straw　**Bouquet:** oily, honeyed　**Taste:** dry appley flavour with a toffee-like finish

---

★½　GEWÜRZTRAMINER HARVEST 1990 (11.3% ALC)

Colour: straw　**Bouquet:** cheesey　**Taste:** dry, appley, lacks varietal character

---

★½　LADY ANN (11.5% ALC)

Colour: straw　**Bouquet:** sweetish nose　**Taste:** sweet, grapey, heavy melon flavours

---

★★½　MORIO MUSCAT 1991 (12.7% ALC)

Colour: pale straw　**Bouquet:** raisiny, orange　**Taste:** very dry, exotic, lean, acidic with an orange and rose character. Not enough extract.

★★½   MORIO MUSCAT 1990 (11.8% ALC)

Colour: straw   **Bouquet:** perfumed, rose-like   **Taste:** exotic, spicy orange. Very dry, tart finish with some astringency.

★★★½   RIESLING HARVEST 1990 (12.4% ALC)

Colour: straw   **Bouquet:** fresh lime   **Taste:** fine varietal character, lime and raisins, hint of sweetness. Well balanced, good length.

★★ (>★★★)   RIESLING CLASSIC 1990 (10.9% ALC)

Colour: palest straw   **Bouquet:** closed in   **Taste:** green, light, austere. Tart appley finish. Fruit locked in, needs bottle age.

★★★   RIESLING INSPIRATION 1988 (10.5% ALC)

Colour: pale gold   **Bouquet:** sweet hay and petrol   **Taste:** floral-grapefruit, lots of apricot flavour. Fine acidity, tart finish.

★★½(>★★★½) TRIUS RIESLING DRY 1990

Colour: yellow straw   **Bouquet:** dry honey and apricot nose **Taste:** lemony, very closed, high acidity, tart finish. Good length. Needs bottle age.

★★   SEYVAL BLANC 1990 (11.7% ALC)

Colour: straw   **Bouquet:** shy nose   **Taste:** dry, not much character. Acidic, lemony finish.

★★½   VIDAL 1989 (12% ALC)

Colour: straw   **Bouquet:** zesty citrus nose   **Taste:** dry, spritzy, lively fruit. Tart finish.

★½   VIDAL EISWEIN 1987 (10% ALC) Half bottle

Colour: copper   **Bouquet:** burnt sugar   **Taste:** sweet, soft, lacking acidity; chalky, chemical finish.

★★★★   VIDAL EISWEIN 1990 (9% ALC) Half bottle

Colour: copper   **Bouquet:** spicy orange with a hint of ginger
Taste: lively, burnt orange peel, smoky. Heavy on the palate, but well balanced and lingering.

RED

★★½   BACO NOIR 1988

Colour: mature ruby   **Bouquet:** meaty, plums   **Taste:** light, very dry, smoky blackberry and plum flavours. Lean fruit, acidic finish.

★★½   LE BARON ROUGE (11% ALC)

Colour: cherry   **Bouquet:** smoky plum   **Taste:** smoky, fruity, light Beaujolais style but short. Good value.

★★½(>★★★½) CABERNET FRANC 1991

Colour: dense purple   **Bouquet:** black currant, orange peel
Taste: dry, lively black currant fruit, medium bodied. Strong spine of acidity.

★   CUVÉE 1812 CANADIAN BURGUNDY (12.5% ALC)

Colour: purple   **Bouquet:** earthy, smoky   **Taste:** dry, smoky blackberry. Somewhat medicinal. Short with an astringent, tannic finish.

★★★(>★★★½) COLLECTOR'S CHOICE CABERNET SAUVIGNON/MERLOT 1989 (12.3% ALC)

Colour: ruby-purple   **Bouquet:** cherry, black currant
Taste: medium weight, black currant and cranberry. Touch of tannin. Well balanced.

★★★½ (>★★★★)	TRIUS 1989 GLENLAKE VINEYARD (12.5% ALC)

(Cabernet Sauvignon, Merlot, Cabernet Franc; 13 months in French oak)

Colour: dense purple **Bouquet:** bramble and black currant, vanilla **Taste:** black currant and pomegranate, fine extract, well balanced, good acidity. Touch of tannin, spicy finish.

★★	GAMAY NOIR HARVEST 1990 (11.4% ALC)

Colour: cherry **Bouquet:** not much on the nose
Taste: light, dry strawberry character. Not much varietal character. Short on fruit.

★★★	MARÉCHAL FOCH 1989 (11% ALC)

Colour: purple **Bouquet:** violets, hint of barnyard
Taste: dry, medium-bodied, red berry flavours, good length, touch of tannin.

ROSÉ

★★	ELIZABETH ROSÉ (11.5% ALC)

Colour: orange-salmon **Bouquet:** sweet raspberry candy
Taste: candied raspberry flavour rescued by its acidity

SPARKLING

★★★	CANADIAN CHAMPAGNE (11% ALC)

(Charmat process)

Colour: pale straw **Appearance:** active mousse **Bouquet:** sweetish melon nose **Taste:** soft mouthfeel, good length, attractive acidity. Good value.

★★★   MOUNIER BRUT (12% ALC)

(Champagne method)

Appearance: active mousse, small bubbles   **Colour:** pale straw
Bouquet: shy nose   **Taste:** dry, appley. Creamy on the palate, good length, good acidity.

★★★   RIESLING CUVÉE (12% ALC)

(Charmat process)

Appearance: medium mousse   **Colour:** straw lime
Bouquet: lime, petrol   **Taste:** crisp, clean, tart lime. True Riesling character. Refreshing.

FORTIFIED

★★½   CANADIAN PALE DRY SHERRY (18.5% ALC)

(aged in oak casks)

Colour: golden bronze   **Bouquet:** volatile, acetone nose
Taste: soft, fleshy, sweetish, biscuity-nutty flavour. Good length.

★★★   CANADIAN CREAM SHERRY (18.5% ALC)

(aged in oak casks)

Colour: rich amber-topaz   **Bouquet:** raisin, caramel
Taste: soft, sweet, toffee-like. Good length, good value.

INNISKILLIN   WHITE

★★½   AUXERROIS 1991 (11.3% ALC)

Colour: almost water white   **Bouquet:** vanilla, orange peel
Taste: fresh, citric and anise flavour. Dry finish.

★★½   BRAE BLANC (11.8% ALC)

(Seyval Blanc, Chardonnay, Chilean Sauvignon Blanc)

Colour: pale straw   **Bouquet:** grassy, dry hay
Taste: dry, herbaceous, austere. Entre Deux Mers style.

★★   BRAEBURN (11.3% ALC) Screwtop litre

(Vidal, Riesling)

Colour: pale straw   **Bouquet:** briny   **Taste:** sweet, appley, apple peel finish with a hint of bitterness

---

★★ (>★★½)   CHARDONNAY 1990 (12% ALC)

Colour: pale straw   **Bouquet:** lemon, toffee, touch of sulphur
Taste: dry appley with a suggestion of oak, light in middle fruit, caramel on the finish

---

★★½ (>★★★)   CHARDONNAY 1991 (12.5% ALC)

(aged in stainless steel)

Colour: pale straw   **Bouquet:** yeasty, grapefruit   **Taste:** crisp, lean green apple flavour, sour milk finish

---

★★★½   CHARDONNAY MONTAGUE VINEYARD 1989 (12.8% ALC)

Colour: pale straw   **Bouquet:** caramel, butter   **Taste:** spicy, appley. Full-bodied. Fruit carries through to a dry toffee-like finish.

★★★½
(>★★★★)   CHARDONNAY RESERVE 1991 (12.7% ALC) Barrel sample

(aged in new Nevers, Allier and Troncais barrels)

Colour: pale straw   **Bouquet:** vanilla, melon   **Taste:** spicy pear flavour, good intensity of fruit. Lingering.

★★★½   CHARDONNAY RESERVE 1988 (12.8% ALC)

Colour: pale straw   **Bouquet:** toasty, barnyard, vanilla   **Taste:** crisp, elegant, very Burgundian. Long spicy, lemony finish.

★★★½
(>★★★★)   CHARDONNAY 1989 SCHUELE VINEYARD (12.9% ALC)

Colour: pale straw   **Bouqet:** apple, caramel   **Taste:** soft appley fruit, clean, lean and well balanced with a hint of vanilla. Good length. Macon style.

★★★½   CHARDONNAY 1990 SCHUELE VINEYARD (12.7% ALC)
(>★★★★)

Colour: pale straw   **Bouquet:** delicate apple and vanilla
Taste: elegant, beautifully harmonious. Lean fruit with good
acidity.

★★★(>★★★★) CHARDONNAY SEEGER VINEYARD 1991 Barrel sample

(aged in new Nevers oak)

Colour: straw   **Bouquet:** cinnamon, caramel   **Taste:** soft,
round fruit giving way to spicy flavours and lively acidity. Needs
time.

★★★(>★★★½) CHARDONNAY 1989 SEEGER VINEYARD

Colour: pale straw   **Bouquet:** smoky, appley, oaky   **Taste:**
spicy apple fruit currently masked by oak

★★★   GAMAY BLANC 1990 (12.3% ALC)

Colour: straw   **Bouquet:** buttery   **Taste:** soft, lactic,
Chardonnay-like. Dry with good middle fruit. Full-bodied.

★   GEWÜRZTRAMINER 1989 (12.5% ALC)

Colour: palest straw   **Bouquet:** honeysuckle and apple
Taste: oxidized fruit, short and bitter. Hot finish, too much
alcohol.

★★   GRÜNER VELTLINER BRAE BURN ESTATE 1990 (12% ALC)

Colour: pale straw   **Bouquet:** sweetish nose, honey tones and
lime   **Taste:** drier on the palate than the nose suggests, medium sweet, appley, hint of red licorice. Acidic finish.

★★★½   PINOT GRIGIO 1990 (11% ALC)

Colour: pale straw   **Bouquet:** pineapple, smoky tea leaf
Taste: drier on the palate than the nose suggests. Well structured, herby, Italianate.

★★   RIESLING 1989 RESERVE (12.3% ALC)

Colour: pale, almost water white   **Bouquet:** kerosene
Taste: peachy, high acidity. Rather clumsy. Sweetish middle taste, long acidic finish.

★★★½   RIESLING/CHARDONNAY (PROPRIETOR'S RESERVE) (12.8% ALC)

Colour: straw   **Bouquet:** oily, citric nose   **Taste:** dry, appley with a lime and caramel finish. Very dry. Good value.

★★★   RIESLING 1990 (11% ALC)

Colour: pale straw   **Bouquet:** spicy apricot   **Taste:** sweetish, lots of fruit with underlying acidity. Good length.

★★★★   LATE HARVEST RIESLING 1989 (11.8% ALC)

Colour: pale straw   **Bouquet:** lime, petrol, touch of Botrytis
Taste: sweet lime and apricots. Well made, great balance and lingering taste.

★★½   SEYVAL BLANC 1989 (12.3% ALC)

Colour: pale straw   **Bouquet:** hay and dry honey   **Taste:** full-bodied, appley taste. Dry with an acidic finish.

★★★½   VIDAL 1989 (11.8% ALC)

Colour: pale straw   **Bouquet:** pear   **Taste:** sweet fruit, but good underlying acidity. Greengage flavour. Well balanced. Clean finish.

★★★   LATE HARVEST VIDAL 1989 (11.8% ALC)

Colour: palest straw   **Bouquet:** custard apple   **Taste:** sweet, soft, apple-like finish, good acidity

---

★★★   VIDAL EISWEIN 1984 (9.1% ALC) Half bottle

Colour: old gold   **Bouquet:** caramel   **Taste:** light mouthfeel, sweet orange, beginning to dry out

★★★½   VIDAL ICEWINE 1986 Half bottle

Colour: deep copper   **Bouquet:** orange, tea   **Taste:** great depth of flavour, marmalade and barley sugar. Drops out in the middle suggesting drying fruit, otherwise well balanced.

★★★★   VIDAL ICEWINE 1989 Half bottle

Colour: gold   **Bouquet:** lively, orange and apricot   **Taste:** wonderfully balanced fruit and acid, toffee finish, great length

★★★   VIDAL ICEWINE 1990 Half bottle

Colour: pale amber   **Bouquet:** gooseberry jam   **Taste:** toffee, high acidity, lacks middle fruit. Not as intense as 1989.

RED

★★½   BACO NOIR 1988 (13% ALC)

Colour: browning ruby (showing age)   **Bouquet:** sweet pruney nose   **Taste:** complex smoky, stewed plums with high acidity. Full-bodied with a fresh finish.

★★   BRAE ROUGE (12.3% ALC)

(Maréchal Foch, Chilean Cabernet Sauvignon)

Colour: purple-ruby   **Bouquet:** vanilla, red berries
Taste: herbaceous, dry raspberry. Foch predominates in final taste. Tannic. Good value.

★★   CABERNET RESERVE 1988 (12.5% ALC)

Colour: ruby-purple   **Bouquet:** shy nose   **Taste:** lean fruit, very dry, dusty and acidic

★★★½   CABERNET SAUVIGNON/CABERNET FRANC 1989 (12.5% ALC)

Colour: rich ruby   **Bouquet:** rose, sweet cake   **Taste:** good extract, fine black currant and cherry flavours. Chocolatey finish, soft tannins.

★★   GAMAY NOIR 1990 (12.9% ALC)

Colour: raspberry   **Bouquet:** dumb, alcoholic   **Taste:** cooked red fruits. Heavy. Not much fruit extract, chaptalized.

★★★   MARÉCHAL FOCH 1987 (12.7% ALC)

Colour: tawny plum   **Bouquet:** flinty, earthy   **Taste:** smoky, red berries. Very dry almost Pinot Noir taste. Cooked plum finish.

★★★½   MARÉCHAL FOCH 1988 (12.3% ALC)

Colour: ruby, browning edges   **Bouquet:** black raspberry **Taste:** good fruit, dry, smoky taste with an acidic finish and some tannin. Good value.

★★★½   MILLOT-CHAMBOURCIN 1989 (12.3% ALC)

Colour: purple   **Bouquet:** smoky, flinty, blackberry, vanilla **Taste:** sweet raspberry, fresh, lively. Medium-bodied, good length, good acidity.

★★   PINOT NOIR RESERVE 1988 (12% ALC)

Colour: cherry   **Bouquet:** oak, raspberry candy   **Taste:** light, lean, austere fruit, slightly green finish (young vines?)

★★★(>★★★½) PINOT NOIR 1989 (12.5% ALC)

Colour: ruby-plum   **Bouquet:** plum, licorice   **Taste:** soft red berry fruit. Good extract, acidic, touch of tannin.

★★★   PROPRIETOR'S RESERVE CABERNET SAUVIGNON/CABERNET FRANC (12% ALC)

Colour: ruby   **Bouquet:** spicy, light black currant **Taste:** good berry fruit, light Bordeaux style. Touch of tannin. Good value.

★★   ZWEIGELTREBE 1988 (12.2% ALC)

Colour: raspberry-ruby   **Bouquet:** raspberry candy
Taste: light fruit, cocoa-like finish. Tannic and astringent.

SPARKLING

★★★   L'ALLEMAND CANADIAN CHAMPAGNE (12% ALC)

Appearance: good, active mousse   **Colour:** pale straw
Bouquet: earthy nose   **Taste:** soft, grapey. Hint of sweetness.
Well balanced. Good value.

FORTIFIED

★★★½   FLEUR D'ONTARIO 1988 (17.5% ALC)

(Pineau des Charentes style)

Colour: straw   **Bouquet:** lime, vanilla, caramel   **Taste:** honeyed lime, ginger taste, well balanced, good acidity and length.
Interesting aperitif.

KONZELMANN   WHITE

★★★½   CHARDONNAY 1991 (12% ALC) Barrel sample

(partially aged in Allier and Nevers oak)

Colour: straw   **Bouquet:** vanilla, apple   **Taste:** well balanced,
clean lemony fruit

★★★½
(>★★★★)   CHARDONNAY RESERVE 1991 (12.5% ALC) Barrel sample

(barrel fermented, Allier and Nevers oak)

Colour: straw   **Bouquet:** apple, peach   **Taste:** drier on the
palate than the nose suggests; grapefruit, well balanced

★★½   CHARDONNAY 1990 RESERVE (12.5% ALC)

Colour: yellow straw   **Bouquet:** olives, incense   **Taste:** oaky,
exotic, apple. Soft, spicy. Short on fruit for the amount of
alcohol.

★★★ GOLDEN VINTAGE 1990 (11.3% ALC)

(Geisenheim Riesling and Vidal)

Colour: straw **Bouquet:** sweet; sultanas, marshmallow
Taste: soft, sweet grapefruit. Well balanced with good fresh
finish. Spätlese quality. Good value.

★★★½ LATE HARVEST GEWÜRZTRAMINER 1990 (11.5% ALC)

Colour: straw **Bouquet:** spicy, orange, rose petal, lychee
Taste: spicy, sweet Muscat-like flavour. Light in the mouth.
Good length, delicate, good acidity.

★★★ PINOT BLANC 1990 (11.5% ALC)

Colour: straw **Bouquet:** spring flowers **Taste:** perfumed,
peachy, hint of sweetness. Soft on the palate with good final
acidity.

(>★★★★)
★★½ JOHANNISBERG RIESLING 1989 (11.3% ALC) Orange label

Colour: pale straw **Bouquet:** green apple **Taste:** soft, perfumed, sweetish melon flavour. Round on the palate. Good
length.

★★½ JOHANNISBERG RIESLING 1989 (11% ALC) Green label

Colour: straw **Bouquet:** shy nose **Taste:** sweet, round,
grapefruit taste. Delicate, lacking definition. Drops out in the
middle. Good apple, acidic finish.

★★★ LATE HARVEST RIESLING (12% ALC) Orange label

Colour: straw, hint of lime **Bouquet:** petrol, lime
Taste: crisp, lime and green plum. Lacks middle fruit. Grapefruit-like finish. Spätlese trocken style.

★★½ LATE HARVEST RIESLING 1989 (11.2% ALC) Green label

Colour: straw **Bouquet:** discreet **Taste:** sweet, soft, perfumed apple flavour. Good length with a chocolate-like finish.

★★★★   RIESLING TRAMINER ICEWINE 1989 Half bottle

Colour: copper orange   **Bouquet:** apricot with a hint of botrytis   **Taste:** rich orange, apricot, toffee, tea and vanilla. Very sweet and rich with great length. Well balanced with a marshmallow-like finish.

★★★   LATE HARVEST VIDAL 1990 (12% ALC)

Colour: pale straw   **Bouquet:** earthy nose   **Taste:** dry, grassy, grapefruit peel. Full in the mouth. Well balanced.

RED

★★   BACO NOIR LATE HARVEST 1990 ESTATE BOTTLED (12% ALC)

Colour: purple   **Bouquet:** earthy, tobacco   **Taste:** dry blackberry, lean and acidic with a smoky finish

★★½   GAMAY NOIR 1988 (11.5% ALC)

Colour: tawny plum   **Bouquet:** licorice   **Taste:** dry, wild strawberry flavour. Drying out. Elegant and austere.

★★½   PINOT NOIR 1989 (11.5% ALC)

Colour: purple ruby   **Bouquet:** jammy strawberry nose with hints of tobacco   **Taste:** light fruit character, not much extract. Very dry with obvious tannin and slightly bitter finish (young vines?).

★★   LATE HARVEST ZWEIGELT 1990 (12% ALC)

Colour: cherry   **Bouquet:** smoky plum   **Taste:** light, fruity cherry taste. Not much extract. Hint of oak, slightly bitter finish, some tannin.

SPARKLING

★★★   RIESLING CANADIAN CHAMPAGNE (12% ALC)

Appearance: not much mousse   **Colour:** pale gold
Bouquet: baked apple   **Taste:** soft, sweetish, foamy. Lots of apple flavour. Well balanced with good length.

LAKEVIEW
CELLARS   WHITE

★★★½   RIESLING 1991 VINC VINEYARD (11.3% ALC)

Colour: palest straw   **Bouquet:** sweet floral nose   **Taste:** soft, delicate, sweet red grapefruit taste. Clean, good length, well made.

★★★   GURINSKAS VINEYARD CHARDONNAY 1991 (11.9% ALC)

(aged in American and old French oak)

Colour: pale straw   **Bouquet:** shy nose   **Taste:** good fruit, pear flavour

★★½   VIDAL 1991 (10.6% ALC)

Colour: pale straw   **Bouquet:** sweet banana, pear   **Taste:** soft, delicate, sweetish marshmallow and grapefruit character

★★½   VIDAL ICEWINE 1990 (9% ALC) Half bottle

Colour: old gold-copper   **Bouquet:** slightly musty
Taste: intensely sweet, glycerol; barley sugar and toffee

RED

★★   CABERNET SAUVIGNON 1990 (10.9%)

(Nevers and old American oak barrels; 50% carbonic maceration)

Colour: plum   **Bouquet:** plummy, spicy   **Taste:** ripe red berries, hint of oxidation. Short.

LAURO & BURDEN	WHITE

★★   DRY WHITE (12% ALC) Screwtop 750 mL

(Californian Thompson Seedless, 30% Ontario Seyval Blanc)

Colour: straw   **Bouquet:** sulphur, shy   **Taste:** soft, easy drinking, unripe peach flavour. Crisp finish. Good value.

★★½   SEYVAL BLANC (12% ALC)

Colour: straw   **Bouquet:** stony, apple   **Taste:** crisp, green apple taste. Italian style. Good value.

★★★   BIANCALINA (12% ALC) Screwtop 750 mL

(33% Ontario Chardonnay, California Thompson Seedless, some Vidal)

Colour: pale straw   **Bouquet:** apple   **Taste:** soft, fruity with apple and pear flavours. Well balanced. Good value.

ROSÉ

★★½   CABERNET ROSÉ (12% ALC) Screwtop 750 mL

(California Cabernet Sauvignon, Ontario Maréchal Foch and De Chaunac)

Colour: pale cherry   **Bouquet:** boiled raspberrry candy
Taste: perfumed with a sweetish cooked raspberry flavour. Good value.

RED

★★   DRY RED (12% ALC) Screwtop 750 mL

(California Cabernet Sauvignon, Cabernet Franc, with Ontario Maréchal Foch and De Chaunac)

Colour: pale plum   **Bouquet:** sweetish raspberry
Taste: perfumed, rose-like, light, off-dry with a cooked raspberry flavour. Not much intensity.

★★½   CABERNET SAUVIGNON (12% ALC) Screwtop 750 mL

(70% California Cabernet Sauvignon, Ontario Maréchal Foch and De Chaunac)

Colour: ruby   **Bouquet:** vegetal, leather   **Taste:** light, perfumed sweetish, red currant flavour. Orangey finish with a hint of tannin. Good value.

LONDON   WHITE

★½   CANADIAN CHABLIS (11.5% ALC) Screwtop litre

Colour: pale straw   **Bouquet:** sweetish, citric   **Taste:** medium-dry, heavy. Synthetic flavour, metallic finish.

★★½   CUVÉE SUPÉRIEUR WHITE (11.5% ALC)

Colour: pale straw   **Bouquet:** earthy, citric   **Taste:** off-dry, herbaceous, green plum flavour. Good acidity. Good value.

★★½   VIDAL 1989 (11.5% ALC)

Colour: straw   **Bouquet:** sweet rhubarb   **Taste:** soft, fruity, mouth-filling. Sweetish after taste, obvious acidity.

★★   VIDAL EISWEIN 1990 (11.7% ALC) Half bottle

Colour: gold   **Bouquet:** salty apricot   **Taste:** sweet celery, astringent finish

RED

★★★   CUVÉE SUPÉRIEUR RED (11.5% ALC)

Colour: deep cherry-plum   **Bouquet:** oak, strawberry
Taste: light, dry, Valpolicella style. Cherry flavour, fresh acidity. Good value.

★★½   CHARDONNAY (11.5% ALC)

(75% Australian Chardonnay, 25% Ontario Chardonnay)

Colour: straw   **Bouquet:** ripe apples   **Taste:** dry, appley, well balanced but a little short on middle fruit

MAGNOTTA   WHITE

★★   BIANCO DEL PAESE (11% ALC)

Colour: straw   **Bouquet:** stoney, herby, alcoholic   **Taste:** dry, Soave syle. Crisp acidic finish. Good value.

★★½   CHARDONNAY (12% ALC)

Colour: pale straw   **Bouquet:** apple, sulphur   **Taste:** dry, soft, apple and pear flavours, hint of anise. Hot finish.

★★★   CHARDONNAY SPECIAL RESERVE 1990 (12% ALC)

Colour: pale straw   **Bouquet:** pear   **Taste:** rich, spicy fruit, apple and pear flavours. Good length, well balanced. Good value.

★½   FESTA BIANCO (11% ALC)

Colour: straw   **Bouquet:** heavy, melon   **Taste:** dry, full in the mouth, green plum flavour. Short.

★★   INTERNATIONAL VINTAGES CHABLIS (11% ALC)

(75% California, 25% Niagara)

Colour: straw   **Bouquet:** vegetal, hay   **Taste:** dry, melon flavour. Full in the mouth. Asparagus-like finish.

★★½   INTERNATIONAL VINTAGES PINOT BIANCO 1991

(75% DOC Pinot Bianco from Northern Italy, 25% Niagara white)

Colour: pale straw   **Bouquet:** resinous   **Taste:** dry, piney and browning apple flavour, crisp finish. Touch of oxidation.

★★★   INTERNATIONAL VINTAGES PINOT GRIGIO 1991 (12% ALC)

(75% DOC Pinot Grigio from Northern Italy, 25% Niagara white)

Colour: pale straw   **Bouquet:** honey, herby   **Taste:** dry, green melon, full in the mouth. Crisp finish. Good value.

★★★½   ICEWINE 1991 (8% ALC) Half bottle

Colour: amber-gold   **Bouquet:** honeyed apricot
Taste: sweet, delicate, peachy with good acidity but ultimately a little short

ROSÉ

★   FESTA ROSÉ (11% ALC)

Colour: pink with blue tints   **Bouquet:** sulphur
Taste: sweetish, candied raspberry, synthetic

★★   INTERNATIONAL VINTAGES CABERNET ROSÉ 1991 (11.5% ALC)

Colour: pale cherry, blue highlights   **Bouquet:** raspberry
Taste: raspery candy, hint of sweetness off-set by an acidic finish

RED

★★   CABERNET SAUVIGNON (12% ALC)

Colour: ruby   **Bouquet:** thin   **Taste:** sweetish, chunky, tannic. Not much varietal character, chaptalised taste.

| ★★½ | CABERNET SAUVIGNON RISERVA 1990 (12.5% ALC) |

Colour: purple-ruby   **Bouquet:** little character on the nose
Taste: dry, heavy, sweetish. Smoky blackberry flavour, some tannin.

★★★½
(>★★★★)

CABERNET SAUVIGNON SPECIAL RESERVE 1990 (12.5% ALC)

Colour: purple-ruby   **Bouquet:** iris, black currant   **Taste:** dry, rich extract, damson-like flavour. A big wine. Tannic finish.

★½

FESTA ROSSO (11% ALC)

Colour: light ruby   **Bouquet:** sweetish, slightly vegetal
Taste: dry, light, sweetish, not much flavour. Some tannin on the finish.

★★½

ROSSO DEL PAESE (12% ALC)

Colour: ruby   **Bouquet:** floral, grapey   **Taste:** sweetish, good fruit, round on the palate. Touch of tannin on the finish. Good value.

★★★

INTERNATIONAL VINTAGES BARDOLINO 1991 (12% ALC)

(75% DOC Bardolino, 25% Niagara reds)

Colour: deep cherry   **Bouquet:** plum and cherry pit   **Taste:** soft, fresh acidity. Peppery finish. Chillable. Good value.

★★★★

INTERNATIONAL VINTAGES CABERNET SAUVIGNON 1990 (12.5% ALC)

(40% Sonoma, 35% Maipo, Chile, 25% Niagara)

Colour: dense purple   **Bouquet:** spicy, chocolate
Taste: thick, full-bodied, chocolatey. Almost Rhone-like in structure. Touch of oak, dusty tannins.

★★½

INTERNATIONAL VINTAGES CALIFORNIA BURGUNDY (11% ALC)

(75% California reds, 25% Niagara reds)

Colour: light ruby   **Bouquet:** yeasty, carbonic maceration nose. **Taste:** sweetish, light, cranberry and raspberry flavour

★★★ INTERNATIONAL VINTAGES MERLOT 1991 (12% ALC)

(75% DOC Merlot from Italy, 25% Ontario Merlot)

Colour: ruby **Bouquet:** light, jammy **Taste:** raspberry and pomegranate

---

★★★ INTERNATIONAL VINTAGES VALPOLICELLA 1991 (12% ALC)

(75% DOC Valpolicella, 25% Niagara red)

Colour: ruby **Bouquet:** raisiny, floral **Taste:** dry, lively plum flavour. Good extract, touch of tannin on the finish.

MARYNISSEN
ESTATES WHITE

★★½ (>★★★) CHARDONNAY 1991 (12.5% ALC) Barrel sample

(aged in stainless steel)

Colour: pale straw **Bouquet:** grapefruit **Taste:** very dry, lean fruit, tart finish. Needs time.

★★★★ CHARDONNAY 1991 BARREL FERMENTED (12.5% ALC) Barrel sample

Colour: pale straw **Bouquet:** smoky, grapefruit **Taste:** rich grapefruit flavour, hints of spice. Full in the mouth.

★★★½ CHARDONNAY 1990 BARREL FERMENTED (11.5% ALC)

Colour: pale gold **Bouquet:** spicy oaky nose, buttered popcorn and banana **Taste:** creamy apple flavour, full-bodied, rich. Good length, nutty finish. Touch of bitterness on the finish.

★★ RIESLING 1990 (11.5% ALC)

Colour: deep straw **Bouquet:** oily, leathery **Taste:** lively rhubarb and green plum flavours, acidic finish

★★★½   RIESLING ICEWINE 1990 (11% ALC) Half bottle

Colour: straw-gold   **Bouquet:** apricot, chocolate   **Taste:** soft, light on the palate, pear and honey. Not too sweet, good acidity with a delicate orangey finish.

★★★½   ESTATE VIDAL ICEWINE 1990 (11% ALC) Half bottle

Colour: straw   **Bouquet:** peachy, apricot   **Taste:** sweet, light, good acidity and length

RED

★★★½   MERLOT 1990 BARREL SELECT (11.5% ALC)

Colour: purple ruby   **Bouquet:** barnyard, earthy, flinty
Taste: spicy blackberry and black currant, medium weight with a touch of vanilla. Elegant sweet fruit, some tannin. Drink now.

★★★★   CABERNET SAUVIGNON/MERLOT 1990 (11.5% ALC)

Colour: purple ruby   **Bouquet:** spicy baked apple and blackberry   **Taste:** light, smoky, sweet fruit with a touch of spice. Soft tannins. Drink now.

★★★   CABERNET SAUVIGNON BARREL SELECT 1990

Colour: ruby   **Bouquet:** black currant and dill   **Taste:** light extract, anise with evident tannin. Drink now.

PELEE ISLAND   WHITE

★★★   CHARDONNAY HULDA'S ROCK 1991 (12.6% ALC) Barrel sample

(barrel fermented)

Colour: straw   **Bouquet:** vanilla, ripe peach   **Taste:** lots of extract, hint of pineapple. Caramel and fresh acidity on the finish, but marred with a touch of bitterness.

★★★   CHARDONNAY HULDAH'S ROCK (12.6% ALC)

Colour: straw   **Bouquet:** vanilla, apple   **Taste:** dry, appley. Good fruit extract, full-bodied, long finish.

★★★   PINOT CHARDONNAY 1991 (12.1% ALC)

Colour: pale straw   **Bouquet:** closed in   **Taste:** crisp fruit, citric, appley finish. Good length.

★★½   DUCKS UNLIMITED CHARDONNAY 1991 (12.2% ALC)

(25% Californian Chardonnay)

Colour: straw   **Bouquet:** fresh, grassy   **Taste:** apple and honeysuckle. Soft initial taste but astringent finish.

★★   GEWÜRZTRAMINER 1990 (11.4% ALC)

Colour: pale straw   **Bouquet:** shy nose   **Taste:** soft, tangerine-like flavour. Not much varietal character. More like Riesling. Good length.

★★ (>★★½)   RIESLING ITALICO 1990 (12.4% ALC)

Colour: pale straw   **Bouquet:** green, stemmy nose
Taste: tart, spicy flavour, lean fruit. High acidity .

★★½   RIESLING DRY 1990 (11.4% ALC)

Colour: straw   **Bouquet:** citrus, rubbery   **Taste:** dry, lime flavour. Good acidity. Tart finish.

★★★   LATE HARVEST RIESLING 1990 (11.1% ALC)

Colour: straw-lime   **Bouquet:** honeyed apple   **Taste:** peachy, initial sweetness gives way to a long acidic, fresh finish. Spätlese quality.

★★★½ SCHEUREBE 1990 (11.2% ALC)

Colour: pale straw **Bouquet:** aromatic, grapey **Taste:** exotic, orange and cardomom. Sweetish middle taste of licorice. Long crisp finish.

RED

★★★½ PINOT NOIR 1990 (12.3% ALC)

Colour: tawny plum **Bouquet:** black raspberry **Taste:** dry, red berry flavour, clean with a touch of vanilla. Well balanced, medium bodied, some tannin on the finish. Well made.

REIF WHITE

★★★½ CHARDONNAY 1991 (12.5% ALC) Barrel sample

Colour: straw **Bouquet:** smoky, grapefruit, barnyard
Taste: good fruit extract, sweet grapefruit

★★★(>★★★½) CHARDONNAY 1990 (12.5% ALC)

Colour: straw **Bouquet:** apple, lemon peel **Taste:** fresh, very dry, Chablis style. Acidic finish. Will age well.

★★½ CHARDONNAY 1989 (12.4% ALC)

Colour: pale straw **Bouquet:** grapefruit **Taste:** very dry, appley, lean, crisp finish. Too much alcohol for the fruit.

★★★★ CHARDONNAY RESERVE 1991 (12.7% ALC) Barrel sample

Colour: straw **Bouquet:** vanilla, ripe tropical fruit
Taste: spicy pineapple, rich fruit, good balancing acidity

★★★★ CHARDONNAY RESERVE 1990 (13% ALC)

(aged in Allier and Nevers oak)

Colour: yellow straw **Bouquet:** rich, apple, hay **Taste:** More intense fruit, nutty with a fine spine of acidity. Very Burgundian in style. Drinks well now, will improve with age.

★★★(>★★★½) CHARDONNAY RESERVE 1989 (11.8% ALC)

Colour: deep straw **Bouquet:** lemon, oak, vanilla **Taste:** spicy, citric, long acidic finish with oak currently masking fruit.

★★½ GAMAY BLANC 1990 (12% ALC)

Colour: straw with a pinkish blush **Bouquet:** dates, woody **Taste:** very dry, austere, clovey middle taste with a tart finish

---

★★★ GEWÜRZTRAMINER MEDIUM DRY 1990 (11.5% ALC)

Colour: straw-gold **Bouquet:** orange, slightly vegetal **Taste:** off-dry, aromatic, spicy Muscat flavour. Good extract, good acidic finish, but a little short in the middle.

★★½ GEWÜRZTRAMINER 1989 (11.5% ALC)

Colour: straw **Bouquet:** cidery, spicy **Taste:** sweet, spicy, Late Harvest Riesling character. Easy drinking.

★★★½ JOHANNISBERG RIESLING DRY 1990 (11.7% ALC)

Colour: straw **Bouquet:** biscuity **Taste:** lean, crisp, mineralish. Rheingau Kabinett style.

★★★★ JOHANNISBERG RIESLING MEDIUM DRY 1990 (11.7% ALC)

Colour: straw **Bouquet:** floral, apricot **Taste:** soft middle palate, peaches and apricots, long acidic finish. Spätlese quality.

★½ KERNER 1989 (12% ALC)

Colour: pale straw **Bouquet:** petrol, floral **Taste:** sweetish, gummy. Some oxidation in the back taste. Tinny finish.

★★★★ JOHANNISBERG RIESLING LATE HARVEST 1990 (11.7% ALC)

Colour: straw-lime **Bouquet:** biscuity, petrol **Taste:** tropical fruits, lingering and lime finish

★★½   VIDAL LATE HARVEST 1989 (12% ALC) 1989

Colour: pale gold   **Bouquet:** baked apple, citrus, dried peach
Taste: tropical fruits, soft, light on the palate. Not too sweet, acidic, blunt finish.

★★★   GEWÜRZTRAMINER ICEWINE 1990 (10.5% ALC) Half bottle

Colour: old gold   **Bouquet:** apricot and peach   **Taste:** sweet peachy flavour, but low acid renders it short. Dry apricot finish.

★★★★   VIDAL ICEWINE 1990 (11.5% ALC) Half bottle

Colour: copper gold   **Bouquet:** toffee and orange   **Taste:** well balanced, honeyed and spicy, intense orange and lively acidity. Elegant.

RED

★★★   CABERNET SAUVIGNON 1991 (12.2% ALC)

Colour: plum   **Bouquet:** fruity, raspberry   **Taste:** dry, light fruit character, vanilla and blackberry, tangerine peel finish

---

★★½   CABERNET SAUVIGNON 1990 (11% ALC)

Colour: plum   **Bouquet:** rhubarb, tobacco, earthy   **Taste:** light cherry character, soft, lacks middle fruit. Low tannins. Young vines.

★★   PINOT NOIR 1990 (11% ALC)

Colour: tawny plum   **Bouquet:** perfumed, high toned, cooked raspberries   **Taste:** lean sour cherry fruit, light body, acidic, tart finish

SOUTHBROOK FARMS	WHITE

★★★½ CHARDONNAY 1991 (12.8% ALC)

(75% Paso Robles Chardonnay, 25% Ontario Chardonnay, aged in new oak)

Colour: straw **Bouquet:** oaky, coconut **Taste:** spicy, apple and pear flavours, fresh, lively acidity

---

★★★ CHARDONNAY 1991 (12.6% ALC)

(aged in stainless steel)

Colour: straw **Bouquet:** barnyard, toffee **Taste:** soft, spicy apple. Well balanced.

★★★★ OAK CUVÉE CHARDONNAY 1991 (12.6% ALC)

(the same wine as above but given 25 days in new Nevers oak)

Colour: straw **Bouquet:** spicy pear **Taste:** elegant, well balanced, very Burgundian in character

---

★★★ RIESLING 1991

Colour: pale straw with green highlights **Bouquet:** flinty, smoky **Taste:** dry, herbaceous, grapefruit. Full in the mouth.

★★★ VIDAL 1991

Colour: pale straw **Bouquet:** grapefruit peel **Taste:** fresh, spritzy, melon and peach flavours. Well balanced, good length.

RED

★★★½ PINOT NOIR VIN GRIS 1991 (12.5% ALC)

(new American oak)

Colour: pink-amber **Bouquet:** oaky, jammy **Taste:** full-bodied sweetish, smoky floral raspberry with hint of smoked bacon. A red wine masquerading as a rosé.

★★★ BLUSH 1991 (12.5% ALC)

(the same wine as Pinot Noir Vin Gris with 2 grams/litre residual sugar)

Colour: amber-pink **Bouquet:** oaky, jammy **Taste:** sweet strawberry, jammy

★★★½
(>★★★★) CABERNET SAUVIGNON 1991 (12.9% ALC)

(Napa Cabernet Sauvignon 1989 with Ontario Cabernet Sauvignon, two months in old French oak)

Colour: ruby **Bouquet:** vanilla, black currant **Taste:** sweet pomegranate and chocolatey. Soft middle taste with an overtone of licorice. Good acidic finish, light tannin.

STONECHURCH WHITE

★★½ CHARDONNAY 1990 (12.2% ALC)

Colour: deep straw **Bouquet:** cidery, vegetal **Taste:** caramel, soft, sweetish, low acidity, flat finish. Mouth-filling. Hot finish.

★★★½ CHARDONNAY RESERVE 1990 (12.5%)

(five weeks in Allier and Troncais oak)

Colour: deep straw **Bouquet:** smoky, vanilla **Taste:** spicy caramel, sweetish taste. Good length, but could do with more acidity. Mouth-filling.

★★½(>★★★½) BARREL-FERMENTED CHARDONNAY 1991 (12.2% ALC) Barrel sample

Colour: straw **Bouquet:** green plum and caramel **Taste:** closed in, acidity dominated but spice and nuttiness bode well

★★★½
(>★★★★) BARREL-FERMENTED CHARDONNAY 1990 (12.7% ALC)

Colour: deep straw **Bouquet:** vanilla, ripe pear **Taste:** sweet, soft, oaky. Spicy finish. Well balanced, good length.

★★★   SELECT CHARDONNAY 1991 (11.9% ALC) Barrel sample

Colour: straw   **Bouquet:** ripe peach   **Taste:** sweet peach and apricot with a spicy overlay. Lacking acidity.

★★½   ESTATE BLANC 1990 (11.5% ALC)

Colour: straw   **Bouquet:** aromatic, raisiny   **Taste:** good fruit, lots of flavour, spicy. Drier on the palate than the nose suggests. Good length, slightly sour note on the finish. Good value.

★★★   EXPORT BLANC 1990 (11.7% ALC)

(60% Seyval Blanc, 40% Vidal)

Colour: pale straw   **Bouquet:** apple   **Taste:** dry, firm appley, full in the mouth. Good length.

★★★★   MORIO MUSCAT 1990 (11.8% ALC)

Colour: straw   **Bouquet:** orange blossom, cardomom   **Taste:** very dry, spicy rose water, exotic orangey. Great length. Reminiscent of Gewürztraminer. Light, fresh. Wonderful aperitif.

★★½   RIESLING ICEWINE 1990 (9% ALC) Half bottle

Colour: old gold   **Bouquet:** toffee, orange peel, hint of oxidation   **Taste:** intense sweetness, unctuous, soft and honeyed. Lacks acidity.

★★★   VIDAL ICEWINE 1990 (11.5% ALC) Half bottle

Colour: burnished gold   **Bouquet:** honeyed toffee
Taste: sweet toffee, low acidity

RED

★★½ (>★★★)   CABERNET SAUVIGNON 1990 (12.3% ALC)

(75% old French oak and 25% American oak)

Colour: ruby   **Bouquet:** yeasty, roses, bramble   **Taste:** red currant, pomegranate and sour cherry, crisp finish. Some tannin.

★★   PINOT NOIR 1990 (11.2% ALC)

Colour: cherry   **Bouquet:** stewed berries   **Taste:** light, plummy, minty, touch of tannin. Prune-like finish.

★★   RED 1990 (11.5% ALC)

Colour: dense purple   **Bouquet:** smoky blackberry
Taste: lean, unripe blackberries, acidic finish

STONEY RIDGE
CELLARS   WHITE

★★★½   CHARDONNAY 1991 PUDDICOMBE VINEYARD (12% ALC) Barrel sample

(aged in stainless steel and American oak)

Colour: pale straw   **Bouquet:** sweet apple   **Taste:** sweet fruit, peach and apple. Well balanced.

★★★   CHARDONNAY 1990 PUDDICOMBE VINEYARD (11% ALC)

(barrel fermented and aged)

Colour: yellow straw   **Bouquet:** coconut, lemon   **Taste:** light, soft fruit. Sweetish coconut flavour. Well made.

★★½   CHARDONNAY 1989 GUTTLER VINEYARD

Colour: pale straw   **Bouquet:** barnyard, lanolin, lemon
Taste: apple, sweetish but not much length

★★★★   CHARDONNAY 1991 EASTMAN VINEYARD (12% ALC) Barrel sample

(aged in new Troncais, Allier and Voges oak)

Colour: pale straw   **Bouquet:** pineapple   **Taste:** sweet fruit, exotic, well balanced. Great length.

★★★★   CHARDONNAY 1990 EASTMAN VINEYARD (12% ALC)

(barrel fermented and aged)

Colour: straw   **Bouquet:** grapefruit, buttery, spicy   **Taste:** complex, sweet passion fruit, peppery, spicy. Well balanced. Great length.

★★★★   CHARDONNAY 1991 LENKO VINEYARD (12% ALC) Barrel sample

Colour: pale straw   **Bouquet:** melon, mango   **Taste:** spicy, concentrated soft fruit. Lingers on the palate. Very evolved for such a young wine.

★★★½
(>★★★★)   CHARDONNAY 1990 LENKO VINEYARD (12% ALC)

Colour: pale straw   **Bouquet:** spicy, cinnamon   **Taste:** soft, sweetish, oaky flavours, focused sweet apple flavour. Good acidity, long finish.

★★★★   CHARDONNAY 1987 LENKO VINEYARD

Colour: deep straw   **Bouquet:** spicy apple   **Taste:** apple and clove, great length, crisp finish

---

★★★½   CHARDONNAY 1991 (11% ALC)

(barrel-fermented and aged)

Colour: straw   **Bouquet:** floral, oaky   **Taste:** spicy, musky, red pepper and melon, hint of sweetness. Good value.

★★★★   MORIO MUSCAT 1990 HUNSE VINEYARD (10% ALC)

Colour: straw   **Bouquet:** orange blossom and cardomom
Taste: soft, off-dry, Turkish Delight flavour with citrus and pineapple tones, good length. Very clean. A little more acidity would have made it outstanding.

★★★½   BENCH RESERVE CHARDONNAY 1991 (12% ALC) Barrel sample

Colour: straw   **Bouquet:** peachy   **Taste:** soft, good extract, apple and peach flavours

---

★★★½   GEWÜRZTRAMINER 1990 (11% ALC)

Colour: straw   **Bouquet:** nutmeg, allspice   **Taste:** intense orange, spice. Off-dry, good acidity. Lingering flavours.

★★★   GEWÜRZTRAMINER ICEWINE 1990 Half bottle

Colour: tawny straw   **Bouquet:** sweet ginger, jasmine
Taste: exotic, gingery, Turkish delight, cardomom. Lively orangey finish. Overblown.

★★★   LATE HARVEST RIESLING 1990 (10% ALC)

(Plekan/Lenko Vineyards)

Colour: pale gold   **Bouquet:** vanilla, orange, pineapple, cinnamon   **Taste:** medium sweet, exotic cardomom and citric flavours. Well balanced with refreshing acidity.

★★★★   SEYVAL BLANC 1990 (11% ALC)

Colour: straw yellow   **Bouquet:** flinty, earthy, grapefruit
Taste: soft, smoky grapefruit flavour. Hint of sweetness. Good length. Well made.

★★★   PREMIUM DRY VIDAL 1990 (11.5% ALC)

Colour: straw   **Bouquet:** tangerine peel   **Taste:** soft, fruity, well balanced, hint of sweetness. Good length.

RED

★★★   ESTATE RED (11% ALC)

(De Chaunac, Villard Noir, Maréchal Foch, Chambourcin, Cabernet Sauvignon)

Colour: light ruby   **Bouquet:** raspberry candy   **Taste:** light, dry, perfumed cherry flavour. Well made. Good value.

★★★   PINOT NOIR 1991

(aged in American oak)

Colour: deep cherry   **Bouquet:** vanilla, red berries
Taste: dry, light raspberry with an oaky overlay. A little shy on extract (young vines?).

★★★½   CABERNET SAUVIGNON 1990 (BUIS VINEYARD)

Colour: light ruby   **Bouquet:** perfumed black and red currants
Taste: remarkably delicate, though good black cherry quality. A lightweight Cabernet, very well made.

★★★½   MERLOT 1990 (12% ALC)

(20% Cabernet Sauvignon)

Colour: ruby   **Bouquet:** jammy, blackberry   **Taste:** dry, medium-bodied, spicy coconut and blackberry fruit. Well structured.

★★★   ROMANCE 1990 (10.5% ALC)

(blush wine from Gamay)

Colour: peachy coral   **Bouquet:** shy nose   **Taste:** off-dry, strawberry. Jammy finish, good length.

★★★½   CHARDONNAY RESERVE 1991 (12% ALC) **Barrel sample**

(partially aged in new Allier and Nevers oak)

Colour: deep straw   **Bouquet:** ripe peach and melon
Taste: mouth-filling, ripe peach, spicy, gingery and soft

★★★(>★★★½) ST. URBAN PREMIUM DRY RIESLING 1989 (10.7% ALC)

Colour: pale straw   **Bouquet:** lime and grapefruit
Taste: crisp, green plum and lime, fresh grassy finish

★★★½   ST. URBAN PREMIUM DRY RIESLING 1988 (10.7% ALC)

Colour: straw   **Bouquet:** petrol and hay with a sweetish overlay   **Taste:** mature Riesling flavour, sweetish with a lemony
grapefruit finish

★★★★   ST. URBAN SEMI-DRY RIESLING 1988 (10.7% ALC)

Colour: pale gold   **Bouquet:** musky, sweet apricot   **Taste:** soft
and peachy with refreshing acidity. Beautifully balanced.

★★★½   ST. URBAN PREMIUM SEMI-DRY RIESLING 1989 (10.7% ALC)

Colour: straw   **Bouquet:** struck flint, petrol, lime   **Taste:** soft,
sweetish floral-grapefruit flavour, good acidic finish

★★★★   ST. URBAN PREMIUM DRY RIESLING 1990 (10.7% ALC)

Colour: straw   **Bouquet:** earthy-floral with citric overtones
Taste: fine varietal character, rich grapefruit flavour, lingering
finish. Will age well.

★★★   ST. URBAN SEMI-DRY RIESLING 1990 (10.7% ALC)

Colour: straw   **Bouquet:** sweetish floral nose   **Taste:** soft
mouthfeel, clean with a hint of sweetness but powerful green
melon acidity. Lacks the structure of the Dry version.

★★★½ RIESLING LATE HARVEST 1989 (10.4% ALC)

Colour: straw **Bouquet:** sweet grapefruit **Taste:** dried apricots, medium sweet. Good acidic finish.

★★★★ RIESLING ICEWINE 1989 (11.3% ALC) Half bottle

Colour: amber gold **Bouquet:** apricot and orange
Taste: barley sugar, marmalade, complex and unctuously sweet

★★★★ VIDAL ICEWINE 1989 (11.5% ALC) Half bottle

Colour: old gold **Bouquet:** heavy toffee and orange peel, tea leaf **Taste:** orange and lemon, lean with great length. Lively acidity. Light on the palate, barley sugar finish. Delicate.

VINOTECA WHITE

★★ ALBINO (11.5% ALC) Half bottle

Colour: palest straw **Bouquet:** sweetish, white chocolate
Taste: initially soft, sweetish and woody on the palate, not much flavour, acidic finish

---

★★★ CHARDONNAY 1991 (12% ALC) Barrel sample

Colour: deep straw **Bouquet:** spicy, cidery **Taste:** soft, apple peel, ginger, toffee. Nutty finish.

★★½ PINOT CHARDONNAY 1989 (12% ALC)

Colour: pale straw **Bouquet:** appley **Taste:** full-bodied, dry appley flavour. Marked acidic finish.

★★★ PINOT CHARDONNAY 1989 (12% ALC)

(partially oak aged)

Colour: straw **Bouquet:** spicy, clovey **Taste:** predominating new oak flavour, smoky finish. Good length though a touch vegetal.

★★   PINOT CHARDONNAY 1989 (12% ALC)

(barrel fermented and aged)

Colour: straw   **Bouquet:** hay and spice   **Taste:** flat, dried peaches. Acidic finish, suggestion of oxidation.

★★   RIESLING 1989 (12% ALC)

Colour: pale straw   **Bouquet:** not much varietal character
Taste: touch of licorice, long acidic finish

★★★   VIDAL ICEWINE

Colour: yellow straw   **Bouquet:** caramel, apricots and dry leaves   **Taste:** burnt sugar, short. Acidic finish.

RED

★★★½   CABERNET SAUVIGNON 1989 (12% ALC)

(barrel fermented and aged)

Colour: ruby   **Bouquet:** vanilla   **Taste:** soft, oaky, light black currant fruit, sweetish. Soft tannins.

★★   CABERNET SAUVIGNON 1989 (12% ALC)

Colour: purple-ruby   **Bouquet:** cherries   **Taste:** sweet chaptalised taste, cherry jam

---

★★½   GAIO 1989 (12% ALC)

Colour: ruby   **Bouquet:** dry, raisiny   **Taste:** sweetish, raisiny, Recioto syle

★★½   PINOT NOIR 1989 (12% ALC)

(Bordeaux bottle)

Colour: deep cherry   **Bouquet:** spicy, earthy   **Taste:** sweetish, flinty, plums. Italianate style.

★★★   PINOT NOIR 1989 (12% ALC)

(Burgundy bottle)

Colour: deep cherry   **Bouquet:** minty   **Taste:** sweet cherries, well structured, good length

BRITISH COLUMBIA WINES

ANDRÉS	WHITE

★★ | PELLER ESTATES EHRENFELSER 1990

Colour: straw **Bouquet:** perfumed celery **Taste:** perfumey, tropical fruits, sweetish, good acidity

BRIGHTS	WHITE

★★½ | VINTAGE SELECT OPTIMA 1990 (12% ALC)

Colour: straw **Bouquet:** ripe melon and peach
Taste: sweetish fruit flavour but finishes dry. Good length.

★★★ | VINTAGE SELECT VIDAL 1990 (9.5% ALC)

Colour: pale straw **Bouquet:** green plum **Taste:** tart, Sauvignon Blanc style, gooseberry and rhubarb. Clean, well made.

★★½ | VASEAUX CELLARS CHARDONNAY 1988 (12% ALC)

Colour: straw **Bouquet:** light, apple **Taste:** dry, not much varietal character but clean. Hint of bubblegum in the middle taste.

RED

★ | VASEAUX CELLARS BACO NOIR 1988 (11.3% ALC)

Colour: cherry **Bouquet:** cherry pit nose **Taste:** yellow cherries, acidic

CALONA	WHITE

★½ | VARIETAL GEWÜRZTRAMINER PROPRIETORS RESERVE 1988 (11% ALC)

Colour: straw **Bouquet:** spicy, cabbagey **Taste:** sweet, perfumed, heaving. Lingers on the palate.

★½   JOHANNISBERG RIESLING 1988 PROPRIETORS RESERVE (11.5% ALC)

Colour: pale straw   **Bouquet:** lemon peel   **Taste:** not much varietal character, citric finish

★★½   PINOT BLANC 1989 (11% ALC)

Colour: almost water white   **Bouquet:** shy   **Taste:** dry, greengage and apple with a hint of vanilla. Some residual sugar, good acidity.

★★★   VARIETAL PINOT BLANC 1988 (11% ALC)

Colour: palest straw   **Bouquet:** shy nose   **Taste:** crisp, appley, delicate. Well balanced, light.

★★   SOVEREIGN OPAL PROPRIETORS RESERVE 1988 (11% ALC)

(Golden Muscat/Maréchal Foch crossing)

Colour: pale straw   **Bouquet:** hybrid nose   **Taste:** off-dry, lavender and tropical fruits, full-bodied. Flavour more interesting than the nose.

RED

★★½   CHELOIS 1988 (12% ALC)

Colour: deep tawny cherry   **Bouquet:** sweet cough drops, leather   **Taste:** dry, austere, drying out fruit. Touch of tannin.

★★★½   VARIETAL CHELOIS 1987 (12% ALC)

Colour: ruby-purple   **Bouquet:** sweet vanilla, red berries **Taste:** dry, raspberry and black currant, good extract, medium weight. Good length, soft tannins.

★★   VARIETAL ROUGEON 1987 (12.5% ALC)

Colour: browning ruby   **Bouquet:** spicy plum   **Taste:** dry, plummy flavour, hint of oxidation. Short, citric finish.

CARTIER	WHITE

★ CHENIN BLANC 1989 PETRONIO VINEYARD (11% ALC)

Colour: straw **Bouquet:** apple sauce, hint of oxidized fruit
Taste: sweet baked apple. Little structure.

★ GEWÜRZTRAMINER 1989 CORNISH VINEYARD (11% ALC)

Colour: dull straw **Bouquet:** sweet browning apple peel
Taste: no varietal character, indeterminate flavour

★ WHITE RIESLING 1990 CLARKE VINEYARD (11.5% ALC)

Colour: deep straw **Bouquet:** gummy **Taste:** sweetish,
indeterminate taste. Lacks fruit character, could be any varietal.

RED

★½ CHANCELLOR 1990 TOKLOS VINEYARD (12% ALC)

Colour: ruby **Bouquet:** woody **Taste:** plummy, short,
astringent finish

CEDARCREEK	WHITE

★★ AUXERROIS RESERVE 1988 (11% ALC)

Colour: gold **Bouquet:** spicy apple **Taste:** dry apple peel,
hint of oxidation

★★★ CHARDONNAY 1990 (11.9% ALC)

Colour: straw **Bouquet:** apple **Taste:** dry, burnt sugar,
caramel. Toffee-like finish. Macon style, low acidity.

★★★ GEWÜRZTRAMINER 1990 (11.5% ALC)

Colour: palest straw **Bouquet:** woody, lychee **Taste:** spicy,
good varietal character. Orange, rose, cardomom flavours.
Astringent finish.

★★★   JOHANNISBERG RIESLING 1990 (11.3% ALC)

(brown bottle)

Colour: pale straw   **Bouquet:** sweetish nose   **Taste:** soft, grapefruit-like character. Crisp apple finish.

★★(>★★★)   JOHANNISBERG RIESLING DRY 1990 (11.5% ALC)

(green bottle)

Colour: pale straw   **Bouquet:** shy   **Taste:** dry, woody, acidic. Apricot finish.

★★★½   JOHANNISBERG RIESLING 1989 (10.5% ALC)

Colour: palest straw   **Bouquet:** apple   **Taste:** sweet apple, soft, light, good length. Nicely balanced.

★★½   PINOT AUXERROIS 1990 (11% ALC)

Colour: almost water white   **Bouquet:** herby, wet stone
Taste: very dry, light caramel flavour. Not much extract. Tart finish. Italianate.

★★★   PINOT BLANC 1990 (10% ALC)

Colour: pale straw   **Bouquet:** fresh, peachy   **Taste:** dry, toffee-like, lactic Chardonnay style. Well made. Sweet peachy finish.

★½   PROPRIETOR'S WHITE (10.5% ALC)

Colour: palest straw   **Bouquet:** lemony   **Taste:** lemon candy, sweetish, soft. Commercial.

★★½   RIESLING BLANC 1989 (11% ALC)

Colour: palest straw   **Bouquet:** green plum, tangerine
Taste: soft, sweetish, baked apple. Peppery fruit. Round on the palate. Commercial.

★★   SEMILLON 1990 HANNAH KIRSCHMAN VINEYARD (10.5% ALC)

Colour: palest straw   **Bouquet:** herbaceous   **Taste:** very dry, light gooseberry. Short on fruit, long acidic finish.

RED

★½   CHANCELLOR 1990 (11.5% ALC)

Colour: ruby   **Bouquet:** earthy, rhubarb   **Taste:** lean fruit, green, tart, acidic finish

★★½   PROPRIETOR'S RESERVE (11.5% ALC)

Colour: ruby   **Bouquet:** vanilla, strawberry, gardenias
Taste: lively red berry flavour, fresh acidity. Light on the palate.

★½   CHANCELLOR 1990 (11.5% ALC)

Colour: ruby   **Bouquet:** earthy, green rhubarb   **Taste:** dry, lean fruit, green taste. Tart, acidic finish.

★★★½   PROPRIETOR'S BLUSH (11% ALC)

Colour: deep salmon   **Bouquet:** cooked strawberries   **Taste:** lively red berry fruit, touch of vanilla. Dry, lots of character.

DIVINO   WHITE

★★½   CHARDONNAY CLASSICO 1989 (12.8% ALC)

Colour: straw-lemon   **Bouquet:** appley   **Taste:** dry, not much extract but finishes well with a lemony flavour. Discernible alcohol.

★★★   MALVASIA MEDIUM DRY 1989 (12.2% ALC)

Colour: pale straw   **Bouquet:** green peas   **Taste:** soft, sweet, vanilla and white chocolate. Full-bodied with good acidity.

★★★   PINOT BIANCO 1989 (12% ALC)

Colour: straw   **Bouquet:** oily, citrus   **Taste:** dry, apple, rose, rhubarb. Hint of pepper. Good length. Interesting wine.

★★½   PINOT CHARDONNAY 1988 (12% ALC)

Colour: straw   **Bouquet:** yeasty, grassy   **Taste:** dry, almost Sauvignon Blanc in character. Well balanced, youthful.

★★   PINOT DE PINOT 1988 (11.5% ALC)

Colour: deep straw   **Bouquet:** apple, caramel   **Taste:** oxidized flavour, soft, sweetish. Good acidity.

★★★½   TOCAI LATE HARVEST MEDIUM DRY 1990 (14.9% ALC)

Colour: palest straw   **Bouquet:** appley   **Taste:** sweet, full-bodied, appley. Voluptuous and fleshy, good length, well balanced.

★★★½   TREBBIANO 1990 (12% ALC)

Colour: pale straw   **Bouquet:** herby   **Taste:** spicy, very dry, white pepper. Good length.

RED

★½   AMARONE ROSSO MEDIUM DRY (16.4% ALC)

Colour: tawny ruby   **Bouquet:** geranium   **Taste:** sweet, raisiny, chocolate, pruney. Heavy, astringent. Unbalanced.

★★(>★★½)   CABERNET 1990 (12.5% ALC)

Colour: light purple   **Bouquet:** herbaceous   **Taste:** very dry, light cherry flavour. Very little extract, no real varietal character. Astringent tannic finish.

★★   MERLOT 1990 (12.2% ALC)

Colour: deep cherry   **Bouquet:** high toned berry from carbonic maceration   **Taste:** light, perfumed, Beaujolais style. Little varietal character. Cherry-like flavour, tannic finish.

★½   NOVELLO CLASSICO 1991 (12% ALC)

Colour: purple   **Bouquet:** sweet plum   **Taste:** dry, light, fruity, spritzy. Not much fruit extract. Too much tannin for a new wine.

ROSÉ

★★½   PINOT GRIGIO ROSÉ 1989

Colour: peachy salmon   **Bouquet:** shy nose   **Taste:** dry strawberry flavour, delicate, well balanced. Peppery. Elegant.

DOMAINE DE
CHABERTON   WHITE

★★★★   BACCHUS 1990 (10% ALC)

Colour: pale straw   **Bouquet:** sweet Muscat-like and pine nut nose   **Taste:** well-balanced, floral peach and lime flavour. Great length. Grapefruit and Muscat-like finish. Clean and true.

★★★½   MADELEINE ANGEVINE 1990 (10% ALC)

Colour: palest straw   **Bouquet:** sweet Muscat and baked apple **Taste:** soft, spicy, aromatic flavour. Light, spicy apple, racy acidity. Good length. A cross between Alsatian Muscat and Pinot Blanc.

★★★   MADELEINE SYLVANER 1990 (10% ALC)

Colour: palest straw   **Bouquet:** touch of sulphur   **Taste:** well-balanced, dry grapey flavour. Fresh, well-made. Elegant, crisp finish.

★★★★   ORTEGA 1990 (10% ALC) Half bottle

Colour: pale straw   **Bouquet:** perfumed Muscat, orange blossom   **Taste:** sweet apple, perfumey taste, fresh grapey finish. Well balanced and harmonious. Medium sweet. A delight!

GEHRINGER
BROTHERS   WHITE

★★★★   EHRENFELSER 1991 (11.8% ALC)

Colour: palest straw   **Bouquet:** aromatic   **Taste:** off-dry, rich, spicy fruit, tangerine and floral character. Lingering.

★★★½   EHRENFELSER 1990 (11.2% ALC)

Colour: pale straw   **Bouquet:** aromatic, citric   **Taste:** soft, sweet, peachy. Round on the palate. Lots of fruit extract, good length.

★★★½   JOHANNISBERG RIESLING 1991 (11.5% ALC)

Colour: palest straw   **Bouquet:** aromatic, floral   **Taste:** off-dry, peachy, lemony. Spicy finish, lingering.

★★★½   JOHANNISBERG RIESLING DRY 1991 (12% ALC)

Colour: palest straw, almost water white   **Bouquet:** mealy, floral   **Taste:** off-dry, round, lemony-floral, green plum. Spicy finish.

★★★½   JOHANNISBERG RIESLING ICEWINE 1991 (13% ALC) Half bottle

Colour: pale straw, hint of lime   **Bouquet:** apricot, peach **Taste:** sweet, tropical fruit, dried apricots. Lively acidity, lemony finish.

★★★½   MÜLLER-THURGAU DRY 1991 (11.8% ALC)

Colour: palest straw   **Bouquet:** aromatic, Muscat-like nose **Taste:** spicy, off-dry, grapey flavour. Lively acidity.

★★★   MÜLLER-THURGAU 1991 (11.8% ALC)

Colour: almost water white   **Bouquet:** crisp, herby
Taste: dry, delicate herby-floral flavour, citric. Well made.

★★★   PINOT AUXERROIS 1991 (11.3% ALC)

Colour: palest straw, almost water white   **Bouquet:** minerally
Taste: dry, delicate, peachy. Well balanced, good length.

★★★   SCHONBURGER 1991 (10.5% ALC)

Colour: palest straw, almost water white   **Bouquet:** aromatic,
orange peel, roses   **Taste:** spicy, off-dry, delicate but fades on
the palate

★★★   VERDELET 1991 (11% ALC)

Colour: palest straw, almost water white   **Bouquet:** bran
Taste: off-dry, kiwi fruit flavour. Delicate, clean vanilla bean
finish.

RED

★★½   CUVÉE NOIRE DRY (11.5% ALC)

Colour: plum   **Bouquet:** cooked cherries   **Taste:** smoky
cherry, touch of sweetness. Light fruit extract, slightly astringent, hot finish.

★★½   CHANCELLOR ICEWINE 1991 (13.7% ALC) Half bottle

Colour: plum   **Bouquet:** raspberry   **Taste:** candied raspberry,
syrupy, heavy. Sweet rhubarb finish.

GRAY MONK   WHITE

★★½   EHRENFELSER 1989 KABINETT (11.5% ALC)

Colour: straw with lime highlights   **Bouquet:** grassy grapefruit
Taste: Riesling-like, crisp grapefruit, tart finish

★★★   GEWÜRZTRAMINER 1988 (11.1% ALC)

Colour: straw   **Bouquet:** spicy apple   **Taste:** good fruit extract, clean, well made, good length but lacking in rich varietal character

---

★★½(>★★★)   GEWÜRZTRAMINER RESERVE 1989 (11.6% ALC)

Colour: pale straw   **Bouquet:** aromatic, light varietal character **Taste:** dry, spicy, well balanced, but lacking in intensity for a Reserve wine

---

★★½   GEWÜRZTRAMINER RESERVE 1988 (11.1% ALC)

Colour: straw-gold   **Bouquet:** caramel   **Taste:** hint of oxidation, lychee, apple. Heavy, clumsy.

★★★★   LATE HARVEST KERNER 1990 (11.6% ALC)

Colour: pale straw   **Bouquet:** grapefruit peel   **Taste:** spicy, off-dry, minerally, concentrated grapefruit flavour. Elegant and lingering.

★★½   JOHANNISBERG RIESLING 1989 (11.2% ALC)

Colour: palest straw   **Bouquet:** grapefruit   **Taste:** spritzy, light, elegant. Very dry grapefruit peel flavour, yeasty finish.

★★½   KERNER DRY 1989

Colour: straw   **Bouquet:** grassy, grapefruit   **Taste:** dry, citric, crisp acidity, good length

---

★★★   KERNER SPÄTLESE 1989

Colour: straw   **Bouquet:** grapefruit   **Taste:** round, sweet grapefruit. Great length, well balanced.

★★   LATITUDE 50 1990 (11.8% ALC)

Colour: straw   **Bouquet:** floral, mealy   **Taste:** peachy flavour with a long lemony, acidic finish

★★★½   PINOT AUXERROIS 1991 (11% ALC)

Colour: almost water white   **Bouquet:** sweaty, grapefruit peel
Taste: crisply dry, concentrated grapefruit flavour. Well balanced, lingering flavour.

★★★   PINOT AUXERROIS 1990 (10.5% ALC)

Colour: pale straw   **Bouquet:** sweet, yeasty nose   **Taste:** nose belies the flavour — dry, peachy, hint of spritz on the tongue. Good fruit, well balanced. Peppery finish.

★★★   PINOT BLANC 1989 (10.8% ALC)

Colour: straw   **Bouquet:** fresh, appley   **Taste:** perfumed peachy flavour. Some residual sugar. Good lingering finish.

★★½   PINOT CHARDONNAY 1989 (12.3% ALC)

Colour: pale straw   **Bouquet:** apple blossom   **Taste:** spritzy, buttery, good acidity. Apple and grapefruit peel flavour. Slightly hot finish.

★★½(>★★★½) PINOT GRIS 1990 (11.3% ALC)

Colour: straw with a pinkish hue   **Bouquet:** rhubarb, grassy
Taste: very dry and crisp. Tart grapefruit-like finish. More Riesling in character than Pinot Gris.

HAINLE
VINEYARDS   WHITE

★★½   WHITE RIESLING DRY 1988 (12.8% ALC)

Colour: straw   **Bouquet:** flinty, barnyard   **Taste:** dry, woody, herby. Not much fruit extract. Crisp, lingering finish.

★★   WHITE RIESLING DRY 1989 (12.6% ALC)

Colour: straw   **Bouquet:** dry honeyed nose   **Taste:** full-bodied, lemon, lime flavours. High acidity, underlying woodiness.

PINOT BLANC DRY 1990 ELISABETH'S VINEYARD

Colour: yellow straw   **Bouquet:** volatile, acetone nose
Taste: sweet fruit, heavy, balsamic vinegar taste

RED

★★★   BACO NOIR 1990 (12.5% ALC)

Colour: ruby   **Bouquet:** smoky, perfumed roses
Taste: raspberry, lively acidity, touch of volatility reminiscent of Pinot Noir

HILLSIDE
CELLARS   WHITE

★★   AUXERROIS 1990 (11.3% ALC)

Colour: pale straw   **Bouquet:** caramel, sulphur   **Taste:** hint of spritz, soft, sweetish. Suggestion of red licorice. A little bitter on the finish.

★★★   CLEVNER 1990 (11.6% ALC)

Colour: palest straw   **Bouquet:** vanilla, apple   **Taste:** spicy, dry, hint of spritz. Delicate red licorice flavour. Good length. Slightly hot finish.

LANG   RED

★★½   MARÉCHAL FOCH 1991 (10.7% ALC)

Colour: ruby   **Bouquet:** fresh, grapey   **Taste:** sweet, soft, light. Commercial.

LECOMTE	WHITE

★★★★   GEWÜRZTRAMINER 1990 (12.2% ALC)

Colour: pale straw   **Bouquet:** concentrated varietal character, rose, red pepper, lychee   **Taste:** rich, spicy grapefruit, aromatic, soft and lingering. A fine Gewurz.

★★★   PINOT BLANC 1989 (12.8% ALC)

Colour: pale straw   **Bouquet:** caramel, hint of oak
Taste: dry, full-bodied, herby. Good length, well balanced.

MISSION HILL	WHITE

★★★   BACCHUS PRIVATE RESERVE 1990 (10% ALC)

Colour: palest straw   **Bouquet:** delicate, rose water
Taste: light, elegant, off-dry. Muscat-like, a little short.

★★   BARREL-FERMENTED CHARDONNAY BIN 33 PRIVATE RESERVE 1989 (10.5% ALC)

(has the distinction of being the longest name of any Canadian wine)

Colour: straw   **Bouquet:** spicy, oaky, touch of geranium
Taste: light, dry, little fruit. Not enough extract to support the oak. Bitter lemony, clovey finish.

★★   CHASSELAS PRIVATE RESERVE 1989

Colour: pale straw   **Bouquet:** shy nose   **Taste:** sweetish, full-bodied anise flavour. Grapefruit and licorice finish. Clumsy.

★★★½   GEWÜRZTRAMINER PRIVATE RESERVE 1990 (10.9% ALC)

Colour: straw   **Bouquet:** aromatic, spicy, rose   **Taste:** soft lychee flavour, lots of extract. Hint of sweetness in middle taste, a trifle flabby on the finish, lacking acidity.

★★★½   DRY BOTRYTIS AFFECTED OPTIMA PRIVATE RESERVE 1990 (11.3% ALC)

Colour: straw   **Bouquet:** hint of lime, rose, Gewürztraminer-like nose   **Taste:** off-dry, light, spicy, exotic. Well balanced, good length.

★★★★   BOTRYTIS AFFECTED OPTIMA PRIVATE RESERVE 1989 (10.2% ALC) Half bottle

Colour: straw-lime   **Bouquet:** exotic, orange, cardomom **Taste:** sweet, perfumed, Turkish Delight taste. Lingering exotic flavour of roses, spices, orange. Light on the palate.

★   CLASSIC RIESLING DRY (10.5% ALC)

Colour: palest straw   **Bouquet:** musty, resinous **Taste:** metallic, citrus, short. Little on the finish.

★½   HARVEST RIESLING (10.8% ALC)

Colour: pale straw   **Bouquet:** lime, petrol   **Taste:** sweetish apple and lime. Heavy on the palate. Overly sweet, astringent finish.

★★★½   JOHANNISBERG RIESLING PRIVATE RESERVE 1989 (11.5% ALC)

Colour: straw-lime   **Bouquet:** petrol, lime   **Taste:** very dry, oily on the palate. Well made, good length. Good fruit extract.

★★★½   JOHANNISBERG RIESLING 1988 PRIVATE RESERVE (10.6% ALC)

Colour: pale straw-lime   **Bouquet:** sweet lime and petrol **Taste:** soft fruit, sweetish with a full lime flavour and good length

---

★★★★   LATE HARVEST JOHANNISBERG RIESLING PRIVATE RESERVE 1989 (9.5% ALC) Half bottle

Colour: straw   **Bouquet:** winter apples   **Taste:** unctuous, rich appley flavour. Well-balanced, clean, medium sweet. Lingering taste. Auslese sweetness.

★★★★   SEMILLON PRIVATE RESERVE 1989 BARREL-AGED (10.9% ALC)

Colour: pale straw   **Bouquet:** smoky, grassy   **Taste:** perfumed vanilla, peachy flavour. Good acidity. Well balanced, good length.

★★½   SEMILLON PRIVATE RESERVE BIN 1 1988 (10.5% ALC)

Colour: pale straw   **Bouquet:** gooseberry skin   **Taste:** dry, gooseberry, herbaceous. Short finish.

★★★½   PINOT BLANC PRIVATE RESERVE 1990 BARREL-AGED (10.4% ALC)

Colour: palest straw   **Bouquet:** vanilla   **Taste:** soft, vanilla and peach flavour. Toffee-like finish. Well balanced. Hint of sweetness in middle taste. Good length, custardy finish.

★½   VINTNERS RIESLING DRY (10.5% ALC)

Colour: almost water white   **Bouquet:** spicy, barnyard
Taste: sweetish, short. Biscuity finish. Over-produced.

★★★   VINTNERS HARVEST RIESLING (10.8% ALC)

Colour: almost water white   **Bouquet:** spring flowers
Taste: sweetish apple flavour. Soft, round on the palate. Good length. Good value.

RED

★★★   VIN NOUVEAU 1991 (12.2% ALC)

Colour: deep cherry   **Bouquet:** flinty cherry   **Taste:** fresh lively fruit. Raspberry candy, hint of sweetness.

★★   VERDELET RIESLING 1990 (11.2% ALC)

(organic — 598 cases)

Colour: palest straw   **Bouquet:** undistinguished   **Taste:** sweet grapefruit and apple, long acidic finish. Browning apple after taste of oxidized fruit.

★★   MARÉCHAL FOCH 1990 (ORGANIC) (11.7% ALC)

Colour: ruby-cherry   **Bouquet:** volatile   **Taste:** spicy, plum pudding, clove. Good acidity.

QUAILS' GATE   WHITE

★★½   CHARDONNAY 1990 (11% ALC)

Colour: straw   **Bouquet:** vanilla, citrus   **Taste:** lemon and apple. Good acidity, light fruit character, appley finish.

★★½   CHASSELAS 1990 (11.5% ALC)

Colour: white gold   **Bouquet:** papery, apple   **Taste:** spicy, green peppercorn, good length. Very individual flavour.

★★½   CHASSELAS 1989 (11% ALC)

Colour: straw   **Bouquet:** dry, herby   **Taste:** very dry, crisp, Italinate. Clean, well made.

★½   DRY RIESLING 1990 (11.5% ALC)

Colour: dull peachy gold   **Bouquet:** candied lemon
Taste: lean fruit, green apple flavour with a tart, bitter finish

★★★   RIESLING 1990 (11.5% ALC)

Colour: gold-pinkish   **Bouquet:** oily, peachy   **Taste:** sweet, fruity, lime, canned peaches. Spätlese sweetness.

★★★★   RIESLING 1989 (11.5% ALC)

Colour: straw   **Bouquet:** oily, petrol   **Taste:** concentrated lime and grapefruit flavour. Lots of extract. Wonderfully balanced and mouth-filling.

★★   DECHAUNAC ROUGEON (12% ALC)

Colour: lively plum   **Bouquet:** smoked bacon, perfumed
Taste: lean tart fruit. Acidic. Good length, touch of tannin.

RED

★(>★★)	PINOT NOIR (11.5% ALC)
	Colour: cherry **Bouquet:** sappy **Taste:** unripe raspberry, tart, tannic, acidic

STE. MICHELLE WHITE

★	JOHANNISBERG RIESLING (9.5% ALC)
	Colour: straw **Bouquet:** gummy, resinous **Taste:** sweetish, synthetic marzipan flavour. Perfumed, almond-like finish.

SIMILKAMEEN
CELLARS WHITE

★★½	EHRENFELSER LATE HARVEST BOTRYTIS AFFECTED 1988 (9.5% ALC) Half bottle
	Colour: brassy gold **Bouquet:** raisins, dates **Taste:** sweet, light mouth-feel, peachy, nutty. Low acidity.

SUMAC RIDGE WHITE

★★★(>★★★½)	CHARDONNAY 1990 LACUSTA VINEYARD (12.5% ALC)
	Colour: pale straw **Bouquet:** apple **Taste:** green apple flavour, light, lemony finish. Good length, crisp finish. Chablis style.

★★½	GEWÜRZTRAMINER DRY 1989 (11.4% ALC)
	Colour: straw **Bouquet:** lime, grapefruit **Taste:** dry, lean, spicy. Riesling style. Crisp, appley finish.

★★★	GEWÜRZTRAMINER PRIVATE RESERVE 1990 (11.7% ALC)
	Colour: pale straw **Bouquet:** grapefruit pith **Taste:** spicy grapefruit, good length but more Riesling character than Gewurz

★★   OKANAGAN BLANC 1990 (11% ALC)

Colour: pale straw   **Bouquet:** lemony, earthy   **Taste:** dry, citric, full in the mouth. Acidic, short on fruit. Commercial.

★★★   PINOT BLANC 1990 (12% ALC)

Colour: straw   **Bouquet:** biscuity, mealy   **Bouquet:** gooseberry and grapefruit   **Taste:** lively green fruit, crisp finish

---

★★★(>★★★½) JOHANNISBERG RIESLING 1990 (12.3% ALC)

Colour: pale straw   **Bouquet:** grapefruit peel   **Taste:** dry with aromatic fruit. Full-bodied, grapefruit flavour. Lots of extract.

★★★   VERDELET 1990 (11% ALC)

Colour: pale straw   **Bouquet:** pink grapefruit   **Taste:** sweetish apple and grapefruit flavour, fine acidity. Clean, soft middle palate, popcorn-like finish.

RED

★★★   OKANAGAN BLUSH 1990 (11% ALC)

Colour: deep salmon   **Bouquet:** strawberry   **Taste:** off-dry, sweet strawberry with a fine spine of acidity. Well balanced.

★★½(>★★★) CHANCELLOR 1990 (11.5% ALC)

Colour: ruby   **Bouquet:** cherry, plum   **Taste:** dry, medium-bodied, austere. Black cherry flavour, hint of tannin on the finish.

★★   CHANCELLOR 1989 (11.5% ALC)

Colour: ruby   **Bouquet:** flinty, cherry-like   **Taste:** crisp fruit, lively acidity. Chillable.

★★½   CHANCELLOR 1989 PRIVATE RESERVE 1989 (11.5% ALC)

Colour: ruby   **Bouquet:** earthy, cake-like   **Taste:** wild strawberry, light. Touch of tannin.

★★½ BLANC DE NOIR BRUT EXTRA DRY (11.5% ALC)

Appearance: lazy mousse **Colour:** pearly-straw (some deposit) **Bouquet:** yeasty, appley **Taste:** soft, mouth-filling, good length

---

★★ STELLA'S JAY CUVÉE DRY (11.5% ALC)

(Champagne method)

Appearance: light mousse **Colour:** straw **Bouquet:** apple **Taste:** dry, foamy, gingery. Tart acidic finish, ultimately astringent.

WILD GOOSE
VINEYARDS WHITE

★★½ JOHANNISBERG RIESLING DRY 1990

Colour: straw **Bouquet:** lanolin **Taste:** peachy, spicy with a crisp acidic finish

RED

★★ BACO NOIR 1990 (12% ALC)

Colour: purple ruby **Bouquet:** fruity cherry **Taste:** bitter cherry, acidic, long finish

---

★★ MARÉCHAL FOCH 1990 (12% ALC)

Colour: purple-ruby **Bouquet:** fruity, cherry **Taste:** dry, sour cherry, acidic, long finish

QUEBEC WINES

| DIETRICH-JOOSS | Rosé |

★★★   VIN ROSÉ 1991 (11% ALC)

Colour: raspberry   **Bouquet:** clean, red berries   **Taste:** light, raspberry flavour, good length. Refreshing green plum acidity on the finish.

| DOMAINE DES CÔTES D'ARDOISE | White |

★★★½   CARTE D'OR SEYVAL 1990

Colour: palest straw   **Bouquet:** spicy, perfumed apple
Taste: crisp and dry with an appley taste. Evident oak.

Red

★★   PINOT NOIR/GAMAY 1990

Colour: cherry   **Bouquet:** red berries   **Taste:** light mouthfeel, raspberry flavour

| LA VITACÉE | Red |

★★   BARBE-ROUGE 1990 (11% ALC)

Colour: deep ruby   **Bouquet:** barnyard, leather   **Taste:** very dry, wild strawberries, cidery, spicy. Good extract, but spoiled by a sour finish and harsh tannins.

LES BLANCS CÔTEAUX	WHITE

★★   LA TASTE SEYVAL 1990 (11% ALC)

Colour: almost water white   **Bouquet:** banana   **Taste:** delicate, crisp, clean, good acidity

VIGNOBLE DE LA BAUGE	WHITE

★½   SEYVAL BLANC 1990 (10.4% ALC)

Colour: water white   **Bouquet:** discreet, fresh   **Taste:** light, crisp, clean

VIGNOBLE DE L'ORPAILLEUR	WHITE

★★★   VIN BLANC 1990 (11% ALC)

Colour: very pale   **Bouquet:** fresh, grassy   **Taste:** very dry, light and crisp with a Sauvignon Blanc character

★★★   VIN BLANC 1991 (11% ALC)

Colour: pale straw   **Bouquet:** fresh   **Taste:** light grapefruit and vanilla flavour. Banana-like finish, well balanced.

★★½   L'ORPAILLEUR 1989 OAK AGED (11% ALC)

Colour: pale straw   **Bouquet:** oaky   **Taste:** spicy oak character, lean, fresh, licorice flavour. Oak overpowers the fruit.

★★★½   APÉRID'OR (15% ALC)

(aperitif wine)

Colour: golden   **Bouquet:** appley   **Taste:** reminscent of Pineau des Charentes but not as sweet; good acidity

VIGNOBLE LE CEP D'ARGENT WHITE

★★★ SEYVAL BLANC (11% ALC)

Colour: peachy-straw   **Bouquet:** floral, delicate   **Taste:** light in the mouth. Good middle fruit, grapefruit peel, peppery. Very crisp finish.

RED

★★ DÉLICE DU CHAIS 1991 (12% ALC)

Colour: pale ruby   **Bouquet:** strawberries   **Taste:** plummy, some oxidation of the fruit. Bitter almond finish, acidic.

VIGNOBLE LES ARPENTS DE NEIGE WHITE

★★ SEYVAL 1990

Colour: almost water white   **Bouquet:** smoky   **Taste:** very dry, grassy taste, soft middle palate

VIGNOBLE MOROU RED

★★½ MOROU VIN ROUGE 1991 (11% ALC)

Colour: good ruby   **Bouquet:** smoky cherry   **Taste:** light fruit, candied cherry. Well balanced, fresh flavour, slightly bitter on the finish.

NOVA SCOTIA WINES

GRAND PRÉ	WHITE

★★★   AVON BLANC (10.4% ALC)

Colour: pale straw   **Bouquet:** apple, perfumed   **Taste:** off-dry, soft Vouvray style. Well balanced.

★★½   CUVÉE EVANGELINE (10.5% ALC)

Colour: pale straw   **Bouquet:** earthy, minty   **Taste:** sweetish, soft, good length. Good value.

★★★   L'ACADIE BLANC 1989 (11% ALC)

Colour: straw   **Bouquet:** apple, hint of leather   **Taste:** crisp, peppery, lively acidity

---

★★½   SEYVAL BLANC 1989 (11% ALC)

Colour: very pale straw   **Bouquet:** green plums   **Taste:** dry, medium bodied, lemony. Tart finish.

           RED

★★   CUVÉE D'AMUR 1986 (11.5% ALC)

Colour: tawny cherry   **Bouquet:** oaky, cooked plums
Taste: dry, acidic, losing fruit, touch of tannin

★★½   L'ACADIE ROUGE (11.3% ALC)

Colour: deep cherry   **Bouquet:** oak, red berries   **Taste:** very dry, raspberries, cranberries. Acidic, lean.

★★½(>★★★½) AMUR PORT 1987 (20% ALC)

Colour: tawny ruby **Bouquet:** chocolate, black cherry
Taste: chocolatey, peppery, spiritous. Some tannin.

JOST
VINEYARDS WHITE

★★★ HABITANT BLANC 1990 (11% ALC)

(Named after Habitant Vineyards in the Annapolis Valley. A
Vineland clone known as V 53261.)

Colour: palest straw **Bouquet:** fruity, sultanas **Taste:** dry,
full in the mouth, citric. Well balanced, good length.

★★★★ SONNENHOF VIDAL 1988 (11% ALC)

(aged 18 months before bottling)

Colour: straw **Bouquet:** delicate, dried fruits **Taste:** round,
unctuous, off-dry, peachy. Good length.

★★ CHRISTIANE MARIA GEWÜRZTRAMINER 1989 (11% ALC)

Colour: pale straw **Bouquet:** vegetal-volatile **Taste:** soft,
off-dry, peach and rose petal. Heavy in the mouth.

★★★½ ROVING PRINCESS GEISENHEIM 1990 (11% ALC)

(Geisenheim clone GM 6494-3)

Colour: old gold **Bouquet:** grapefruit, mineralish
Taste: soft, off-dry, melon and peach flavour. Good length.

★★★(>★★★½) GRAND CRU ROUGE 1989 (12.5% ALC)

(Maréchal Foch and Severnyi)

Colour: purple-ruby **Bouquet:** peppery blackberry
Taste: less extract than the nose suggests; dry, medium-bodied,
blackberry and black currant flavour. Touch of tannin.

★★   MARÉCHAL FOCH 1989 (12% ALC)

Colour: purple-ruby   **Bouquet:** sappy, raspberry   **Taste:** not a lot of flavour, tannic

SAINTE FAMILLE WHITE

★★★½   CHARDONNAY 1990 (12.5% ALC)

Colour: pale straw   **Bouquet:** pear   **Taste:** dry, apple and pear flavour with a fine citric finish. Good varietal character.

★★★   ESTATE SEYVAL (12% ALC)

Colour: water white   **Bouquet:** grassy, rhubarb   **Taste:** off-dry, anise and gooseberry flavour. Well-made.

★★   GOLD BELL HOUSE WINE (12% ALC)

Colour: palest straw   **Bouquet:** fruity, lemony   **Taste:** semi-dry, Germanic. Citric finish, a little short.

★★★   DRY RIESLING 1990 (12% ALC)

Colour: palest straw   **Bouquet:** peachy, floral   **Taste:** light, dry, clean peachy flavour. Good length. Alsatian style.

★★★   JOHANNISBERG RIESLING (12% ALC)

Colour: palest straw, hint of lime   **Bouquet:** lime, hint of petrol   **Taste:** off-dry, apricot, lemony finish. Good length. Germanic style.

★★½   PREMIUM CHABLIS (12% ALC)

Colour: almost water white   **Bouquet:** earthy, citric
Taste: off-dry, green plum flavour, clean, round on the palate

Red

★★★   LA PAROISSE ROUGE (12% ALC)

(Michurinetz and Maréchal Foch)

Colour: tawny ruby   **Bouquet:** smoky, cherry   **Taste:** dry, good fruit extract, black cherry flavour. Touch of oak and tannin. Chocolatey finish.

★★★   MARÉCHAL FOCH (112% ALC)

Colour: ruby-plum   **Bouquet:** vanilla, apple, earthy
Taste: dry, blackberry flavour, medium bodied. Touch of tannin.

Vintners Quality Alliance

*E*very wine growing country has its own appellation system — a body of regulations that governs the viticultural
and vinicultural aspects of wine. These rules tell farmers
where they can grow grapes, set minimum standards in the vineyard and the cellar and determine what goes on the label. France
has *Appellation d'Origine Controlée* (AOC); Italy has *Denominazione
di Origine Controllata e Garantita* (DOCG); Germany has
Qualitätswein mit Prädikat (QMP). The regulations in these countries are quite similar, dictating to winemakers what grapes they
can grow (with minimum sugar levels and maximum yields), how
much wine they can make from a given weight of grapes and how
they should age the product.

For the 1988 vintage, Ontario introduced its own appellation
called The Vintners Quality Alliance (VQA). (The name was
"lifted" from an association in California called "The Carneros
Quality Alliance," a group of wineries in Napa and Sonoma.) Originally, the VQA rules were formulated by a group of Ontario
wineries so that they could apply to all wine growing provinces in
Canada but to date only British Columbia has bought into the
concept, following the Ontario model to the letter from their 1990
vintage.

A year after the formal introduction of VQA in Ontario, the
VQA published its *Rules and Regulations* which are set out here.

1. **Statement of Goals & Purposes**

   The Vintners Quality Alliance (VQA) is an independent
   body responsible for introducing and maintaining standards
   and appellations adopted by members of the Ontario wine
   industry. The VQA has established the following goals for its
   organization:

(1) To develop and implement educational material in order to inform the public and interested members of the wine community about Ontario's wine growing regions.

(2) To coordinate and exchange research in areas of temperature, clonal selections, training methods, viticultural practices and wine varieties for the mutual benefit and development of Ontario's wine growing regions.

(3) To disseminate information with regard to the uniqueness of Ontario's wine growing regions in order to define the characteristics and qualities of the wines that are produced in those regions.

(4) To coordinate marketing efforts in order to create a quality image for all Ontario wines that bear the trademark of the Vintners Quality Alliance.

(5) To establish standards covering general areas such as vintage dating, estate bottling, viticultural areas, etc., which will compare favourably with similar standards established elsewhere in the wine world, e.g. California and France. Further development of standards will be established as a better understanding of the characteristics and production standards for the region is advanced.

2. Appellations of Origin

The VQA has divided appellations of origin into two categories: provincial and geographic designations.

(1) Provincial Designation

A provincially designated wine will bear the appellation of origin 'Ontario' provided that it meets the following standards:

(i) It is produced one hundred percent (100%) from grapes grown within the provincial boundaries of the Province of Ontario.

(ii) It is produced from one or more of the authorized grape varieties listed in Section 9 below, Authorized Grape Varieties, including both *Vitis vinifera* and *Vitis vinifera* hybrid varieties.

(iii) In the case of varietal wines, *Vitis vinifera* or hybrid, seventy-five percent (75%) of the wine must be made from the designated variety and the wine must have the pre-dominant character of variety, as determined by the VQA tasting panel.

(iv)   In the case of hybrid varietal wines, the other varieties used may not be indicated on the front label.

(2)   Geographic Designation

(i)   **Definition**

The Designated Viticultural Areas (DVAs) recognized by the VQA are:

> Niagara Peninsula
> Lake Erie North Shore
> Pelee Island

The Niagara Peninsula is defined as that area bounded by Lake Ontario on the north, the Niagara River on the east, the Welland River on the south and Highways 56 and 20 on the west.

Lake Erie North Shore is defined as that area contained within the political boundaries of Essex, Kent and Elgin counties, save and except that part of Kent county lying to the north of the Thames River.

Pelee Island is defined as that area contained within the geographic limits of Pelee Island, bounded by the waters of Lake Erie on all sides.

(ii)   **Standards**

A geographically designated wine may bear one of the appellations of origin set out in Section 2 (2) (i) provided that it meets the following standards:

(a)   It is produced one hundred percent (100%) from grapes grown within the political boundaries of the Province of Ontario.

(b)   At least eighty-five percent (85%) of the grapes were grown in the named viticutural area.

(c)   It is produced from authorized *Vitis vinifera* grapes only, listed in Section 9 (1) below.

(d)   In the case of varietal wines, eighty-five percent (85%) of the wine must be made from the desig-nated grape variety and the wine must have the predominant varietal character of that designated grape variety, as determined by the VQA Tasting Panel.

(e) In the case of blended wine, where a variety is stated on the label, the wine must contain a minimum of ten percent (10%) of that variety.

3. Varietal Wine

A varietal wine is one which:

(i) Bears the name of a grape or varieties authorized by the VQA.

(ii) Has the predominant character of the named variety of the appropriate character of the named varieties as determined by the VQA tasting panel.

(iii) Conforms to the standards set out in Section 2 (1) (iii) or 2 (2) (ii) (d).

4. Blended Wine

The only non-varietal wines allowed in the VQA must be one hundred percent (100%) vitis vinifera, except for specialty wines.

(1) In addition to the criteria set out in this section, to qualify for a VQA Designation a blended or non-varietal wine must conform with the standards required for the appropriate designation, set out in Section 2 above.

(2) With the exception of Specialty Wines listed in Section 8 below, the only blended or non-varietal wines allowed in the VQA are those which are produced one hundred percent (100%) from authorized *Vitis vinifera* grapes, listed in Section 9 (1) below.

(3) A maximum of three grape varieties may be identified in a blend, provided that:

(i) When two grapes are identified in a blend, the total volume of the second variety must be greater that 15%. In addition, the total sum of the two varieties must not be less than 85% of the total volume, and the total sum of all non-stated varieties cannot be greater than the total sum of the second variety.

(ii) When three grape varieties are identified in a blend, the total volume of the second variety must be greater than 15%, and the total volume of the third variety must be greater than 5%. In addition, the total sum of the three varieties must not be less than 85% of the total volume, and the total sum of all non-stated varieties cannot be greater than the total sum of the third variety.

(iii) All grape varieties identified in the blend must be listed on the front label, in descending order as measured by volume percent.

(iv) All grape varieties identified in the blend must employ the identical colour, style and size of lettering on the front label.

(v) Blended wines identified by a proprietary name which do not specify the grape varieties used in the blend are exempt from the provisions of this sub-section.

5. Vintage Dated Wines

Where a vintage date is stated on the label, at least ninety-five percent (95%) of the wine must derive from the designated vintage.

6. Vineyard Designated Wines

(1) Where a vineyard is designated on the label, one hundred percent (100%) of the wine must derive from the designated vineyard, which must be located within a Designated Viticultural Area.

(2) For the purposes of this section, either the word "vineyard" or "estate" can be used to identify a specific vineyard on the label.

(3) The vineyard designation shall appear directly beneath the stated variety and in the same size of type, and in letters as conspicuous as, the appellation of origin.

(4) The DVA within which the vineyard is located must be declared on the label and the wine must comply with all standards set out in Section 2(2) above.

7. Estate Bottled Wine

(1) An Estate Bottled wine is defined as a wine which derives one hundred percent (100%) from grapes grown on land owned or controlled by the bottling winery, and which has not left the winery prior to bottling.

(2) For the purposes of this section, "controlled by" refers to property on which the bottling winery has the legal right to perform, and does perfom, all the acts common to viticulture under the terms of a lease or similar agreement of at least ten years duration. During the first three years of any such leasehold term the bottling winery will not be entitled to use the term "Estate Bottled." That entitlement will be reserved for the fourth and subsequent years of the leasehold term.

(3) No term other than "Estate Bottled" may be used on a label to indicate combined growing and bottling conditions.

(4) The "Estate Bottled" designation denotes the origin of the grapes, not the location of the processing facility, provided that the processing facility is located within the political boundaries of the Province of Ontario (British Columbia).

(5) The DVA within which the land is owned or controlled by the bottling winery must be declared on the label and the wine must comply with all standards set out in Section 2(2) above.

8. Specialty Wines

To qualify for a VQA Designation, a Specialty Wine must comply with the standards required for the appropriate designation, as set out in Section 2 above.

(1) Icewine

Icewine means any wine produced one hundred percent (100%) from Ontario grown grapes of an authorized grape variety, as set out in Section 9 below, that have been harvested naturally frozen on the vine at minus 7 degrees or colder. The pressing must take place immediately following the harvest in a continuous process, within the recognized viticultural area in which the grapes were grown. Artificially induced freezing is prohibited at any point in the process and a minimum of at least 32 Brix (132 Oechsle) is required as a computed must average. In addition to those grape varieties specified in Section 9 (1), the Vidal grape variety shall qualify to be labelled in conjunction with a Designated Viticultural Area, vineyard or estate designation, for the purposes of Icewine only.

The addition of sugar to any VQA Icewine is prohibited.

(2)   Botrytized Wine

Any wine using the designation "Botrytis Affected" or other synonym must have been made one hundred percent (100%) from Ontario grown grapes of an authorized grape variety, as set out in Section 9 below, that were affected by *Botrytis cinerea* in the vineyard, and the resulting wine must have the predominant character of naturally botrytized grapes, as determined by the VQA Tasting Panel.

The addition of sugar to any VQA Botrytized wine is prohibited.

(3)   Late Harvest Wines

A Late Harvest wine means any wine produced one hundred percent (100%) from Ontario grown grapes of an authorized grape variety, that have been naturally harvested on the vine after achieving the minimum must average of 22 Brix. The addition of sugar to any VQA Late Harvest wine is prohibited.

(4)   Select Late Harvest

A Select Late Harvest wine means any wine produced one hundred per cent (100%) from Ontario grapes of an authorized grape variety that have been naturally harvested on the vine and achieve a minimum must average of 28 Brix. The addition of sugar to any VQA Select Late Harvest wine is prohibited.

(5)   Special Select Late Harvest

A Special Select Late Harvest wine means any wine produced one hundred percent (100%) from Ontario grown grapes of an authorized grape variety that have been naturally harvested on the vine and achieve a minimum must average of 35 Brix. The addition of sugar to any VQA Special Select Late Harvest wine is prohibited.

(6) *Vin du Curé*

Vin du Curé means any wine produced one hundred percent (100%) from Riesling or Vidal grapes grown in Ontario according to the following procedures:

(i) Riesling grapes must attain a minimum of 18 Brix at harvest.

(ii) Vidal grapes must attain a minimum of 20 Brix at harvest.

(iii) After harvest, the grapes must be left to dry on frames, mats, small boxes, or any other similar structure with a perforated bottom in a dry, ventilated place until such time as they yield a must of at least 32 Brix (132 Oechsle) as an average. The addition of sugar to any VQA *Vin du Curé* is prohibited.

(iv) The resulting wine must have a predominant botrytized character, as determined by the VQA Tasting Panel.

(7) *Nouveau* Red Wine

A *Nouveau* Red wine means any wine produced one hundred percent (100%) from Ontario grown grapes of one or more authorized grape variety according to the following procedures:

(i) Grapes must attain a minimum of 18 Brix at harvest.

(ii) Vinification must involve at least partial carbonic maceration.

(iii) The wine must be produced and labelled as a varietal wine, e.g. "Gamay Nouveau," with the grape variety printed in letters at least half the size but no larger than those specifying "Nouveau," directly below or following the grape variety.

(iv) For the purposes of the VQA Tasting Panel and the VQA Appeal Panel, the wine will be assessed as a *Nouveau*, in addition to being assessed as a varietal.

(8)   *Blanc de Noir*

Blanc de Noir means any wine produced one hundred percent (100%) from Ontario grown grapes of one or more authorized variety according to the following procedures:

(i)   Grapes must attain a minimum of 18 Brix at harvest.

(ii)   The juice must be separated from the skins prior to fermentation and must be vinified using techniques which are suitable for the production of white wine.

(iii) The wine must be produced as a varietal wine, in accordance with the standards set out in Section 3 or as a blended wine in accordance with the standards set out in Section 4.

(iv)   The term "Blanc de Noir" must appear on the label directly above or below the grape variety, grape varieties or proprietary name, in letters at least half the size of but no larger than twice the size of those specifying the grape variety, grape varieties or proprietary name.

(v)   For the purposes of the VQA Tasting Panel and the VQA Appeal Panel, varietal character will not be an important component of the overall grade.

9.   **Authorized Grape Varieties**

(1)   Varieties of *Vitis vinifera*

Prime Name	Synonyms
Aligoté	
Auxerrois	Pinot Auxerrois
Cabernet Franc	
Cabernet Sauvignon	
Chardonnay	
Chasselas	Chasselasdore, Gutedelweiss
Chenin Blanc	Pineau de la Loire
Ehrenfelser	
Furmint	
Gamay	Gamay Noir
Gamay de Chaudenay	
Gewürztraminer	
Goldburger	
Grüner Veltliner	
Kerner	

Limberger	Lemberger, Blaufrankisch
Malbec	
Malvasia	Malvasia Bianca
Matsvani	
Melon	
Merlot	
Morio-Muscat	
Muscat Blanc	
Muscat Ottonel	
Müller-Thurgau	
Optima	
Oraniensteiner	
Ortega	
Perle of C'saba	Pearl of Casaba
Pinot Blanc	Weissburgunder, Pinot Bianco
Pinot Gris	Ruländer, Pinot Grigio
Pinot Meunier	Meunier
Pinot Noir	Spätburgunder
Riesling	White Riesling
Sauvignon Blanc	
Scheurebe	
Sémillon	
Serekseya chornaya	
Siegerrebe	
Sylvaner	Silvaner
St. Laurent	
Trebbiano	Ugni Blanc
Welschriesling	Riesling Italico
Yellow Muscat	Gelber Muscateller
Zweigeltrebe	

(2) Varieties Produced by Inter-Specific Crossbreeding

(i) Varieties Allowed for Varietal Designation

Prime Name	Synonyms
Baco Noir	
Blauburgunder	
Castel	Castel 19637
Chambourcin	
Chancellor	
Chelois	
Couderc	

Leon Millot	Millot
Maréchal Foch	Foch
Pollux	
Siegfried Rebe	Siegfried
Seyval Blanc	Seyval
Vidal Blanc	Vidal
Villard Noir	

(ii)   Varieties Allowed for Blending Purposes

Prime Name	Synonym
Aurore	
DeChaunac	
Landal	
Michurinetz	
Verdelet	
Vignoles	Ravat 51
Vincent	
Vivant	
GM 311-58	
GM 318-57	
GM 322-58	
SV 23-512	

10. Quality Standards

(1)   Amelioration

(i)   Addition of Water

The addition of water to any VQA wine is prohibited.

(ii)   Chaptalization

Chaptalization is defined as the addition of sugar to the grape must prior to or during fermentation. Chaptalization is permitted in all VQA wines, provided that it is not used to achieve minimum brix levels for Vineyard Designated, Estate Bottled or Specialty Wines, as set out in Sections 8 and 10 (2).

(2)   Minimum Brix Levels

Estate Bottled and Vineyard Designated varietal wines must meet the following minimum brix levels:

Variety	Minimum Brix
Chardonnay	19°
Riesling	18°
Gamay (red wine)	18°
Gewürztraminer	18°
Aligoté	17°
Pinot Noir	18°

(3) Audit Procedure to Certify Appellation of Origin

(i) In addition to the normal information required by the LCBO audit department, the following information shall be provided for all VQA wines:

(a) varieties stipulated by individual tank;

(b) quantities for Vineyard Designated Wines duly identified;

(c) quantities for Estate Bottled Wines duly identified;

(d) quantities for Provincially Designated Wine duly identified;

(e) quantities for Specialty Wines duly identified.

Quantities indicated in these various categories will be reconciled with recorded grape purchases to assure reasonable feasibility of reported recoveries.

(ii) Tank records and racking orders for all VQA wines setting out the complete processing record up to and including the bottling stage must be available for audit purposes. When racking orders are not used, the maintenance of a "Day Book" indicating quantities processed to bottling will be acceptable for audit purposes.

(iii) In the course of the normal LCBO audit, notification will be provided to the VQA Board of Directors indicating either compliance with these Rules and Regulations or outlining the circumstances of exceptions or inauditable conditions. The Director of General Audit will advise the Chairman, LCBO, and the VQA Board of Directors of non-compliance with these Rules and Regulations.

(4) Tasting Panel

(i) Composition

The VQA Tasting Panel shall consist of the Supervisor of Quality Control, Liquor Control Board of Ontario, or his/her designate, plus a minimum of six (6) other permanent members. To qualify for membership on the VQA Tasting Panel, candidates must be Wine Consultants employed by the LCBO who have passed a written test and tasting conducted by the Supervisor of Quality Control at the LCBO.

(ii) Sensory Evaluation

(a) All products shall be tasted blind in their respective groups, e.g. varietal, geographic designation, vintage year, sugar code, specialty wine, etc.

(b) The scoring system used shall be a 20 point scale as set out on the Grading Sheet attached hereto as Schedule B.

(c) Tastings shall be held when twenty wines are available, but a minimum of once per month.

(d) All tastings shall be conducted in the early morning of the day appointed.

(e) In the case of varietal wines, varietal character shall be an important component of the overall grade, to be noted under the score for aroma. Varietal wines are to be judged and scored as varietals. For example, a fine, well-made Grüner Veltliner may score only 12 out of 20 judged as a "wine," but judged as a Grüner Veltliner it may be near the top of its class and merit a 15. In the case of blended wines, varietal character shall not apply unless specific varieties are identified on the label.

(f) In order to monitor the margin of error on the VQA Tasting Panel, duplicate samples shall be introduced to the Tasting Panel as a check on scores.

(g) In the event that a wine is defective, a second bottle will be opened and tasted by the VQA Tasting Panel. If the second bottle contains a similar defect, the mark assigned to the first bottle will stand.

(iii) **Laboratory Analysis**

(a) All products which pass the sensory evaluation outlined in Section 10 (4) (ii) shall be forwarded to the LCBO laboratory for regular analysis. Upon laboratory analysis, any VQA wine found to be in violation of the Federal Food & Drug Act and Regulations and the LCBO's pre-established guidelines shall have its VQA revoked.

(b) An additional sample of all wines which pass sensory evaluation shall be maintained in a library for future reference.

(c) All products shall be checked by the Gas Chromatograph and Mass Spectrometer to ensure that *Labrusca* grapes are not being used.

(iv) **Score Notification**

The LCBO shall notify the Wine Council of Ontario (WCO) of scores along with a summary of reasons for rejected wines. The WCO shall then notify individual wineries of their respective scores.

(5) **Appeal Panel**

(i) **Composition**

Members of the VQA Appeal Panel shall be appointed by the VQA Board of Directors from time to time. The VQA Appeal Panel shall be comprised of the Executive Director of the VQA, or his/her designate, plus a minimum of three representatives of the academic community and/or the hospitality industry, and a minimum of three VQA qualified winemakers. Winemaker participation in the VQA Appeal Panel shall be on a rotating basis as determined from time to time by the Executive Director of the VQA or his/her designate.

Under no circumstances shall a winemaker sit on the VQA Appeal Panel if his or her wine is being tasted.

(ii) **Criteria For Submission**

    (a) Any product not approved for appellation or not obtaining 13.5 at the VQA Tasting Panel shall be eligible for submission to the VQA Appeal Panel.

    (b) Any product which is approved by the VQA Appeal Panel shall be eligible for re-submission to the VQA Tasting Panel. However, appealed wines which have already received appellation approval may only be returned to the Tasting Panel is a score of 13.5 or higher is received at the Appeal Panel.

    (c) Appeals shall be allowed once only.

    (d) If an appellation has been granted by the Tasting Panel, it cannot be rescinded. Tasting Panel scores shall supercede Appeal Panel scores.

(iii) **Sensory Evaluation**

    (a) All products shall be tasted blind in their respective groups, e.g. varietal, geographic designations, vintage year, sugar code, specialty wine, etc.

    (b) The scoring system used shall be a 20 point scale as set out on the Grading Sheet attached hereto as Schedule B.

    (c) Tastings shall be held at the direction of the Executive Director of the VQA.

    (d) Tastings shall be conducted in the early morning of the day appointed.

    (e) In the case of varietal wines, varietal character shall be an important component of the overall grade, and will be noted under the score for aroma and flavour. Varietal wines are to be judged and scored as varietals. In the case of blended wines, varietal character shall not apply unless specific varieties are identified on the label.

(f) In order to monitor the margin of error on the VQA Appeal Panel, a duplicate sample may be introduced at each appeal tasting, as a check on scores. In addition, several approved VQA wines and non-approved Ontario wines may be introduced at each appeal tasting.

(g) In the event that a wine is defective, a second bottle will be opened and tasted by the Appeal Panel. If the second bottle contains a similar defect, the higher mark will be accepted.

(iv) Score Notification

The Executive Director of the VQA or his/her designate shall notify the Wine Council of Ontario (WOC) and the Supervisor of the LCBO Quality Control Department of the scores along with a summary of the reasons for rejected wines. The Wine Council of Ontario shall then notify individual wineries of their respective scores.

If granted an appeal by the VQA Appeal Panel, the appellant winery may resubmit the wine to the VQA Tasting Panel to be re-evaluated.

11. Packaging

(1) Cork Finish

Any bottle size with a natural cork finish shall be allowed the VQA designation.

12. Labelling

For the purposes of this section, a wine must be approved by the VQA Tasting Panel in order to acheive a VQA appellation of origin. This approval shall be granted if a majority of the Tasting Panel feels that the wine's attributes fairly reflect the viticultural and enological quality standards established in these Rules and Regulations. In addition, the wine must be without fault and representative of quality wines of the stated types (e.g., Botrytized) or the stated grape variety or varieities.

(1) VQA Appellation of Origin Wines

Any wine which meets the minimum production and appellation standards set out herein and which is also passed by the VQA Tasting Panel must display the "VQA" Trademark (gold on black) as part of its package and the letters VQA on the label, provided that:

(i)   The type size is equal to, but not greater than, the type size used to designate the provincial or geographic designation, as the case may be; and

(ii)   The letters "VQA" appear on the same line as, and on either side of the provincial or geographic designation, but nowhere else on the label.

(iii)   The letters "VQA" appear without artistic embellishment and in the same colour and typeface as that used for the provincial or geographic designation.

(iv)   Reproductions of the VQA Trademark must conform in all particulars with the designs and specifications itemized on Schedule A attached hereto.

(v)   The following forms of the VQA Trademark are permitted:

    (a)   self-adhesive sticker, which must be placed on the front shoulder of the bottle or on the front neck only (see Schedule A); or

    (b)   printed on a paper neck or shoulder label, which must be placed on the front should of the bottle or on the front neck only (see Schedule A); or

    (c)   evenly spaced and printed three times on the capsule (see Schedule A).

(2) VQA Medallion Wines

Any wine which meets the minimum production and appellation standards set out herein and which also scores 15 or more at the VQA Tasting Panel shall be entitled to display the

VQA Medallion as part of its package. Reproductions of the VQA Medallion must conform in all particulars with the designs and specifications itemized on Schedule A attached hereto.

(i)   The following forms of the VQA Medallion are permitted:

    (a)   self-adhesive sticker, which must be placed on the front shoulder of the bottle or on the front neck only (see Schedule A); or

    (b)   printed on a paperneck or shoulder label, which must be placed on the front shoulder of the bottle or on the front neck only (see Schedule A); or

    (c)   evenly spaced and printed three times on the capsule (see Schedule A).

(3)   Wines not approved by the VQA Tasting Panel

Any wine which fails to be approved by the VQA Tasting Panel or is in violation of the rules and regulations set out herein, shall be prohibited from displaying the following on its label:

(i)   Appellation of Origin as defined in Section 2 above;

(ii)   VQA Medallion or Trademark;

(iii)   The term Icewine or any synonym or translation thereof;

(iv)   Vineyard Designation;

(v)   Estate Bottled Designation.

(4)   Synonyms

The use of synonyms or translations to describe any terms or references set out herein is strictly prohibited. All terms and references are to be transcribed as they appear within these Rules and Regulations.

13. Board of Directors

The VQA Board of Directors shall consist of six winery representatives, one representative of the LCBO, one representative of the academic community, one representative of the research sector and one Ontario grape grower.

An alternate academic representative has been appointed to be on the VQA Board of Directors. In the event that both representatives are in attendance at a meeting of the VQA Board of Directors, only one of them shall be allowed to cast a vote.

14. Changes to Rules and Regulations

Any proposal for changes to these rules and regulations, including any change in the financial obligations of the VQA beyond normal operating expenses, must be circulated in writing to the Directors of the VQA Board at least thirty days prior to any meeting of the VQA Board of Directors called to consider such things.

15. Funding

Upon approval by the VQA Tasting Panel, the producing winery shall be assessed a bottle fee to be determined from time to time by the VQA Board of Directors. The bottle fee shall be payable for both VQA Appellation of Origin and VQA Medallion wines.

Schedule A

VQA Medallion

The VQA medallion must be reproduced on the capsule as shown (black print and gold background). The stripes and the words Vintners Quality Alliance must appear as shown and must be reproduced in black print; the exception being when the background colour is black, whereupon the words and stripes must appear in gold. The background colour of the capsule may be any one solid colour.

(The above wording applies to the VQA Trademark as well.)

SCHEDULE "A"

(a) Self - Adhesive Sticker

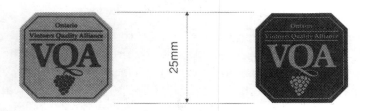

25mm

Black on Gold
VQA Medallion

Gold on Black
VQA Trademark

(b) Neck or Shoulder Label

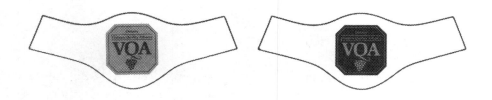

(NOT TO SCALE)

Black on Gold
VQA Medallion

Gold on Black
VQA Trademark

SCHEDULE "A" (continued)

(c) Printed on the Capsule

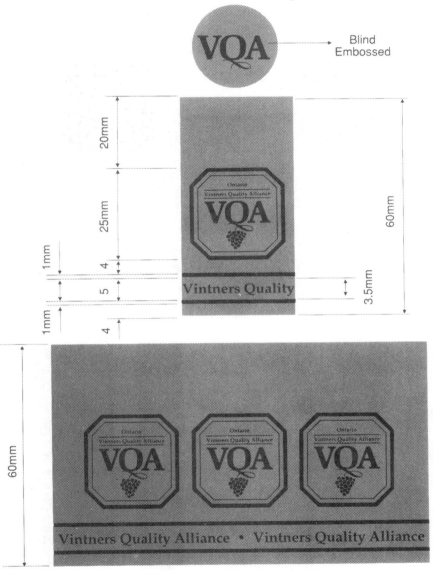

Blind
Embossed

20mm

25mm

1mm

4

5

1mm

4

60mm

Vintners Quality

3.5mm

60mm

Vintners Quality Alliance • Vintners Quality Alliance

Black on Gold
VQA Medallion

SCHEDULE "A" (continued)

(c) Printed on the Capsule

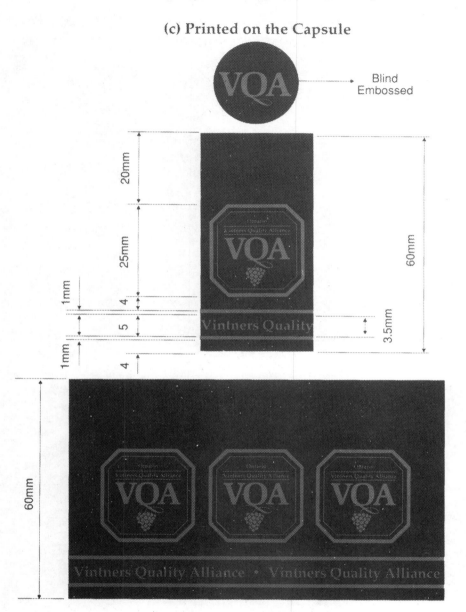

Gold on Black
VQA Trakemark

Schedule "B"

Vintners Quality Alliance
Product Application

1. Designation Applied for ☐ Provincial ☐ Geographic	2. Brand Name		LCBO Use Only
			Sample # _____
3. CSPC Number	4. Vintage Year	5. % Alcohol/Volume	Category # _____

6.Blended Wine (Major Varieties with Percentages)

_____ %   _____ %

_____ %   _____ %

7. Varietal Wine - Grape Variety
           %
	8. Brix at Harvest	9. Residual Sugar
		        g/100mL

10. Remaining Grape Varieties (if applicable)	11. Estimated Retail Price	
12. Estimated Total Production (in cases)	13. Amount available to LCBO (in cases)	

I hereby warrant that all of the above statements are true and all grapes used to produce this wine were grown in Ontario.

Name (please print) _____ Signature _____ Date _____

Name and Address of Supplier	Name and Address of Agent
Fax: Contact:	Fax: Contact:
Telex: Phone No.:	Telex: Phone No.:

LCBO Use Only

Quality Assessment Information

Initial Tasting Score _____ Date _____	Comments	☐ Appellation ☐ Medallion ☐ Rejected	I Forward to Lab _____ QC Signature
Retaste (if Required) Score _____ Date _____	Comments	☐ Appellation ☐ Medallion ☐ Rejected	I Forward to Lab _____ QC Signature
Laboratory Analysis ☐ Acceptable ☐ Not Acceptable	Sugar Content	Alc. Found	Alc. Declared

Date: _____ Laboratory Signature: _____

SCHEDULE "B"

Liquor
Control Board
of Ontario

"Grading Sheet"

Name										Date	Comments	Varietal Character Nil Good	Weak Distinct	
Sample Number	Appearance & Colour (3)	Aroma & Bouquet (6)	Total Acidity (1)	Balance (2)	Body (1)	Flavour (3)	Finish (2)	General Quality (2)				Varietal Character	Appellation	Total
V-												N W G D	Y / N	
V-												N W G D	Y / N	
V-												N W G D	Y / N	
V-												N W G D	Y / N	
V-												N W G D	Y / N	
V-												N W G D	Y / N	
V-												N W G D	Y / N	
V-												N W G D	Y / N	
V-												N W G D	Y / N	
V-												N W G D	Y / N	

SCHEDULE "C"

VINTNERS QUALITY ALLIANCE

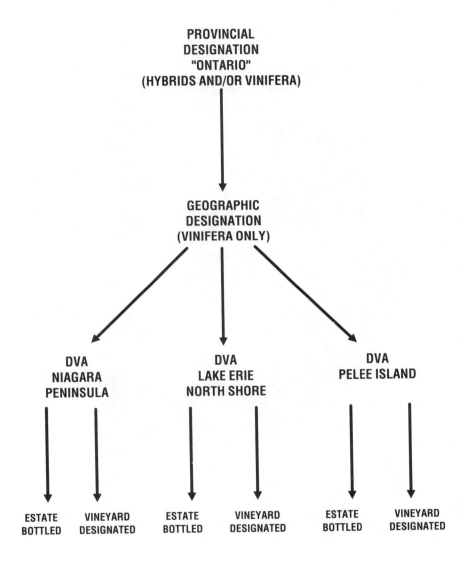

PROVINCIAL
DESIGNATION
"ONTARIO"
(HYBRIDS AND/OR VINIFERA)

GEOGRAPHIC
DESIGNATION
(VINIFERA ONLY)

DVA
NIAGARA
PENINSULA

DVA
LAKE ERIE
NORTH SHORE

DVA
PELEE ISLAND

ESTATE
BOTTLED

VINEYARD
DESIGNATED

ESTATE
BOTTLED

VINEYARD
DESIGNATED

ESTATE
BOTTLED

VINEYARD
DESIGNATED

SCHEDULE "C" (continued)

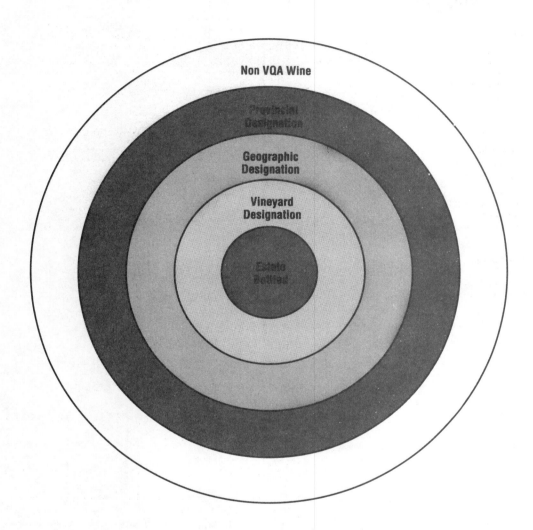

SIGHT

3 – Excellent — Brilliant with outstanding characteristic color.
2 – Good — Clear with characteristic color.
1 – Poor — Slight haze and/or slight off color.
0 – Objectionable — Cloudy and/or off color.

AROMA AND BOUQUET

6 – Extraordinary — Unmistakable characteristic aroma of grape variety or wine type. Outstanding and complex bouquet. Exceptional balance of aroma and bouquet.
5 – Excellent — Characteristic aroma. Complex bouquet. Well balanced.
4 – Good — Characteristic aroma. Distinguishable bouquet.
3 – Pleasant — Slight aroma and bouquet, but pleasant.
2 – Acceptable — No perceptible aroma or bouquet or 6, 5 or 4 above with slight off odors.
1 – Poor — Rating 3 above with slight off odors.
0 – Objectionable — Objectionable and offensive off odors.

TASTE

6 – Extraordinary — Unmistakable characteristic flavor of a grape variety or wine type. Extraordinary balance. Smooth, full bodied, mouth filling and overwhelming.
5 – Excellent — All of the above but a little less. Excellent but not overwhelming.

4 – Good — Characteristic grape variety or wine type flavor. Good balance. Smooth. May have minor faults. Good wine.
3 – Pleasant — Undistinguished wine but pleasant.
2 – Acceptable — Undistinguished wine with minor imperfections and/or more pronounced faults then 5, 4 or 3 above.
1 – Poor — Offensive flavors. May be drinkable with strong foods.
0 – Objectionable — Undrinkable.

FINISH

3 – Excellent — Lingering outstanding aftertaste and slow finish.
2 – Good — Pleasant aftertaste, medium finish.
1 – Poor — Little or no distinguishable aftertaste or fast finish.
0 – Objectionable — Unpleasant aftertaste.

BALANCE

2 – Excellent — Very harmonious in all characters.
1 – Good — One or more characters expressed slightly too forcefully or too little.
0 – Poor — Several characters very inappropriately expressed.

SCORES

18 - 20	Extraordinary	9 - 11	Pleasant
15 - 17	Excellent	6 - 8	Acceptable
12 - 14	Good	0 - 5	Poor and objectionable

Taster's Name: _____ Place: _____ Date: _____

	WINE	PRICE	SIGHT 3 MAX.	AROMA BOUQUET 6 MAX	TASTE 6 MAX.	FINISH 3 MAX.	BALANCE 2 MAX	TOTAL 20 MAX.	RANK	FINAL RANK	COMMENTS
1											
2											
3											
4											
5											
6											
7											
8											
9											
10											

NOTES

NOTES

NOTES

NOTES

NOTES

NOTES

NOTES

NOTES

NOTES

NOTES

NOTES

NOTES